THE JACOBITES
—— *and their* ——
DRINKING GLASSES

Geoffrey B. Seddon

Antique Collectors' Club

ISBN 1 85149 207 0

British Library Cataloguing-in-Publication Data
A catalogue record for this book is available from the British Library

The author and publishers are indebted to the Drambuie Liqueur Company for their generous support in subsidising the colour photographic content of this book.

Frontispiece: The Spottiswoode 'Amen' glass. H. 20.8cm. (COURTESY SOTHEBY'S, LONDON)

Printed in England by the
Antique Collectors' Club Ltd., 5 Church Street, Woodbridge, Suffolk IP12 1DS
on Consort Royal Art paper supplied by the
Donside Paper Company, Aberdeen, Scotland

CONTENTS

LIST OF COLOUR PLATES

WITH CAPTIONS

PREFACE

'Rosie', to whom this book is dedicated, is our first grandchild. She arrived in the September of the year I started writing. Now four years old it may yet be a few years before she thinks to glance through her copy of the book. When she does so she may well come to ponder upon the strange ruling passion of her eccentric grandfather. Should she have a mind to ask me about it I will need to try to explain, having first reassured her that my daughter and son-in-law had no thoughts of pandering to my obsession when they chose her name.

In my own defence it is fair to say that few who venture into the Jacobite period escape the fascination; the mystery and the unanswered questions make for exciting, compelling history. I fell prey to the enchantment over twenty years ago when, as a new and enthusiastic member of the Glass Circle, I chanced upon a modest eighteenth century drinking glass thought to be of Jacobite significance. The overwhelming sense of history cast its spell and this book is the story of what followed.

I began to acquire the equipment necessary to take detailed close-up photographs of engravings on glass. This included devising a reliable means of lighting the subject and of processing the films to give consistently good results. Then, over a period of many years, I visited museums and private collections from the heart of London to the furthermost corner of the Isle of Skye.

A valid criticism of any book such as this, containing as it does many detailed photographs, is that it gives the unscrupulous craftsman a recipe for forgery. This is quite true, as will be seen from the way in which the photographs in Joseph Bles's book were used in the 1930s to copy some of the 'Amen' glasses. However, unless this type of detailed study is undertaken, scholarship never advances. In any event, the problem of forged Jacobite glasses already exists because it seems likely that between ten and fifteen per cent of the engravings on Jacobite glasses are fakes. The risk of encouraging further forgeries has to be balanced against the benefit of giving those who have the responsibility of authentication a detailed guide to the genuine engravings. Only in this way will the false come to be recognized. As with the 'Amen' glasses, sooner or later the forgeries are exposed because the counterfeit, no matter how skilfully executed, can never quite live up to the original, and the more detailed the information which is available the better.

I am especially grateful to Robert Charleston who, as President of the Glass Circle and Keeper of the Department of Ceramics at the Victoria and Albert Museum, took an interest in my study in the early 1970s and allowed me to photograph the Museum's Jacobite glasses. To my publisher, Diana Steel, goes my appreciation for her courage in chancing her arm with an unknown author.

I am also grateful for the support and forbearance of my family as I understand that I have oft-times been observed roaming the house with my lips moving to no apparent effect, and this must have caused concern. To my son, Andrew, my special thanks; his interest in history enabled him to read and correct all my draft manuscripts and I found his help and advice invaluable.

On my travels I was always treated with the utmost courtesy and kindness. The unstinting generosity of all those who permitted me to photograph their valuable glasses made this book possible. The many private individuals are too numerous to mention, and most would prefer to remain anonymous, but I hope the mounted copies of the photographs, which I always tried to send to them, served as some small token of my appreciation.

I am most grateful to the Drambuie Liqueur Company for their generosity in contributing towards the costs of the colour photography, and I am particularly indebted to George Neilson, Drambuie's curator, for all his helpful assistance. The superb coloured photographs of the glasses and paintings in the Drambuie collection were taken by Eddy Fawdry.

I am very grateful to Charles Hajdamach for helpful advice, and to Peter Lole for his kindness and his lively, informative correspondence. A debt of gratitude is also owed to Rachel Russel of Christie's and to Simon Cottle of Sotheby's.

The Jacobite glasses photographed that are on view to the public are noted below.

The Victoria and Albert Museum, London; The Fitzwilliam Museum, Cambridge; The Ashmolean Museum, Oxford; The Harding Collection of glasses, Christ Church, Oxford; Mompesson House, Salisbury; The Cecil Higgins Museum, Bedford; Pilkington Glass Museum, St Helens; Traquair House, Innerleithen; Glasgow Art Gallery and Museum; The West Highland Museum, Fort William; National Museum of Antiquities, Edinburgh (now part of the National Museums of Scotland); The Royal Scottish Museum, Edinburgh (now part of the National Museums of Scotland); Huntley House, Edinburgh; Dundee Museum and Art Gallery; Dunvegan Castle, Isle of Skye.

Redditch 1994

For Rosemary Clare Sandford

NOTES

(1) A constant source of confusion for events in the first half of the eighteenth century is the question of Old Style and New Style dating. The Catholic continental countries adopted the New Style Gregorian Calendar at the beginning of the eighteenth century. Britain retained the Old Style Julian Calendar, which was eleven days behind the Gregorian Calendar, until 1752 when it too adopted the New Style dating. British sailors at sea would use the Old Style dates, while soldiers and diplomats on the Continent would usually adopt the New Style. I have endeavoured to follow the customary practice when writing about the Jacobite period before 1752, which is to use Old Style for events in Britain and New Style for events on the Continent.

(2) In chapters 1, 2, 3, 4, 5, 6 and 7 many of the illustrations have a capital letter in square brackets at the end of the caption. This indicates the engraver, [A, B, C, D, E, F, G, H or I], to which that particular glass has been attributed. If there is no such letter then attribution has not been possible.

INTRODUCTION

Writing history is attended by many hazards. The accurate interpretation of events after the passage of time is open to all manner of distortion: eye witness accounts may differ; contemporary sources can be difficult to assess, because any observation inevitably reflects the sympathies of the observer and too much emphasis may be placed on a source without taking this into account. The total knowledge of a period or incident is always incomplete. The historian selects what is perceived to be correct but, in so doing, is influenced by previous assessments; ideas can become entrenched and false interpretations perpetuated. Worse still the historian may identify with a certain perception of events and then have a vested interest in presenting all findings in such a way as to support that perception. Every effort should be made to retain unbiased judgement, to be fair and accurate, but great integrity may be required to maintain complete objectivity.

The history of any period is always dominated by the party in power; there is much truth in the saying that history is written by the winning side. The first half of the eighteenth century was the era of Whig supremacy and the recorded history is likely to have a Hanoverian bias. Students of Jacobite history have to penetrate any veil of misrepresentation to try and find the true Jacobite perspective. When assessing the impact of the 1745 rebellion or the real character of Charles Edward Stuart there are additional problems because the events of the 'Forty-five and the life of Bonnie Prince Charlie have been romanticized in fiction and folk-lore and the historian has to separate true facts from romantic myth.

These difficulties have been ably demonstrated by A.J.Youngson.[1] He examines the 1745 rising, first from the Hanoverian point of view and then, using the same facts, from the Jacobite standpoint. It is alarming how easy it is to describe the same characters and interpret the same events in such a way that the two opposing perceptions become equally plausible. He shows that even good history is fallible - there can never be any absolute certainty -and bad history may be little better than propaganda.

In the last fifteen years or so there has been a resurgence of interest in Jacobite history. Studies and biographies have appeared in profusion. Modern historians are coming to believe that the impact of Jacobitism in the eighteenth century was probably greater than has previously been supposed. They are looking again at the character of Charles Edward. Was he the dashing young prince of legend, or the rash adventurer recklessly disregarding the lives of others in pursuit of his own ends? And was his enterprise, the 'Forty-five, a desperate ill-conceived venture, doomed from the start, or was it the product of a courageous, innovative mind, and did it come much nearer to succeeding than has hitherto been supposed? Did the government of the day really regard the rising as little more than an irritation, or were they badly shaken? Winston Churchill describes the 'Forty-five as 'one of the most audacious and irresponsible enterprises in British history'.[2] Audacious it may well have been, nevertheless, many authorities now believe that it came within a whisker of succeeding. The historians who subscribe to these 'revisionist' theories of Jacobite significance in the eighteenth century have succeeded in reopening the whole debate and anything which sheds a little light may be of value.

For England the eighteenth century was a period of great constitutional and social change. The so-called Glorious Revolution of 1688 and James II's flight into exile saw, not only the start of the Jacobite movement, but also the beginning of the transition from absolute monarchy to the constitutional monarchy that exists today.

When James II ascended the throne, in 1685, on the death of his brother, Charles II, few would have guessed that in less than four years he would be fleeing for his life (Colour Plate 2). As Duke of York, James married twice. His first wife, Anne Hyde, was a Protestant. She gave him two daughters, Mary and Anne, both of whom were destined to be queens of England. In 1669 James underwent a religious conversion and became a Roman Catholic. He had no means of knowing at the time that what to him was a simple act of faith would, ultimately, bring about the downfall of the Stuart dynasty and cause the deaths of thousands of his fellow countrymen. Two years after the death of Anne Hyde in 1671, James married Mary of Modena (Colour Plate 3). The Whigs, fearing Popery and slavery under a Catholic king, tried to exclude James from the succession but the Tories, upholding the rule of law, hereditary monarchy and Divine Right, won the day. Meanwhile his elder daughter Mary, remaining true to her mother's religion, had married William of Orange, the Protestant champion of Europe.

When James became king and started to pursue his Roman Catholic ambitions the Tories became as alarmed, if not more so, than the Whigs. James II might have been tolerated in the knowledge that when he died the throne would pass to his Protestant daughter, Mary, but when Mary of Modena, after a long period of infertility, produced a healthy male infant and the Roman Catholic succession was seen to be secured, it was too much for Whigs and Tories alike. William, who all along had been worried that James might try to deprive his wife of her rightful inheritance, made his move. His invasion fleet arrived at Torbay proclaiming for 'Protestants and Liberty'.

The Whigs were victorious and, relishing the Tories' disillusionment, they made sure they gained the advantage with the new monarch. Neither Whigs nor Tories had wanted a revolution in the usual sense of the word; they were not seeking radical political reforms; they wanted a return to the old order and to be free from the threat of Popery. These days when Catholics and Protestants seem, to some extent, to be trying to find common ground, it is difficult to appreciate the depth of anti-Catholic feeling in England at this time. Protestants believed that Catholics plotted ruthlessly to gain power and, if they achieved their aims, would then subject non-believers to the most cruel suppression. It was a very real fear.

William came to protect Protestantism and his wife's right to the succession. He had no wish to harm James but, of course, he had no means of knowing what his father-in-law would do. When James, mindful of the fate of his father, Charles I, decided to flee into exile no attempt was made to stop him; it was even better than had been hoped because the Whigs were able to claim that James had abdicated and to offer William the crown, with conditions. A constitution was agreed excluding Catholics from the throne and advocating a 'free' parliament with frequent elections. They also ensured that henceforth the monarch would be financially dependent upon parliament. In so doing the foundations of constitutional monarchy were laid. The Whigs managed to hold the reins of government for most of the first half of the eighteenth century while the Tories, especially after the 1715 rebellion, were identified with the Jacobites.

The eighteenth century also saw the beginnings of industrialization and the emergence of a new wealthy, influential middle class: men like Josiah Wedgwood and the other great craftsmen of the day. The towns began to grow and seethe with humanity. A new age of enterprise and invention dawned: the use of coke in the smelting of iron, Arkwright's inventions in the cotton industry, James Watt's steam engine, better communications with improved roads and a canal system, and enormous improvements in the efficiency of agriculture with the enclosure of farming land.

While the Glorious Revolution was shaping Britain's future constitution a quieter revolution was taking place within the English glass industry. In 1675 George Ravenscroft had discovered lead-glass and this gradually replaced the lighter, rather dull, Venetian-type soda-glass and the Northern European potash-glass. This new brilliant English crystal with its extraordinary ability to refract the light was heavy, clear and durable. It was also ideal for cutting and engraving. New styles had to be developed to suit the properties of lead-glass and the English glassmakers of the eighteenth century were not found wanting. They used this new material to produce some of the finest glass available anywhere in the world.

By the end of the century Britain was in a position to expand her industrial base and extend her influence abroad. The British people had come to realize that the Divine Rights of monarchs were of little consequence compared to the democratic rights of the people and parliament. The constitutional reforms were such that the monarchy was in the process of becoming a focus for national identity instead of a vehicle for executive power. Britain had managed to keep its monarchy, albeit in a constitutional form, unlike the French whose kings retained their grip on absolute power until their country went plunging headlong into the chaos of a bloody revolution. The Englishman had not achieved the total 'liberty and equality' proclaimed in the revolutionary fervour spreading from France across Europe, but he had a kind of freedom that he cherished. Although hidebound by an antiquated class system the different classes did intermingle to a certain extent and it was becoming possible to move from one class to another.

The nineteenth century saw Britain becoming a major world power and herein lies one of the fascinations of Jacobite history. What would have been the effect if a Stuart had returned to power in the middle of the eighteenth century with the emphasis on all the old values, especially if that restoration had only been possible with French assistance? And just how close did the Jacobites get to effecting a Stuart restoration? The 1715 rebellion was the attempt which should really have succeeded yet it was the 1745 rising which came nearest to success and it was this attempt which was the real watershed in Jacobite fortunes.

And what of the Jacobites themselves and their so-called secret societies? The Duke of Berwick writing to Bolingbroke prior to the 1715 rebellion said: 'The majority of the English nation is so well affected that we may venture to say five out of six are for the King'.[3] 'The King' being, of course, the Old Pretender, James. Five out of six may have been an exaggeration, even so, where were they when they were needed? There is little doubt that the number of Jacobites prepared to risk everything was quite small. Certainly the Jacobites who liked to raise their glasses in a treasonable toast to the 'King over the Water' greatly outnumbered those prepared to raise their swords when the time came.

The government's attitude to these fireside Jacobites is also unclear. The rebel leaders who were executed or had their property confiscated are known, but what of the ordinary citizen who enjoyed a drink with like-minded friends using a specially engraved wine glass for an illicit but otherwise harmless toast? How did he or she fare? The impression has always been that such indulgence, however harmless was, nevertheless, dangerous and always conducted in great secrecy, the possession of a Jacobite glass being tantamount to treason. Again, some of these ideas may need to be revised.

And the drinking glasses themselves, so highly prized by students of Jacobite history and collectors of glass. Beautiful eighteenth century glasses engraved with a variety of obscure emblems, glasses which clearly meant a great deal to their original owners. Even today many of the emblems are still a matter of controversy. But, more than this, where were these glasses engraved and by whom? More important still, when were most of these glasses engraved? Were they, as is usually supposed, sentimental glasses the majority being engraved between 1750 and 1760, that is five to fifteen years after the last Jacobite rebellion, when any real threat of a Stuart restoration had receded? Or, were they highly political glasses engraved and used at the time of the 'Forty-five, when the threat to the established order was greatest? None of these questions has ever been answered satisfactorily (Colour Plates 1, 14, 15 and 16).

Contemporary sources form the basis of all historical research; they are the raw materials which the historian uses to fashion our concept of the past. Usually they take the form of the written word: government records, personal memoirs, contemporary accounts, diaries, letters etc. Less frequently some artefact or archaeological relic will seek to reveal something about the history and so it is with Jacobite glass. Using close-up photography a detailed study has been made of nearly 500 Jacobite glasses from museums and private collections all over the country. An overall picture emerges which throws some light on the mystery surrounding the glasses, the craftsmen who engraved them, and the people who used them. The object of this book is to show how history can help unravel some of the mystery of the glasses and, perhaps more important, how the glasses themselves can tell us something about the history. They are a valuable primary source. Apart from the written word Jacobite glasses are, with the possible exception of contemporary paintings, the most important surviving historical relics of this period. They may not speak with the same clarity as the written word but they have a story to tell, a story which can add a few details to the picture of everyday life in the middle of the eighteenth century at a time when the future of the country was in the balance.

Finally, Jacobite glasses, because they have such strong historical sentiments, have always commanded high prices and have therefore had their fair share of attention from unscrupulous forgers who have engraved fake Jacobite emblems on to genuine eighteenth century glasses. No foolproof method has ever been devised for detecting these spurious engravings and many of them still change hands in the salerooms and elsewhere as genuine Jacobite glasses, simply because it cannot be proved otherwise. Although it may not be possible to prove, positively, that a wheel-engraving of a Jacobite glass is a fake, now at least, using the close-up photographs, it is possible to authenticate most of the genuine glasses, isolating the fakes and leaving them exposed to a measure of reasonable doubt which is long overdue.

When considering the most highly prized of all Jacobite glasses - the 'Amen' glasses - it is a different story. These glasses are engraved by the diamond-point technique

Colour Plate 1. Jacobite loving cup. H. 22cm. (COURTESY DRAMBUIE LIQUEUR CO.)

with verses of the Jacobite hymn and the handwriting can be subjected to expert analysis allowing, as will be seen, the positive identification of some very clever forgeries.

It is often more enjoyable to travel hopefully than to arrive, and it would be a pity if the historians ever manage to dispel every myth of the Jacobite movement, or if all the mystery were to go out of Jacobite glass. But, it is important to realize that Jacobitism in the first half of the eighteenth century was not an irrelevance, an inconsequential ideology pursued by fanatics; it was deep-rooted, widespread, and posed, probably, the greatest threat to English society in the eighteenth century. Nor were all the Jacobite attempts lost causes, condemned to failure before they started; the 1715 and 1745 risings could very easily have gone the other way. This book attempts to throw a little light on a few of the unanswered questions.

CHAPTER 1
The Cause

Gentlemen, you are come hither this day to fight, and that in the best of causes; for it is the battle of your King, your religion, and your country, against the foulest usurpation and rebellion; ... I ask nothing of you, that you shall not see me do before you; and, if any of us shall fall upon this occasion, we shall have the honour of dying in our duty, and as becomes true men of valour and conscience: and such of us shall live and win the battle, shall have the reward of a gracious King, and the praise of all good men.

Viscount Dundee to his men before the Battle of Killiecrankie, in which he was mortally wounded, 27 July 1689.[1]

The Stage is Set

On Christmas morning 1688 an English yacht, the *Henrietta*, having crossed the Channel under cover of darkness made landfall on the French coast at the small village of Ambleteuse. It had been snowing and was cold. On board the *Henrietta*, cramped in a tiny cabin, was James II. For the second time in his life James was an exile from his country and the Jacobite movement was about to begin.

James had been a boy not yet fifteen when he made his first escape to France to avoid Cromwell's roundheads in 1648. Then, in May 1660, when the royal party was rowed ashore at Dover, after the collapse of the Commonwealth, James was at his brother's side as Charles II knelt on the shingle and gave thanks to God for his restoration, and the guns along the coast roared in salute. When he became king in 1685 James was fifty-one and, by seventeenth century standards, already on the brink of old age. Even so the throne he inherited from Charles II seemed as secure as any in Europe, yet here he was, less than four years later, fleeing from his own son-in-law. What had he done wrong?

One can only guess at James's bewilderment as the coach and the escort of French officers took him to join his wife and the infant Prince of Wales who had made their escape to France two weeks before. Some historians have been at a loss to account for the incompetent mismanagement during his short reign. In truth James lacked imagination and he tended to miss the subtleties of complex political situations. He was also a poor judge of character and exposed himself to betrayal by those in whom he had placed his trust. As his reign proceeded he found himself unequal to the burden of supreme command; his confusion increased until, unable to cope, and aware in his own words that 'there is but a short distance between the prisons and graves of kings', he lost his nerve.

Plate 1. The Château Saint-Germain-en-Laye

Saint Germain

James's cousin, Louis XIV, had placed the château at Saint-Germain-en-Laye at his disposal (Plate 1). A large forbidding edifice, on a promontory above the Seine and overlooking the Plain of Paris, the château was more magnificent than the palace of Whitehall which James had forsaken. With it went a guard of honour and a retinue of courtiers and attendants together with a handsome annual pension. The Jacobite court which assembled there was a mixture of exiles from various parts, and the streets of the quiet village of Saint-Germain soon bustled with a variety of uniforms and accents.

Whig historians were to accuse James of fleeing for fear of his life but this was unjust. It is true that he was undoubtedly influenced by what had happened to his father, Charles I, but James was no coward; he left England because he perceived his position to be untenable in the existing circumstances. He may have been bewildered but he was not wholly dispirited and he saw his arrival in France as an opportunity to get to grips with the situation and plan his next move. The atmosphere at Saint-Germain was one of excitement and expectation. Within a few months James, with Louis's blessing and a large supply of arms, had embarked for Ireland. He regarded Ireland as the stepping stone to England; but, while Dundee was bravely forfeiting his life, in a glorious victory at Killiekrankie to preserve Scotland for his king, James himself, after some initial successes, suffered ignominious defeat at the Battle of the Boyne.

On his return to Saint-Germain James's mood changed to one of apathy. He loved France and seemed content to remain there. In 1692 Mary Beatrice gave him another child, this time a daughter. Louis XIV was godfather and in his honour she was christened Louise Marie; James nicknamed her his 'Solace'.

There were the ritual exchange visits between the courts at Versailles and Saint-Germain but, with the exception of Louis who was always kind to his cousin, the French had little time for the exiled king. He was regarded as a pathetic failure. His lack of wit, his ponderous rather hesitant speech and the total absence of any sense of humour, did little to endear him to the sparkling court at Versailles. The persistence with which he retained the ancient title of 'King of France' was, in the circumstances, ludicrous to say the least. Even his constant pious devotions failed to gain him the respect which, being in a Catholic country, one might have thought to be his due; the Archbishop of Paris observing sarcastically: 'There is a very good man; he has given up three kingdoms for a mass.' In contrast his wife, Mary Beatrice, was loved by all.

James remained active well into his sixties. He was fond of hunting in the Great Park of the château, but he became increasingly preoccupied with thoughts of his own mortality and devoted more and more time to securing the salvation of his soul. Surrounded by his priests he immersed himself in prayer. Never a merry monarch, his outlook became more dismal than ever. In 1701, while in chapel, he collapsed into the arms of Mary Beatrice. He was taken to his room and for two weeks drifted in and out of coma. His demeanour became serene and saintly, the manner of his dying gaining the admiration of all who visited him. Smiling and at peace with his God he prepared to leave his troubled world. He blessed the tearful Prince of Wales and his 'Solace', Louise. Mary Beatrice was inconsolable.

When Louis XIV visited James for the last time he made a momentous announcement from James's bedside to all those in the crowded room: 'I am come, Monsieur, to acquaint you that whenever it shall please God to take your Majesty from this world, I shall take your family under my protection, and will treat your son, the Prince of Wales, in the same manner as I have treated you, and recognize him, as he will then be, King of England.'··· [2] The assembled company wept with relief and joy. While James struggled to express his feelings Jacobites threw themselves at Louis's feet in gratitude. A few days later, on 16 September, James died.

Perhaps in death he found the peace he had been seeking. If his melancholia in life was due to guilt it was not without good reason, for he had blundered on a grand scale, and the consequences of his policies, however sincere his motives, were far-reaching. Many lives were to be lost in the rebellions which followed as his supporters tried to regain the throne he so wantonly abandoned.

James had courage and he was not without ability, but he had failed as a monarch; his own character and the age in which he lived had conspired against him. He had neither the wit nor the wisdom for the formidable task which he had undertaken: to rule as a Roman Catholic king in a Protestant country which had still to discover religious toleration. An essentially honest man he was intensely loyal to his friends but naïve in his expectations. In exile he had been unable to inspire the Jacobite cause and had made the mistake of expecting history to repeat itself; the formula which had restored the Stuart monarchy in 1660 did not work for James.

He has been described as a misunderstood martyr, the first real champion of religious freedom. There can be no doubting his sincerity; it shines throughout but, when religious sincerity becomes bigotry minds close against it. The assessment of a lady at the French court is probably apt: 'To tell the truth our good King James is a brave and honest man but the silliest I have ever seen in my life.'

Jamie the Rover

James Francis Edward Stuart, thirteen years old, was proclaimed King on the same day that his father died. The proclamation, read in English, French and Latin, to the courtiers and townspeople assembled at the gates of Saint-Germain, declared the new sovereign to be James III of England and James VIII of Scotland.

The new king was quickly recognized by France, Spain and the Papacy. Louis's recognition of James as *de jure* king of England was in breach of the Treaty of Ryswick which he had signed in 1697. This had been to make peace with the Dutch and by this treaty he had agreed to recognize William III as king. Fulfilling his pledge to look after the young boy Louis saw that he was provided with an adequate household and supervised his education. James loved hunting, fencing and dancing and he had a social grace and a sophistication of manner which pleased the French, but there was a nervousness and an introspective sadness about him which were to be the hallmarks of his character in later life when the flush of youth had passed.

On his deathbed James II had presented his son with a manuscript. This was a complete book of instructions on how to be a good Catholic king: everything from how to balance the exchequer to moral advice on the abuse of alcohol and the unlawful love of women. It is impossible to resist the thought that if only James II had been able to follow some of his own good advice he might have had a kingdom to pass on to his son which was larger than that encompassed by the walls of Saint-Germain.

In March 1702, William gave assent to an Act of Attainder and Abjuration which held James Francis Edward to be guilty of high treason and liable to execution without trial. It was also high treason to communicate with James or help him in any way. William was on his deathbed when he gave the royal assent and he died the following day. Two weeks previously he had been thrown from his horse fracturing his collar bone. His horse had stumbled on a molehill and the mole in question was subsequently celebrated in a favourite Jacobite toast to 'The little gentleman in black velvet'. This ended the reign of William and Mary, Mary having died of smallpox in 1694. Queen Anne, James II's younger Protestant daughter, now came to the throne.

William had expressed a dying wish to see England and Scotland united by Act of Parliament. Scotland was a separate country with its own parliament and the fear was that the Scots might be tempted to accept the Stuart pretender as their ruler. England would then have had a hostile neighbour to the north, ruled by a Catholic king and allied to her traditional enemy, France, in the south.

Notwithstanding fierce opposition in Scotland the Treaty of Union was finally passed in 1707. There were celebrations in England but for many Scots the loss of sovereignty was a humiliation.

The 1708 Attempt

It was this discontent which, in 1708, caused Louis XIV to consider that a rising in Scotland might be feasible. In supporting such a venture Louis's motives were not wholly altruistic; he hoped the English would be obliged to withdraw forces from Europe where his armies in Flanders were being hard pressed by Marlborough.

A fleet of five warships and over twenty privateers was assembled at Dunkirk under Admiral Forbin. Forbin was convinced from the start that the expedition was foolhardy. He was also constantly at loggerheads with the Comte de Gacé who commanded the infantry. The ships carried 6,000 troops and a large supply of arms for the Scottish loyalists who were expected to rise once a landing was made. James arrived to join the expedition but was unwell with a rising fever. Unbeknown to him his young sister, Louise Marie, had fallen ill with measles shortly after he had kissed her farewell at Saint-Germain. Now James was stricken at this crucial time.

The activities at Dunkirk did not go unnoticed on the other side of the water and before long a fleet of English warships was patrolling the Channel and awaiting events. Gales delayed departure but eventually James, still weak from his illness, was carried on board Forbin's flagship and the fleet set sail. Further gales damaged a number of the French ships but they managed to avoid the English warships and on the evening of 12 March Forbin anchored off the Isle of May in the Firth of Forth.

A landing was made at Pittenweem but there was only a small welcoming party; the army of Scottish Jacobites that had been expected was nowhere to be seen. The following morning they were alarmed to see the English fleet, which had pursued them up the coast, anchored at the mouth of the Firth of Forth. Under full sail Forbin managed to outrun his enemy with the loss of only one ship. James pleaded to be landed with some of his companions but Forbin, whose orders were to protect the King at all costs, insisted on a return to Dunkirk. It was a sad and dejected Pretender who eventually returned to Saint-Germain.

The Succession

Three months before the death of James II parliament had approved the Act of Settlement which stated that, failing legitimate issue to William III or his sister-in-law Princess Anne, the crown was to pass to the Electress Sophia of Hanover, grand-daughter of James I. Thus the Protestant succession had been assured.

Queen Anne was now in poor health. She was only in her forties and, after no fewer than seventeen pregnancies, had no heir. She was unhappy about the succession passing to the Electress of Hanover and she was rumoured to be sympathetic towards the possibility of James III succeeding her. However, when James wrote to her in 1711, expressing the hope that some compromise might be reached, she did not reply.

Nevertheless, about this time the Jacobites had good reason to be hopeful of a restoration. In 1710 there had been a change of government in England and the Tories had gained power. There was strong Jacobite support in the government and the Earl of Oxford and Viscount Bolingbroke, Anne's principal ministers, were both pro-Jacobite. On the Pretender's birthday, 10 June, 'White Rose Day', there were open demonstrations of support for James.

Towards the end of 1711 James returned from a tour of central France to greet his mother and sister who were staying at the Convent Chaillot close by Saint-Germain. James was then twenty-three and Louise Marie delighted in the company of her brother (Colour Plates 4 and 5). Spirits were running high at Saint-Germain and there was a possibility of marriage between Louise and Charles XII of Sweden. The armed strength of Sweden would have been further welcome support for James. Winter passed. Then, one day during Easter 1712, James was returning from a day's hunting when he felt unwell. It soon became apparent that he had smallpox and fear for the King's life mounted as James became critically ill. A few days later Louise Marie also contracted the disease. The young princess deteriorated rapidly and, after little more than a week, she made her confession and died. James slowly recovered to mourn the loss of his dear sister.

Louis XIV was anxious to end the European war but the English insisted that, as part of a peace treaty the Pretender should remove himself from the French court. James was obliged to move to Lorraine, a nearby province, while his mother and the Jacobite court remained at Saint-Germain. His exile in Lorraine became permanent when, in 1713, Louis signed the Peace of Utrecht and reluctantly agreed to recognize the Protestant Hanoverian succession.

Queen Anne's reign was clearly drawing to a close. She became even more opposed to a Hanoverian succession when the Hanoverians openly joined forces with the Whigs whom she viewed with equal dislike. If James could have been persuaded to become a Protestant the only real obstacle to his succession would have been removed. In February 1714 Oxford communicated with James telling him that if he would just declare himself to be a Protestant he, Oxford, would see to it that Queen Anne named James as her successor. James, who was too honest to be party to such hypocrisy, restated his intention to ensure religious freedom but reserved the same freedom for himself and remained steadfast in his faith.

Two months before the death of Queen Anne in 1714 the Electress Sophia of Hanover died and the succession passed to her son George. Then Oxford had a fierce argument with Bolingbroke in the presence of Queen Anne a few days before her death and was dismissed. Bolingbroke, in trying to form his cabinet, sought to create a coalition with the Whigs and, to his dismay, the Whigs gained control. When Queen Anne died the Whigs dominated the Cabinet and, although it was rumoured that the Queen had left a letter beneath her pillow naming James as her successor, messages went out from the Privy Council to all parts of the kingdom that George of Hanover was to be king. The Whigs had taken the initiative and the Jacobites had lost any chance of a peaceful restoration.

The 1715 Rebellion

The Whigs may have carried the day and achieved a Hanoverian succession but, with the crowning of George I, there were many who came to feel that the Protestant faith of the new monarch was possibly his sole redeeming feature. During 1715 support for the Jacobites grew and 'White Rose Day' again saw demonstrations for the Pretender in many parts of the country. There were several riots and James's health was drunk openly.

There were plans for a Jacobite rising in England and preparations had reached an advanced stage in the West Country, the intention being that James would land near Plymouth. However Bolingbroke and his fellow Tory, the Duke of Ormonde, both fled to France when they came under suspicion. The Earl of Oxford maintained his innocence but was imprisoned in the Tower.

The Earl of Mar then took centre stage. Many prominent Jacobites had been arrested but, in August, Mar managed to return to Scotland, to his estates in the Cairngorms. He invited all the well-known Jacobite clan chiefs to attend a large annual hunt at Braemar where he made an eloquent speech denouncing the Hanoverian succession and upholding James's right to the throne. Just over a week later, on 6 September, James's blue and gold standard was raised at Braemar.

Mar was not prominent as a Jacobite, indeed his nickname, 'Bobbing John', while due in part to a nervous head movement, also referred to his ability to change his political loyalties when it suited him. Although James had sent a message to him declaring 10 August to be the date for the rising and promising to come in person as soon as possible, Mar was, nevertheless, acting without consultation with the Jacobite leaders in France when he raised the standard at Braemar. He had ability as a diplomat but, as events were to prove, Mar was not a military leader. By inflaming Jacobite passions with his eloquence he started a blaze he was not competent to control. To give Mar his due, however, he was not unaware of his limitations and he probably never expected to have full responsibility for the military leadership of the rebellion he had precipitated. Help from France was expected and Mar probably thought the Duke of Berwick would be assuming military command.

Berwick was James's half brother, the illegitimate son of James II and Arabella Churchill. He had been with his father on board the *Henrietta* when James II had escaped to France. Eighteen years older than his half-brother, he had devoted his life to the service of France. In 1704 Berwick, with James's approval, had become a French citizen and in 1706 Louis XIV had made him a Marshal of France. By 1715 he ranked with Marlborough as one of the foremost military leaders of his day. Head and shoulders above any other likely candidate he was the obvious choice to take command of the Jacobite forces. But, in 1715, Berwick found himself in a moral dilemma. The French government could not allow a Marshal of France to lead a rebellion to topple a monarchy which, by the Treaty of Utrecht, they had agreed to uphold. Thus, when Berwick sought permission to accompany James it was declined, and when James commissioned Berwick to take command of the Jacobite forces he refused. It was a terrible blow and this was one of the few occasions when James revealed any bitterness. He was deeply wounded for he had always taken it for granted that his half-brother would be at his side when the time came and he felt, with some justification, that allegiance to the Stuart cause and family loyalty should take precedence over French citizenship.

To add to the problems of the Jacobites, and to James's personal distress, Louis XIV died on 1 September 1715. His successor, Louis XV, was only five years old and France was ruled by a Regent, a nephew of Louis XIV, the Duc d'Orleans. The French Regent, while maintaining a friendly interest in James's wellbeing, had no intention of compromising France to support the Stuarts.

Notwithstanding these setbacks the Jacobites must have been encouraged initially because Mar soon found himself at the head of an army some 5,000 strong. The government troops opposing Mar were under the Duke of Argyll. They numbered less than half the Jacobite force but they were seasoned regular troops and Argyll himself was an experienced commander. Argyll stationed his forces at Stirling which gave him control of the bridge over the Forth making it difficult for Mar to join up with the Jacobites in the Lowlands. Mar simply occupied Perth and seemed content to remain there for several weeks. More recruits flocked to his standard and his army grew to over 10,000. The Jacobites controlled all of Scotland north of the Tay yet Mar seemed reluctant to move against Argyll who, little more than thirty miles away, was sending urgent requests for reinforcements.

A small group of Jacobites attempted to capture Edinburgh Castle but this went sadly amiss. The castle would have been a valuable prize; the Jacobites would have had the strongest fortress in Scotland as well as control of the capital. The castle also contained large stores of arms and considerable wealth in gold. The plan could have succeeded if some of the party had not stopped to fortify their spirits in an Edinburgh tavern, delaying the group's departure. Some soldiers in the garrison had agreed to help but by the time the attempt to scale the walls got under way the guard was changing and the intruders were discovered.

When the Jacobites learnt of the death of Louis XIV and realized that French support might not be forthcoming, Mar knew he had to act before his men started to lose heart and drift away; but he still rejected a straightforward confrontation. Instead he detached a force of some 2,500 under a Brigadier MacIntosh with orders to make a crossing of the Forth, then move south to join the Jacobites in the Lowlands and the North of England. The combined force was then to turn north again to threaten Argyll from the rear. MacIntosh got his men across the Firth of Forth in small boats under cover of darkness by cleverly diverting three English men-of-war patrolling the area. He then moved south to the border. There the Jacobites consisted of two groups: the Lowland Scots under Lords Kenmuir, Nithsdale, Carnwath and Wintoun; and the North of England Jacobites under Lord Derwentwater and Thomas Forster, MP for Northumberland. When they joined forces with MacIntosh there was disagreement. The Scots wanted to follow Mar's plan and return north to try and draw Argyll out of Stirling, while the English wanted to march south against General Carpenter who had left Newcastle and was riding at the head of a force of government cavalry to engage them. In the event they did neither and moved across the border, through Jedburgh, then down through Penrith, Kendal and Lancaster. They had hoped to gain more recruits on crossing the border but their number was actually depleted when a substantial body of the Highlanders, disagreeing with the move into England, deserted.

On 9 November the Jacobite horse rode into Preston a day ahead of the infantry. James was proclaimed King at the market cross and the town was occupied. Without making any attempt to fortify Preston against a surprise attack the troops relaxed. On Saturday 12 November the Jacobite army was preparing to evacuate the town and march on Manchester when they suddenly discovered that a government army, under General Wills, had passed through Wigan early that morning and was already moving on Preston.

Forster, who had assumed command of the army once it crossed into England, must take responsibility for this failure of military intelligence. The surprise was almost complete. By midday the government cavalry was within sight of the town and Forster did not even have time to defend the bridge over the Ribble.

The Jacobites withdrew into the town barricading the streets and occupying strategic houses. Unprepared and bottled up in this manner the rebels still retained the advantage because they outnumbered the government force and Wills could not use his cavalry in the narrow streets of Preston. In the houses and behind the barricades the Jacobites had good cover and were able to deliver a murderous volley of small arms fire. By evening they had successfully repelled three government attacks inflicting heavy losses.

Sunday morning found the rebels in a confident mood having sustained only minor casualties, but at midday the odds lengthened dramatically. General Carpenter, who had followed the Jacobites down from the north arrived to reinforce Wills's army and the town was completely sealed.

At this point Forster began to delude himself into thinking he might be able to negotiate favourable surrender terms and, even worse, sent Colonel Oxburgh to parley with Wills on behalf of the English Jacobites, excluding the Scots. Wills, however, would have none of it and was not prepared to bargain for the lives of the rebels. The King's mercy, which gave precious little comfort, and the promise to prevent his troops from extracting revenge on the rebels, was the most Wills would offer in return for unconditional surrender. MacIntosh, disgusted by Forster's betrayal, was for making a stand but, on being informed by Wills that no quarter would be shown to any of the Scots, he was obliged to comply with the same terms. The Jacobite army surrendered on 14 November. Some 1,600 men were disarmed and taken prisoner.

While General Carpenter was riding into Preston on Sunday 13 November to seal the fate of the Jacobites in Lancashire, the first shots were being fired in the Battle of Sheriffmuir north of the border.

Mar and Argyll had both been playing a waiting game; Mar waiting in vain for the arrival of the King with assistance from France, and Argyll, more realistically, waiting for reinforcements. On 10 November Mar moved south leaving a force behind to hold Perth. He planned to cross the Forth to the west of Stirling, occupy the Lowland counties, and presumably join up with the Jacobites in the North of England. He was more than usually vague about his precise intention because he had had no news of the movements of the Jacobite army south of the border.

Argyll, although outnumbered two to one, knew that he had to prevent Mar from crossing the Forth at all costs. He moved his army north across the river and, on the evening of 12 November, occupied Dunblane, covering the road along which the Jacobites would advance.

Meanwhile Mar, having no knowledge of Argyll's movements, was drawing near. The advance guard returned with the news that Dunblane was already occupied; Argyll had gained the advantage of being able to select his ground at Sheriffmuir, north east of Dunblane. That night Mar camped two miles from the town while Argyll's men had orders to remain at their posts throughout the night. There was a sharp frost and it was bitterly cold.

On Sunday 13 November, after a morning of cumbersome manoeuvring the armies engaged just after midday. Argyll's left wing immediately felt the full fury of a Highland charge and, within minutes, had been overwhelmed. Mar pursued the survivors of the onslaught almost as far as Stirling, thinking he had won the day.

However his left wing had not been so successful against Argyll's right. Argyll used his cavalry to good effect outflanking the Jacobites and slowly driving them back some three miles. When he realized the fate of his own left wing Argyll, like Mar, regathered his troops and marched back to the battlefield. His force had been reduced to about 1,000 infantry and five squadrons of dragoons, while the Jacobites numbered around 4,000. Realizing he was heavily outnumbered Argyll took up a defensive position and waited for the attack. Mar faltered yet again and failed to take the initiative, allowing what should have been a certainty to dwindle into stalemate. As evening came both armies began to disperse and the battle was over.

The following day Argyll returned to the field prepared to fight but Mar had left and was making his way back to Perth. Argyll claimed victory; he had captured the Jacobite supply wagons and several of their colours. Mar, likewise, claimed victory but the plain fact was that he had failed to cross the Forth and he was back where he had started with a demoralized and much reduced force. The old Jacobite song tells the story:

> There's some say that we wan,
> And some say that they wan,
> And some say that nane wan at a', man;
> But one thing, I'm sure,
> That at Sheriffmuir
> A battle there was, that I saw, man.
> And we ran, and they ran,
> And they ran, and we ran,
> And we ran, and they ran awa', man.

James sailed from Dunkirk on 16 December. One has to admire his devotion: beset with disappointments and difficulties he was determined to join his demoralized supporters in Scotland. His ship sailed through stormy seas for five days, under constant threat of being spotted by an English frigate, before entering Peterhead harbour in Aberdeenshire.

James's arrival in his ancient kingdom on 22 December was not occasioned by any ceremony. He was received in Aberdeen and then moved on to Dundee, arriving there on 6 January. He decided to establish his headquarters at the Palace at Scone and on 9 January entered Perth.

He was not encouraged by what he saw of the Jacobite army nor was the army encouraged by what they saw of James. One anonymous rebel writing: 'A True Account of the Proceedings at Perth', says: '… his person is tall and thin, seeming to incline to be lean rather than to fill as he grows in years. His countenance is pale and perhaps he looked more pale by reason he had three fits of an ague, which took him two days after coming on shore. Yet he seems to be sanguine in his constitution, and has something of a vivacity in his eye, that perhaps would have been more visible, if he had not been under dejected circumstances, and surrounded with discouragement; which it must be acknowledged, were sufficient to alter the complexion even of his soul, as well as of his body. His speech was grave, and not very clearly expressing his thoughts, nor overmuch to the purpose; but his words were few; his behaviour and temper seemed always composed; what he was in his diversions, we know not; here was no room for such things; it was no time for mirth, neither can I say that I ever saw him smile. ... I must not conceal that when we saw the person who we called our King, we found ourselves not at all animated by his presence, and if he was disappointed in us, we were tenfold more so in him.'[3]

Mar may have been flattered by the dukedom conferred on him by James but he could offer little in return which gave any hope of a reversal in the Jacobite fortunes. It had been two months since he returned to Perth during which time he had been at the centre of a deteriorating situation. The army that returned from Sheriffmuir had been reduced to near half its previous strength. When news arrived of the fate of the Jacobites at Preston, the sense of despair deepened and the Highlanders started to drift away. While Mar's force was dwindling Argyll's was steadily growing as more reinforcements arrived. Argyll, however, was anything but happy; he was being accused of showing undue sympathy towards his fellow countrymen and it had been decided that he should share the command of the government army with General Cadogan who was not handicapped by any such sympathies.

James had set aside 23 January 1716 as the date for his coronation, but it never took place because by this time Argyll was planning to advance on Perth. It was mid-winter and there was deep snow on the ground. In an attempt to slow down the government advance, by depriving them of shelter, James reluctantly signed an order to burn the houses in the villages between Stirling and Perth. Many of the poor villagers left standing in the snow subsequently died from exposure. This act of brutality was out of character for James, and it served little purpose because Argyll left Stirling on 29 January and was on the outskirts of Perth by the 31st. The Jacobites evacuated the town and crossed the frozen River Tay.

With the lack of direction in the Jacobite camp came an increasing awareness that some treachery was afoot. Mar was arranging James's safe return to France, and James was forced to admit that there was no real alternative; his continued presence was likely to do more harm than good.

The Jacobite army arrived in Dundee on 1 February and Montrose on the 3rd, but, when they left to march to Aberdeen on the 4th the Highlanders were unaware that Mar and James had slipped away and boarded a French ship. The loyal remnants of the army were under the command of General Gordon who, on arrival in Aberdeen, had the unpleasant duty of informing his men that the rebellion was over and their king was already on his way back to France. Argyll was close on their heels and, a few days later when the army disbanded, the Highlanders melted into the mountains.

General Cadogan was given the job of extracting retribution from the Highlands but few prisoners were taken and affairs in Scotland soon returned to normal. Many of the Scottish nobility implicated in the rebellion escaped to the Continent and no death sentences were carried out on any of the Jacobites taken prisoner in Scotland. The prisoners at Preston did not fare so well. The peers and clan chiefs were taken to stand trial in London. The impeached Lords were all condemned to death but Lords Wintoun and Nithsdale managed to escape, as also did Forster and MacIntosh. Lords Widdrington, Carnwath, and Nairn were eventually released under the Act of Grace in 1717, and only Lords Derwentwater and Kenmuir paid the ultimate penalty on the executioner's block. As for the less prominent Jacobites: in Lancashire four officers were tried by court martial, for desertion, and shot; while twenty six Jacobites were hanged for treason: twenty-two in Lancashire and four in London. In addition several hundred were shipped as slaves to the American colonies.

The '1715' rebellion was the Jacobites' missed opportunity. If Mar had moved against Argyll in the early days, especially when MacIntosh got his men across the Forth, it is difficult to see what could have stopped him. The Jacobites would have swept through the Lowlands and the North of England gathering support. But, as with all the Jacobite attempts, there was something missing, and on this occasion it was a military leader with flair. The sun had not yet set on Stuart aspirations but, for James, the circumstances for a successful restoration would never again be as favourable.

The 1719 Attempt

Back in France James found himself even less welcome than before. His previous abode in Lorraine was no longer acceptable to the French Regent and James was obliged to move to Avignon, which was then in Papal territory. There he remained for several months and Avignon became the rallying point for Jacobites escaping the aftermath of the 'Fifteen. Before long, however, threats from the British government caused the Pope to ask James to move even further from the country of his birth. He crossed the Alps, visiting his mother's old home in Modena, and then passed through Rome before finally arriving in Urbino on 11 June 1717. There the old palace was placed at his disposal.

In adopting his policy of non-cooperation with the Jacobites, and forging an alliance with Britain, the French Regent, Duc d'Orléans, was thinking of his own interests as well as those of France. As Louis XIV's nephew he would succeed to the French throne in the event of young Louis XV's death, which, given the infant mortality rate in the eighteenth century, was always a likely possibility. But, there was an even closer relative of Louis XIV, a grandson, the Duc d'Anjou. He had become Philip V of Spain in 1700 but a condition of his acceptance of the Spanish crown had been that he should relinquish his right to inherit the French throne. Orléans was not so naïve as to believe that Philip would keep this promise if the French throne became vacant and he looked to Britain as an ally in that event.

James too needed an ally. After the failure of the 'Fifteen, Jacobite hopes were not crushed to the extent which might have been expected. They had been encouraged by the support for their cause, much of which, they felt, still remained. James was still young and vigorous, and George I, dependent upon the Whigs, remained as unpopular as ever. But, if the 1715 rising had taught them anything, it was that they needed the support of a foreign power.

Attention focused on Spain where the key figure was Cardinal Alberoni, principal minister to Philip V. In 1718 a Spanish fleet, in the Mediterranean, had been annihilated by Admiral Byng and Alberoni was thirsty for revenge. It was also his ambition to see Philip on the throne of France and, to these ends, he sought to use the Jacobite cause as a means of striking a blow at the Anglo-French alliance.

Although it was clear that James was being used for his nuisance value he was in no position to object because, deprived of French assistance, his financial resources were getting low. Alberoni agreed to an expeditionary force of 5,000 Spanish troops and additional arms. These were to be carried on some twenty transporters with an escort of ten warships.

Ormonde, one of the few Jacobites remaining at Saint-Germain, was brought to Spain to lead the expedition; he and James were to join the fleet at Coruna. By this time France, having uncovered the plot to replace the Duc d'Orleans with Philip of Spain, had declared war.

The main expeditionary force, under Ormonde, was to make a landing in the south-west of England, while a smaller force, under Earl Marischal, consisting of three frigates, 300 Spanish troops, and a quantity of arms, was to descend on Scotland and create a diversion. The main fleet, which had been assembled in Cadiz, left for Coruna in March but was hit by severe storms off Cape Finisterre. The surviving ships staggered into harbour at Coruna and the 1719 rising was in ruins before it had even started. Marischal, who had sailed out of San Sebastian three weeks earlier, of course, knew nothing of this and early in April, after eluding English patrols, arrived in Stornoway.

The ultimate fate of this small force is not difficult to envisage. On the mainland they occupied Eilean Donan Castle and used it as a store for their ammunition. But, on 9 May, a British squadron sailed into Loch Alsh, overpowered the small garrison which had been left to guard the castle, and blew up their stores.

On that same day, far away on the Continent, the young Princess Maria Clementina Sobieska of Poland (Colour Plate 7), having made a perilous journey south to Bologna, was married by proxy to James Francis Edward Stuart (Colour Plate 6) and became *de jure* Queen of England. As though to further emphasize the irony, the end of the 1719 rising came a few weeks later when, at the Pass of Glenshiel, the Jacobites were overwhelmed by government troops. The date was 10 June the King's thirty-first birthday.

The Jacobite Star

James now ceased wandering. He returned to Rome where, for the first time, he saw his pretty seventeen year old bride. The official marriage ceremony took place the same day and the couple settled down to live at the Palazzo Muti in Rome. Life in the city was agreeable for them and the Romans were fascinated by the English king and his young queen. James worked diligently, organizing the new Jacobite court.

On Tuesday 31 December 1720 Clementina gave James a son and news of the Stuart heir was joyously received by Jacobites throughout Europe. Charles Edward Stuart was immediately created Prince of Wales (Colour Plate 8).

However, clouds were gathering over the marriage and there were signs of tension and disharmony. Clementina resented being left alone while James dealt with official business and she became increasingly prone to bouts of depression and outbursts of anger. Even more, she resented the fact that James, in an endeavour to prove the sincerity of his promise of religious toleration, had included a number of Protestant advisers and governesses in his court, and he refused to allow Clementina to interfere in these appointments.

On 6 March 1725 their second son, Prince Henry Benedict, was born and was created Duke of York (Colour Plate 9). Clementina's unhappiness only seemed to increase. When James dismissed one of Clementina's favourites, Mrs Sheldon, Charles's governess, Clementina became distraught. She lashed out with wild accusations of infidelity, which were totally without foundation but which James's enemies fell upon and used to the full. Later the same year she left James with his two sons and retired to a convent.

This marital breakdown did considerable harm to the Jacobite cause and James found it difficult to forgive the disgrace her behaviour brought upon his family. It was over two years before the couple were reunited. James then found that Clementina was spending more and more time in religious devotion and self-mortification. She appeared to find few pleasures in life, would fast for long periods and was locked in her room for much of the time. James was at a loss and could do little but observe as his wife was slowly devoured by religious mania. Clementina was thirty-four when she died in 1735. The marriage, which in the beginning had been so full of promise, had given James two sons but had otherwise brought him nothing but unhappiness.

The birth of Charles and Henry had given Jacobites good reason to be hopeful but the circumstances were not right for another rebellion. The lessons of the previous attempts were clear: for a successful restoration the Jacobites needed either, substantial foreign aid or, a well-organized rising in Britain with a competent military leader. They would have liked both but, for twenty years after the failure of the 'Nineteen, they had neither; the former depended upon Britain being at war with her neighbours, and the latter upon unrest at home. Under Walpole, Britain enjoyed peace abroad, with increasing prosperity at home, and economic stability always militates against successful rebellion.

Against this background James could only wait and bide his time. Then, in 1740, circumstances began to change with the War of the Austrian Succession. As the cracks appeared in the peace between England and France so the hopes of the Jacobites began to rise. Charles was twenty and straining at the leash. He had never doubted that the Stuarts would be restored to their rightful place and he knew that his role would be a vital one. Less inclined towards intellectual pleasures than his brother, Henry, he had made sure of his preparedness by spending his days walking long distances, riding, and hunting.

James was, as ever, cautious. He had received assurances that the Highlands were ready to rise again if this could be combined with a French invasion of England, but he was not going to commit Charles until he felt convinced of the French intentions.

William MacGregor Balhaldy was one of a number of Scots who had arrived in Rome with messages of support from Scotland. In 1740 James sent Balhaldy to Paris to join with Lord Sempill, the Stuart agent, in entreating Louis XV to assist a Jacobite rising. However, the French were also being cautious. The war in Germany was not going well and they were anxious, once more, to play the Jacobite card; but, they wanted to be sure that the English Jacobites, as well as the Scottish Jacobites, would rise when the time came.

In 1743 Louis sent his equerry to England, ostensibly to buy horses but with instructions to gain information on the strength of British forces. The agent returned with glowing reports of Jacobite support and Louis decided upon an invasion of England. However, he realized it would need to be a surprise attack and he knew that the moment Charles Edward arrived in France the English spies would be alerted. On the other hand the English Jacobites had promised support only if the French carried documents from James investing Charles with powers of Regent. Louis wanted to get the documents from James and initiate the invasion of England before Charles arrived to give the game away. Charles could cross to England later. Louis, however, did not know that Charles's leash was near breaking point.

Balhaldy was instructed to return to Rome and bring back the necessary letters of authority from James but Louis purposefully omitted to supply Balhaldy with any written invitation to Charles. James was thrown into confusion: he did not want to miss an opportunity nor did he want to send his son on some haphazard venture without a formal invitation from the French. Louis had sent no details of his intentions and, quite apart from anything else, the journey to Paris was itself hazardous: a sea route was likely to meet with an English patrol, and on land the Mediterranean plague was raging and large areas were subject to quarantine restrictions. Balhaldy said he felt sure some French invasion was afoot and that was enough for Charles; he pressed his father to be allowed to go. In the end James left the decision to Charles and that settled the matter.

The utmost secrecy was vital if Charles was to have any chance of reaching France alive. Even Henry was kept in ignorance of the plans for his brother's departure. On 9 January 1744, before dawn, Charles left the Palazzo Muti with his attendants on the pretext of going boar hunting at Cisterna. He was never to see his father alive again.

A month later Charles arrived in Paris expecting a royal welcome and was perplexed by the cool reception he received from the French. Although England and France had been supporting opposite sides in the War of the Austrian Succession for three years the two countries had still to officially declare war upon each other. However, once Charles's presence became known, it did not take the English agents long to realize that the force that was being assembled at the coast was intended for England.

The French plans were shaken but Charles was summoned to Dunkirk to join Marshal Saxe. Once again the weather took control of Jacobite fortunes. The French transporters embarking Saxe's men were devastated by a severe storm and a number were lost with all hands. In addition the English fleet had been alerted and was now patrolling the Channel. This spelt the end of the French invasion plans. Charles remained in France but was left high and dry, abandoned to his fate. It was not till the summer of 1745 when, having been ignored by the French for over a year, his frustrations were finally relieved. An Irish ship-owner and privateer, Antoine Walsh, provided him with a 16-gun frigate, the *Du Teillay*. In addition he obtained the use of an escort, a 64-gun man o' war, the *Elisabeth*. The escort also carried 700 men from an Irish brigade serving in France and a quantity of arms. Charles and his seven companions, later to be known as the 'Seven Men of Moidart', boarded the *Du*

Teillay and set sail for Scotland. Off the coast of Ireland they were engaged by *HMS Lion*. The *Elisabeth* was badly damaged and forced to return to France. Thus it was that Charles and his small entourage arrived off the Isle of Eriskay, in the outer Hebrides, on 23 July 1745.

The 1745 Rebellion

This famous rebellion has been documented in great detail. In the history of the British Isles, for sheer audacity, it can have few equals; and, like many an audacious act, it enjoyed an undue measure of success. There has been a natural tendency to dwell upon the romantic legend rather than the consequent human suffering, but this is because people like to hear an exciting story, and a daring, close-run venture which just fails is often more gripping than one that succeeds. So it is with the 'Forty-five.

From the moment of his birth, Charles Stuart had been held by every Jacobite to be their shining star of hope. From the first dawning of self-awareness until his death Charles regarded himself as the God-given saviour of the Stuart cause. He was to prove unstable in character, uncaring towards his father, unloving towards his womenfolk, and unsteadfast in his religion but, in this one belief, he never wavered. Throughout he showed himself prepared to sacrifice his own life, and those of his followers, to further the Stuart cause, but he was to die bitter and frustrated by the total failure of all his efforts. However, the failure, the drunkenness and the degradation were in the future and, that day in July 1745, when Antoine Walsh brought the *Du Teillay* to anchor off the Isle of Eriskay, he was the prince of popular legend.

If the need for the *Elisabeth* to return to France, with the Irish troops and the supplies, had been a blow to Charles's confidence, then his reception on Eriskay could have done little to restore it. His first meeting, on board the *Du Teillay*, was with Alexander MacDonald of Boisdale from neighbouring South Uist. He informed Charles that Sir Alexander MacDonald of Sleat and Laird Macleod of Macleod, the Skye clan chiefs upon whom Charles had been relying for support, and who had previously promised to join him, did not intend to stand by the pledge they had made. Having arrived without French aid the advice was plain: 'Go home'. To which Charles replied: 'Home, I am come home, Sir.' He had been invited to Scotland and he had been biding his time in France long enough. In a letter written to his father before setting sail he had resolved 'to conquer or to dye' and, to him, the notion of returning to France was unthinkable.

Two days after arriving in Eriskay the *Du Teillay* set sail for the mainland coming to anchor in Loch-nan-Uamh, between Arisaig and Moidart. His reception here was no more encouraging but Charles's attitude remained the same: he declared his intention to raise his father's standard no matter how meagre the support and, as if to underline his resolve, after two weeks he gave Walsh a letter for Louis XV, announcing his arrival in Scotland, then sealed his fate by ordering him back to France in the *Du Teillay*.

Charles's determination was not altogether lost on the clan chiefs who visited him. They were doubtless encouraged by his assurances that French assistance would be on the way once Walsh got back to France but, it would be stretching credibility too far to imagine that the hard-headed clan leaders who threw in their lot with Charles were simply mesmerized by the young prince's charisma and their loyalty to the Stuart cause. Of course, ideology was important but so was self-interest, and inter-clan rivalry was also a cogent factor.

Although the clan chiefs were still lords of their glens they had come under increasing pressure from central government ever since the Act of Union. Many did not hold any definite legal title to their land, simply claiming the land by right of occupation and, in the eighteenth century, this ancient custom was coming under threat. Lochiel, the Cameron leader, whose support was so vital, only joined after Charles had agreed to indemnify him against future loss of his land.

Duncan Forbes, the Lord President for Scotland, had his agents in the Highlands and many clans had found it in their best interests to conform; there were substantial financial rewards for the clan leaders prepared to toe the government line. This may have been one of the reasons why the Skye clan leaders, Macleod of Dunvegan and MacDonald of Sleat, broke their pledge to Charles and took the Hanoverian side in the 'Forty-five. Forbes had done his work well. On his own conservative estimate the Highlands had the potential to put a rebel army in the field of over 30,000 armed men, yet at no time did Charles's army reach even a quarter of this number.

The clan chief possessed absolute power of life and death over the members of his clan. His authority exceeded that which any government in London might attempt to impose. Beneath the chief were the tacksmen, the gentry of the clan system, to whom the chief leased areas of land. They acted as landlords collecting rents from the tenants. When the chief made a call to arms the tacksmen had to see that their tenants complied on pain of having their bothies burnt down if they refused.

The ordinary Highlander lived a life of grinding poverty. It was a struggle to provide his family with basic nourishment. The land was poor and cattle rustling between neighbouring clans was commonplace. He swore a solemn oath of allegiance to his chief and his loyalty was strengthened by feelings of kinship: the belief that all clan members were blood relatives of the chief. Genealogical studies have shown that this was not universally true. When a Highlander joined a clan he would often assume the name of the clan and would change his name again if he later left to join another.

The Highlander was trained to arms and, fully equipped, might carry a musket, a dirk, a claymore, and possibly a targe. Man for man a regular soldier was no match for a Highlander on his home ground. A full-blooded Highland charge could strike terror into the most hardened trooper. What he lacked in formal training the Highlander made up with sheer ferocity. The technique would be to fire the musket before dropping to the ground while the enemy returned fire. Then, leaving the musket on the ground, he would draw his claymore and, with blood curdling yells, charge before his enemy had time to reload.

Charles came to believe that his Highlanders were invincible, a belief which was ultimately to cost Scotland dear. Many of these poor men were virtually pressed into service by their chiefs in the 'Forty-five and it says much for them that, once committed, they served Charles with such unstinting loyalty.

The clans were to gather at Glenfinnan, at the head of Loch Shiel, on 19 August, where today a commemorative monument stands. Charles left Kinlochmoidart on 17 August with a personal bodyguard of 50 Clanranald Highlanders and 150 men under the old Banffshire laird, Gordon of Glenbucket. While his men marched along the bank of Loch Shiel, Charles arrived at the head of the Loch by boat. This theatrical touch must have misfired somewhat when he stepped ashore for, instead of a cheering multitude, there was just a small band of 150 MacDonalds. Two hours passed while Charles waited despondently. The die was well and truly cast; he already had a price of £30,000 on his head and his promise to raise his father's standard, 'with the few friends that I have', began to have a hollow ring of truth about it. Then they heard the sound of distant pipes gradually getting louder and soon 700 Camerons, led by Lochiel, came zigzag down the hillside, followed shortly by 300 others. The ceremony of raising the standard and reading James's proclamation went ahead, and, once again, the Highlands gave birth to rebellion.

It has been said that Charles conquered most of Scotland by the simple expedient of walking from Glenfinnan to Edinburgh. Scotland's defences were depleted, as most of the government forces were in Flanders, and this had undoubtedly entered into Charles's calculations. The government commander in Scotland, Sir John Cope, was ordered to crush the rebels before the rising could take hold. As the standard was being raised at Glenfinnan, Cope was assembling some 1,500 troops at Stirling. The Jacobites were poorly equipped, virtually devoid of provisions, and totally undisciplined as an integrated army, but even so, Charles was anxious to engage Cope as soon as possible, before he had a chance to gain reinforcements. The rebel army headed north-east from Glenfinnan towards Fort Augustus, and Charles laid his trap in the steep Corriearrack pass. Cope, learning of the rebel plan, and realizing he would be at a disadvantage, wisely avoided an engagement, but, instead of keeping his force between the rebels and Edinburgh, moved north to Inverness. The Highlanders were frustrated; they now had the enemy behind them when they moved south. However, without at first realizing it, Charles had scored against his enemy because it was generally believed that Cope had been outwitted and the Prince, resplendent in a tartan outfit trimmed with gold, was able to ride into Perth in triumph at the head of his army, gathering adherents with every day that passed.

Charles was in Perth for a week and during this time his army doubled in size. New additions included the Duke of Perth himself and, most notably, Lord George Murray. A military man of great ability and high moral principle, Murray was one of the clan leaders acting out of ideological conviction. He had been 'out' in 1715 and 1719 and now, once again, he left his family and estates to follow a Stuart.

The Jacobites had to decide whether to march north and engage Cope or try to seize Edinburgh to the south. It did not take them long to decide upon the latter course, and when news came that Cope was heading for Aberdeen in order to take his army by sea to the Firth of Forth, the race for the capital was on. The rebel army left Perth on 11 September. They now numbered about 2,500 men and were a more coherent, disciplined force. By 16 September the Jacobites were camped outside Edinburgh. The following day they stormed the Netherbow gate when it was opened to let a coach pass, and gained entry to the capital. The local government troops were blockaded in Edinburgh Castle while Charles, with Lord Elcho and the Duke of

Colour Plate 2. James II, c.1690. By unknown artist. (NATIONAL PORTRAIT GALLERY)

Colour Plate 3. Mary Beatrice of Modena. By Wissing. (NATIONAL PORTRAIT GALLERY)

Perth on either side, rode through the city to the palace of Holyrood, the seat of his ancestors (Colour Plate 10). Meanwhile, Cope had arrived in the Firth of Forth and, while Charles was being proclaimed Prince Regent, Cope was completing the disembarkation of his troops at Dunbar.

So far the rebels had made their gains without any real trial of strength, but this was coming. News arrived that Cope had landed at Dunbar, 25 miles to the east, and had already started to close on the capital. His army was about equal in numbers to the Jacobites and, unlike the latter, was well equipped including cavalry and artillery. So it was that, just two days after their arrival in Edinburgh, the Jacobite army moved out to camp at the village of Duddingston east of the capital. On the morning of 20 September Charles addressed his army making an impassioned speech and, finally, drawing his sword, concluded: 'Gentlemen I have thrown away the scabbard; with God's assistance I don't doubt of making you a free and happy people.' The Highlanders flung their bonnets in the air, then, at the head of his men, Charles set out to meet his enemy.

Cope brought his army to occupy an area of low, level ground about nine miles east of Edinburgh, between the villages of Preston and Prestonpans in the west and Seton in the east. The Jacobite army came into view in the afternoon of 20 September and formed up in line of battle half a mile to the south, close by the village of Tranent. Cope immediately swung his front line round to face the Highlanders. The Jacobites were occupying slightly higher ground and, at first, it seemed they might be able to swoop down upon the government forces, but closer inspection revealed the strength of Cope's position. His army was on firm ground, a field of corn stubble, ideal for infantry, cavalry and artillery. Behind was the sea, to his right the protection of the tall walls and hedges surrounding Preston House, and in front of him, separating him from the Jacobite army, first a wide ditch then a deep morass of marshy ground,

Colour Plate 4. James Francis Edward Stuart. James III. By de Troy. (COURTESY DRAMBUIE LIQUEUR CO.)

Colour Plate 5. James's sister, Princess Louise Marie. By de Troy. (COURTESY DRAMBUIE LIQUEUR CO.)

making a Highland charge impossible. Cope stayed where he was and waited.

That evening an incident occurred which was to set the tone of the relationship between Charles and his senior general. Fearing that Cope might try to slip through to Edinburgh under cover of darkness, Charles ordered the Atholl brigade to guard the road. The Athollmen were under Lord George Murray (Colour Plate 11) and, upon hearing that his brigade had been moved without his knowledge, Lord George confronted the Prince, flung down his pistols in a rage, and 'swore God he'd never draw his sword for the cause if the Brigade was not brought back.' Charles, taken aback at this outburst, meekly acquiesced. This was the first of a number of disagreements between Charles and Lord George and it established Murray as the dominant character. He was to be responsible for many of the tactical decisions during the campaign, and many of the Jacobite successes, but, when the rebellion ultimately failed, he was to pay the price because the prince he had served so faithfully was to lay the blame at his door.

At a council meeting that evening Lord George put forward his plan for the forthcoming battle: to march eastward at daybreak, and then attack the enemy's left flank. The Jacobite camp settled for the night but Lord George was roused to be told that one of his men, Robert Anderson, a local man familiar with the area, knew of a track through the bog beyond the left flank of Cope's army. The plan was approved and in darkness the Highlanders silently struck camp, then, three abreast with Anderson leading the way, they started to cross the marshy ground. The horses were left behind so they could move without noise. At daybreak Cope's scouts raised the alarm as the Highlanders appeared, taking up battle positions in two ranks, facing the left flank of the Royal army. Cope rapidly swung his front line through ninety degrees to face the enemy.

The Battle of Prestonpans was fought on the morning of Saturday 21 September. Cope's army must have presented a daunting spectacle to the Highlanders: fully equipped soldiers, supported by cavalry and artillery, facing a Jacobite front rank having only dirks, claymores, and a variety of firearms. Some of the Highlanders had only the blades of scythes lashed onto poles. But, Cope's men were not as seasoned as their glittering accoutrements might have led one to suppose, and the sudden appearance of the Jacobite army on their left flank was unnerving.

The Highlanders, targes on their arms, dirks at the ready, bonnets pulled down and crouching low, started a slow menacing advance in silence. There was a brief exchange of fire, then, letting out a hideous cry, the Highlanders rushed Cope's men before they had time to reload. It was a rapid, murderous charge with claymores, dirks, Lochaber axes, and scythes. The government troops, terrified by the onslaught, turned and fled. The cavalry was thrown into confusion because the Highlanders adopted the tactic of attacking the horses rather than the riders; they lashed at the noses of the horses and the dragoons were helpless to control the poor demented animals as they turned and bolted through the ranks of their own infantry.

In ten minutes it was all over; the carnage was terrible. The fleeing troops found themselves trapped by the walls and hedges of Preston House, and were hacked down by the Highlanders. The Jacobite losses were recorded as 34 killed and 76 wounded, while Cope's were in excess of 300 killed and 400 wounded. Fewer than 200 government troops escaped; the remainder, some 1,500, were taken prisoner. Cope, after making several attempts to rally his men, escaped to Berwick, where he was accused, rather unkindly, of being the only general to bring news of his own defeat.

The Highlanders returned to Edinburgh with the pipes playing: 'The King shall enjoy his own again.' It was less than five weeks since the raising of the standard and the Jacobites had control of Scotland. In London, news of the defeat at Prestonpans was received with consternation; the previously held belief that the rising would be quickly and easily contained was shattered.

Charles was now convinced that he could achieve anything with his Highlanders. He wanted to pursue Cope to Berwick and then press on into England and engage Marshal Wade's army at Newcastle. His goal was London and the restoration of the Stuart dynasty. The clan chiefs, however, were more concerned to see Scotland restored as an independent nation; they were bitterly opposed to the Act of Union and now the Jacobites had control of Scotland, Lord George Murray wanted to remain in Edinburgh and consolidate their position. Charles continued to argue for an invasion of England and, when three French ships arrived with some arms and a few French gunners, he was able to remind his followers that they were not forgotten. In the end he won his way in the council and, after six weeks in the capital, the Jacobite army, numbering about 5,000 foot and 500 horse, moved out on 31 October

Plate 2. During the Jacobite occupation of Edinburgh, the Castle refused to surrender and was put under siege. The commanding officer threatened to open fire on the capital unless communications with the city were restored and provisions allowed into the Castle. This letter is Prince Charles's reply to the City Deputies who delivered the message. (COURTESY DRAMBUIE LIQUEUR CO.)

His Royal Highness the prince of wailess ansure
To the Gentlmen who were Sent Deputies from
the City of Edinbrough with a Letter from General
Guist Threatning. That unless the Cummainication
Betwixt the City and Castle was opened. they wold
fire upon the City

Gentlemen

I am Equaley Suprised and Concerned at the barbarity
of the orders y: have ben signified to you from the Castle
Ano which those who Command in it Say they have
Recived from the Elector of hanover. at the Same time
That they own they have Six weeks provisions Left
if he Look upon you as his subjects he would never
Exact from you what he Knows it is not in your —
poure te do. and Should we. out of Compassion
to you Comply with this Extravagant Demand
of his. he might as well Summon us to Quite the
Soun. and abandon those advantages which providence
has Granted us by Crouning the Valoure of our troops
with Such Signal Sucess. Shall be hartley
Sorey for any Mischief y: May befall the City, and
Shall make it my peculiar Care to Indemnify you in
the most ample Maner. In the mine time. I Shall
make full reprisals upon the Estates of those who are
Known to be open Abettors of the gearman —
Gouerment. if I am forced to it by the Continuance
of Inhumanities — Holy rood house sepbr 30
Charles p: R: 1745

Colour Plate 6. James III & VIII, from contemporary painting by Mengs. (NATIONAL PORTRAIT GALLERY)

Colour Plate 7. Maria Clementina Sobieska by Trevisani. (NATIONAL PORTRAIT GALLERY)

and headed south. On 8 November they forded the Esk and entered England.

Carlisle capitulated with little resistance and, leaving a small garrison behind in Carlisle Castle, the rebel army moved quickly through Penrith, Shap, Kendal and Lancaster, arriving in Preston on 27 November. Although they had encountered no resistance the signs were worrying. Lancashire was known to be pro-Jacobite; this was, after all, one of the reasons why Lord George had chosen this route through England; yet, they had had no more than a trickle of new recruits. Moving through Wigan and Leigh they arrived in Manchester on 29 November. Here the support was a little more promising and a new regiment was formed consisting entirely of Englishmen, to be known as the Manchester Regiment, but at no time did it number more than 300 men. What had happened to Lord Barrymore and the other English Jacobites, and where was Sir Watkin Williams Wynn with the Welsh Jacobites? The clan chiefs were becoming restless and beginning to doubt the wisdom of continuing the advance into England. But Charles, spurred on by the speed of their advance, remained confident. He left Manchester on 1 December, marching at the head of his troops. He was wearing tartan dress with a blue sash and on his head a blue velvet bonnet with a white cockade.

The Jacobite army moved through Stockport to Macclesfield and here Lord George displayed some of his tactical skills. The rebels had left Marshal Wade's army well behind but they were now close to the Duke of Cumberland's army coming up from the south (Colour Plate 12). His forward troops were only a few miles away at Newcastle-under-Lyme. Lord George, taking 1,200 men, moved towards Congleton and engaged Cumberland's advanced guard. Cumberland, believing the Jacobites were either marching to engage him or heading for Wales, withdrew to Stone and waited

Colour Plate 8. Miniature of Prince Charles Edward Stuart. Italian School, c.1735. (COURTESY DRAMBUIE LIQUEUR CO.)

Colour Plate 9. Miniature of Prince Henry Benedict Stuart. Italian School, c.1735. (COURTESY DRAMBUIE LIQUEUR CO.)

to encounter the rebels. This left the road to Derby and the south wide open. Charles moved on to Leek and joined up with Lord George at Ashbourne. On 4 December the first Highland troops entered Derby. Cumberland had been outmanoeuvred and the road to London was open. Charles was exultant; he was within a few days of achieving his goal. Oblivious of the imminent dangers he saw only the fulfilment of his dreams. But Lord George was less sanguine about the Jacobite situation, and the fateful council meeting in the oak panelled drawing room of Exeter House in Derby on 5 December, was to bring Charles's euphoria to an abrupt standstill. The clan chiefs were not prepared to proceed any further. They realized, only too well, that once they left Derby for London it would be all or nothing; the return to Scotland would no longer be an option. Wade's army was coming down from the north and Cumberland's army was 30 miles to the west, each considerably larger than the Jacobite army. And even though the road to London was open they would still have to deal with 4,000 militia on the outskirts of the capital, at Finchley. They were no longer prepared to accept bland assurances of help from the English Jacobites and the French. Another week and it would be too late. What contact had Charles had with the English and Welsh Jacobites since he came to Scotland? What did he actually know of the French invasion plans? They wanted answers and Charles had none.

The retreat started the next day, 'Black Friday', 6 December. The Highlanders who, like Charles, had been at the peak of expectation, found themselves retracing their steps. Charles was almost too despondent to bother, but it was going to need all Lord George Murray's skill to get the army back to Scotland intact. Two days after the Jacobites left Derby a Doctor Barry arrived with messages of support from Sir Watkin Williams Wynn and Lord Barrymore.

Lord George Murray's principal concern was that Wade might cut across the Pennines and block their retreat enabling Cumberland to overhaul them, but Wade was too slow. However, Cumberland's forward troops did engage the Jacobite rearguard under Lord George on the road to Penrith. Murray had been delayed, struggling up Shap Fell with heavy baggage waggons in freezing snow and mud. Charles was already in Penrith with the van of the Jacobite army. Lord George, upon learning that the force which had engaged him represented only a quarter of Cumberland's main army of 8,000 men, saw an opportunity to inflict a defeat on the enemy. He sent an urgent message to Charles to return with the rest of the Jacobite army, but Charles refused and would only supply enough troops to get Lord George out of trouble. An opportunity was missed but this was not the only bizarre decision made by Charles in his apathy.

When the army reached Carlisle a small Jacobite garrison was left behind in Carlisle Castle to face Cumberland. This consisted of some 300 men mainly from the Manchester Regiment. When Cumberland arrived the castle presented him with little difficulty and the men were captured. They were eventually sent for trial and, being an English regiment, they received particularly harsh treatment. Charles is usually blamed for the sacrifice of these men, and as commander-in-chief he has to take ultimate responsibility, but the Manchester Regiment stayed behind at the request of its commander, Colonel Francis Townley.

The Jacobite army left Carlisle on 20 December, the Prince's birthday, and crossed the swollen Esk into Scotland. On 26 December they entered Glasgow where Charles stayed for a week. On 3 January 1746, the same day that the Jacobites moved out of Glasgow, the Duke of Cumberland, having given up the immediate pursuit, left Carlisle and returned to London; the main worry of the government in the south now being the possibility of a French invasion. Meanwhile, on 24 December, General 'Hangman' Hawley, who was with Cumberland in Carlisle, was appointed to succeed Marshal Wade. He moved to Newcastle and took over command of the government forces. Leaving Newcastle on 2 January, his army was in Edinburgh by the 6th.

Two days after leaving Glasgow, Charles was taken ill with influenza and for two weeks languished in Brannockburn House being nursed by Clementina Walkinshaw. When he recovered his next objective was the capture of Stirling and once again the town was no problem but Stirling Castle was a different story. The Jacobites laid seige to the castle but failed to gain any advantage.

Hawley felt nothing but contempt for the Highlanders and when he decided to march to relieve Stirling he fully expected the rebels to turn and run. Far from doing this the Jacobites marched to meet him. The wily Lord George suggested gaining some high ground southwest of Falkirk. This was the Hill of Falkirk, a steep ridge of moorland a mile from Hawley's camp. Hawley was confidently eating his lunch when news arrived that the whole Jacobite army was marching to gain the high ground. He had to rush from the dining table to prepare his troops and urge them to gain Falkirk Hill before the Jacobites. But the Highlanders won the race and, when they came to face the enemy, they found they also had the wind at their backs. The winter rain that had started to fall was driving straight into the faces of Hawley's infantry, soaking their firearms and rendering most of them unserviceable. Hawley ordered his cavalry to charge and his infantry to fix bayonets, but he was soon to learn that the Highlanders he despised so much were no disorderly rabble. With the wind at their backs they were able to keep their powder dry, and Lord George waited until the dragoons were within about twelve paces before giving the order to fire. The effect was devastating, some 80 dragoons falling dead in the instant. The Highlanders, not bothering to reload, fell upon the remaining cavalry attacking the horses and dragging their riders from the saddle. The cavalry turned and fled, riding through their own infantry struggling up the hill. As the Highlanders charged panic set in and Hawley's troops broke and scattered. For Hawley it was a complete fiasco and he was only spared from total humiliation by his second in command, General Huske, who managed to keep the Hanoverian right wing intact.

Cumberland now returned to take command of the government forces, arriving in Edinburgh on 30 January. However, when he reached Falkirk, he discovered that the rebel army had abandoned the seige of Stirling Castle. The Jacobites were heading for Inverness and Cumberland followed Lord George's column as far as Perth. There he halted for a while to obtain provisions for his men. Then he moved to Aberdeen on 27 February and again he halted to build up his supplies. He was to stay in Aberdeen for six weeks making sure that everything was ready for the forthcoming encounter.

Since leaving Glasgow Charles had been plagued with illness. First the influenza at Brannockburn then, at Moy on 16 February, he was forced to flee from the home of Lady Mackintosh in the middle of the night to avoid capture by Lord Loudoun's government troops. Wearing only his night attire he caught another cold and developed a chest infection. He spent most of February recovering in Culloden House outside Inverness. In March he became ill again, this time with scarlet fever.

Inverness had capitulated to the Jacobites and, while Charles was out of action, Lord George made several forays into the neighbouring Highlands achieving some spectacular successes, including the capture of Fort Augustus and the dispersal of Lord Loudoun's forces. He also laid siege to Blair Castle and Fort William. These were the sort of exploits that suited the Highlanders on their home ground and Lord George confidently maintained that with these tactics he could gradually wear down the government forces, over a period of years if necessary.

This was all very well but the Jacobites seemed to be ignoring the immediate threat: Cumberland. With Teutonic thoroughness the Duke had been resting his men, waiting for the better weather, and stocking up with necessary provisions. He now had a number of supply ships ready to follow him along the coastal route and provide for all his needs. In contrast, the Jacobite army as a whole was in a deplorable state. The reality of the decision to return to the Highlands was now coming home. The truth was that the barren Highlands could not support an army of this size. Bottled-up in Inverness, and deprived of the richer pickings in Lowland Scotland, there was neither the money to pay, nor the food to feed, the Jacobite army. It had been a hard winter, provisions were desperately low, and the men had been without pay for several weeks. The shortage of money became so acute that Charles was obliged to instruct a Jacobite engraver, Robert Strange, to design and print some bank notes for him. The Jacobites needed outside assistance, but the government was now in a position to intercept foreign aid destined for the rebels, and the capture by the Hanoverians of a supply ship from France, bringing several thousand pounds in gold for the Jacobites, was a bitter blow for Charles.

In addition, the Jacobite army was depleted. With the coming of spring there had been some desertions but, more serious, was the fact that several units were still scattered in the Highlands on various assignments. Keppoch and Lochiel's men were

Colour Plate 10. Prince Charles entering the ballroom at Holyrood. By John Pettie. (REPRODUCED BY GRACIOUS PERMISSION OF H.M. THE QUEEN)

Colour Plate 11. Lord George Murray. (FROM THE DUKE OF ATHOLL'S COLLECTION AT BLAIR CASTLE, PERTHSHIRE)

Colour Plate 12. William, Duke of Cumberland, c.1748. School of D. Morier. (NATIONAL PORTRAIT GALLERY)

Colour Plate 13. 'A Jacobite Incident: Culloden'. By D. Morier. (REPRODUCED BY GRACIOUS PERMISSION OF H.M. THE QUEEN)

laying siege to Fort William while Mackenzies, MacGregors and MacDonalds were further north pursuing the remnants of Loudoun's force. In all it is estimated that some 2,000 Highlanders were absent from Inverness when the long-awaited encounter became imminent.

News arrived that Cumberland had left Aberdeen on 8 April and was advancing with his entire army. The Duke had waited until the Spey was low enough to get his men across. Even so, his army was vulnerable at this point, yet for some inexplicable reason, Charles failed to contest Cumberland's crossing of the Spey, and by 14 April the government army was camped at Nairn, some seventeen miles from Inverness. That same day Charles led his men out of Inverness to Culloden Park, near to Culloden House where Charles himself was quartered. The armies were twelve miles apart; Cumberland's well fed and rested, the Highlanders half starved with hardly any food left.

Charles, as usual, was anxious to engage Cumberland as soon as possible. Lord George, realizing the situation was becoming desperate, suggested three possible courses of action: to disperse into the Highlands and reform at a later date; to retire to Inverness and occupy a defensive position; or, if Charles insisted on confronting Cumberland in battle, to occupy a site on the opposite side of the River Nairn where the terrain was ideal for the Highlanders, since it was undulating, rough ground which would make it difficult for Cumberland to use his artillery. Charles dismissed all these suggestions. He was adamant that he was going to confront Cumberland in battle, and his chosen ground was Drummossie Moor, a mile south of Culloden House. Lord George pointed out that this ground was firm and flat, ideal for Cumberland's artillery and cavalry, but totally unsuitable for the Highlanders. Charles, however, had made up his mind and refused to listen.

Then, the notion of a night raid arose. The Jacobite army could approach Cumberland's encampment under cover of darkness and fall upon the government troops as they slept in their tents. It seemed a desperate plan but the 'commando style' tactics had an immediate appeal for Charles. To be fair he also realized that his men were starving and that if he did not face Cumberland in the next day or two his Highlanders would be incapable of fighting at all. Lord George and some of the others reluctantly agreed, if only because they could see the folly of the Prince's alternative plan of meeting Cumberland on Drummossie Moor.

The Nairn raid was a total farce. The Jacobite army was delayed setting out on the evening of 15 April because many of the desperate Highlanders went back to Inverness to look for food. The march to Nairn was further delayed by the nature of the ground they had to cover. The Jacobites totally miscalculated the time it would take to move the army the ten or so miles to Nairn in darkness. When they had covered three-quarters of the distance it was quite clear they were not going to reach Cumberland's camp before dawn and they were forced to turn back.

The exhausted Highlanders who arrived back at Culloden in the morning on 16 April were the same men who, a few hours later, had to form battle lines as Cumberland's troops, fresh and fit, advanced in regular ranks on to Drummossie Moor about midday.

It can be said, of course, that all armed conflict is sad and depressing; nevertheless, the detailed accounts of certain battles can make exciting reading. Not so the Battle of Culloden (Colour Plate 13). Whether you happen to support the Hanoverian or the Jacobite point of view, Culloden is a depressing battle. Perhaps it is the inevitability of the outcome or, possibly, the knowledge that it was only the beginning of what was to be brutal suppression. Whatever the rights and wrongs of the 'Forty-five rising the rebel army had always fought with imagination and flair. They now seemed to have burnt themselves out. Given the immense superiority of Cumberland's fire power, and the fact that he was fighting on terrain which gave his artillery free reign, and was ideally suited to his troops, the Jacobites were without hope. Mutilating grape-shot from the Duke's cannon had a devastating effect and the Highlanders fell by the score. Those who escaped the grape-shot had to clamber over the bodies of their fallen comrades to engage Cumberland's bayonets. Once the Jacobites were in retreat Cumberland ordered his troops in pursuit and large numbers of the rebels were cut down on the road to Inverness. Wounded Highlanders were shot or bayoneted and the dead and dying were to be found many miles from the battlefield.

Prince Charles, meanwhile, had been escorted from his chosen field of battle, convinced he had been betrayed, especially by Lord George Murray who, more than anyone, had been responsible for the Jacobite successes.

The Aftermath

The Prince's five months as a fugitive in the Highlands, his adventures in the Outer Hebrides and on the Isle of Skye before his final escape to France, the devoted assistance of legendary figures such as Flora MacDonald and the old boatman, Donald MacLeod; all this is another story. The Battle of Culloden was the last battle to be fought on British soil. For the Jacobites in the 'Forty-five, it was their only defeat, but it was final. It is estimated that over 2,000 Highlanders died at Culloden, Cumberland's casualties numbering some 300 wounded and killed.

The carnage at Culloden could have been avoided. Lord George Murray had favoured dispersal of the Jacobite army in order to fight a guerrilla war rather than the pitched battle against hopeless odds. After Culloden he penned an angry letter to Charles in which he said: 'It was surely wrong to set up the Royal Standard without having positive assurance from his most Christian Majesty that he would assist you with all his might.' This was doing no more than state the obvious but Charles, who had gravely miscalculated the likely response of the French, resented Lord George's forthright assertion and never forgave him.

In an age which was no stranger to cruelty the brutal excesses of the British troops after Culloden were to gain for Cumberland the sobriquet of 'Butcher'. Cumberland held his enemy in contempt and he was clearly disinclined to bring his troops to heel when they lost control. Whether he actually instructed his officers to give no quarter is disputed but at best his orders were ambiguous and as commander-in-chief he is rightly held to be responsible.

If after the 1715 rising there had been a tendency to show leniency, this was certainly not so after the 'Forty-five. In suppressing the Highlands the Duke's men plundered showing no mercy. 'Butcher' Cumberland returned to London in July, leaving behind a strong military presence. At a thanksgiving service in St. Paul's cathedral Handel's 'The Conquering Hero', which had been specially composed for the Duke, received its first public performance.

In May 1746 an Act of Attainder was passed naming forty-one of the more prominent rebels. They lost their titles and their property was taken over by the Crown. They were

Colour Plate 14. Pair of Jacobite wine glasses, each engraved with a rose, two buds and an oak leaf. H. 15.6cm. [A]. (COURTESY DRAMBUIE LIQUEUR CO.)

Colour Plate 15. Jacobite tumbler engraved with a portrait of Prince Charles, a rose, two buds, a thistle and a crown. H. 10.5cm. [B]. (COURTESY DRAMBUIE LIQUEUR CO.)

declared guilty of treason and could be executed without trial if captured. Most, including Lord George Murray, escaped to the Continent. Murray came to Paris in 1747 seeking reconciliation with Charles but the Prince refused to see him.

Four peers stood trial before parliament and all were found guilty. Lord Kilmarnock and Lord Balmerino, who had been captured at Culloden, had no defence and bravely met their deaths on the executioner's block. Likewise, the elderly Lord Lovat, whose fate was sealed when John Murray of Broughton turned King's evidence and testified against him. The fourth peer, Lord Cromartie, had been taken prisoner before Culloden and was reprieved after his wife made an emotional plea for mercy to the King.

Although the government was intent on making sure that there would be no further Jacobite risings, it was more concerned with the ringleaders than the common rebel. As Speck points out: 'The macabre fascination of the state trials, and grim spectacle of death on the block or the gibbet, with its attendant theatre of last meals, mob-lined processions, dying speeches and heads impaled on gateways, can give an undue emphasis to the axe and the rope in the aftermath of the 'Forty-five.'[4] However, there were at least 120 executions, the garrison at Carlisle, which consisted mainly of the Manchester Regiment, faring worst of all: of just over 300 taken prisoner, 70 were executed after trial. In addition. many prisoners died in the overcrowded jails and large numbers were deported to the colonies for life, many of them dying unaccounted for, in the filthy, insanitary, holds of the ships that transported them.

In August 1746 the Disarming Act was passed making it illegal for anyone in the Highlands to carry or conceal any arms, including the broadsword. The wearing of Highland dress also became illegal and many Scots left their homeland to make a new life for themselves in the Colonies.

The Highlanders had displayed great bravery in the 'Forty-five; their cause had been a daring one; their leader, young, inexperienced and impulsive. For an instant it had even seemed possible that they might succeed in overthrowing the Hanoverian regime. But, Jacobitism was now a spent force and the 'cause' was lost irretrievably.

CHAPTER 2
Charles Edward Stuart

Colour Plate 16. Jacobite decanter engraved with a rose, two buds, oak leaves, a compass, a star and 'fiat'. H. 18.5cm. [B].
(COURTESY DRAMBUIE LIQUEUR CO.)

More needs to be said about this man. His brief appearance upon the world stage during the 1745 Rebellion was sufficient to project him into legend. He presented a romantic image in the 18th century and continues to do so today; the gallant loser who has become one of history's enigmatic heroes. In this sense history has been kind to him, because he is still largely remembered for his exploits in the 'Forty-five. In preserving the romantic image a screen is pulled down on the unnecessary loss of life, on the suffering that followed in the wake of his enterprise, and on the subsequent degradation in his own life: the alcoholism; the disruptive, sometimes violent, behaviour; the refusal to reconcile his differences with his father, despite the pleading letters from Rome, and with Lord George Murray, who lost everything in the Prince's cause; the abuse and neglect of Clementina Walkinshaw and their daughter, Charlotte; all of which occurred during a period of over forty years after the rebellion, that is the greater part of his life, until his death as an embittered old man in 1788. No one is more aware of the devastation that followed after the 1745 rising than the Scots,

Colour Plate 17. Prince Henry Stuart, Cardinal Duke of York. See p.54. (NATIONAL PORTRAIT GALLERY)

whose country suffered most on his account, yet, Bonnie Prince Charlie lives on in the Scottish tourist industry and in popular imagination.

On the other hand, serious historians have often dismissed Charles Stuart as an unintelligent non-entity; an unstable, irresponsible egotist, playing with the lives of others; a rash adventurer, using his charisma to lure his followers to their destruction; the subsequent disintegration of his character being proof of his fundamental weakness and the futility of his attempt to restore the Stuart dynasty, an attempt which was doomed to failure before it even started. The 1745 rising is a paradox because, of all the Jacobite attempts, it should have had the least chance of success and yet, despite all the difficulties, it came within an ace of succeeding. But, how much of the surprising success, and how much of the ultimate failure, was due to Charles Stuart? What is the truth about this remarkable man?

When Charles was called to his great adventure he was twenty-five and all authorities agree that he was at the peak of physical fitness. Never studious in the academic sense, he was very much a physical person. As a keen huntsman he was an expert shot and a fine horseman. He was tall in stature with reddish hair, brown eyes, and a ruddy complexion. There is no doubt that he had charisma, such as that found in his great uncle, Charles II, but so lacking in his own father. His appearance and personality had a striking impact on most who met him. His affability also extended to the common man, which is one of the reasons why his Highlanders were so devoted to him. Far from distancing himself from his men, he enjoyed identifying with the ordinary Highlander. Not for him the comfort of the carriage. He marched with his men, often ate the same food, and shared many of their hardships. Nor was he lacking in courage, showing at times an almost reckless disregard for his own safety. His physical fitness was to stand him in good stead during his months in the heather after Culloden when, frequently undernourished and exposed to the elements, he did well to survive, let alone escape. In many ways it was during this extreme hardship that his courage and his character seemed at their best.

Unlike the victor of Culloden, Cumberland, whom history remembers as the 'Butcher', Charles showed himself to have a merciful and compassionate nature, halting the slaughter after Prestonpans -'They are my fathers subjects',- and seeing that the wounded and the prisoners were treated humanely.

All very positive attributes; the archetypal hero. So what was wrong?

Charles had a traumatic, albeit privileged, early childhood. He was only five, and Prince Henry had just been born, when the dispute arose between his parents over the dismissal, by James, of Mrs Sheldon, Charles's governess. Following what, at first, seemed like a marital tiff, Clementina and her retinue took sanctuary in a convent. The incident then hardened into a prolonged rift, as James stubbornly exerted his authority. The marital separation, which became the gossip of Europe and which was so damaging to the Jacobite cause, must have had a detrimental effect upon the young Charles Edward. Clementina returned to James after two years, but, having been deprived of a mother all this time, Charles now found he was faced with a woman who was neurotic and clearly in the grip of some mental illness. Religious mania and fasting reduced Clementina to a chronic invalid before she died in 1735. She was thirty-four, Charles just fourteen. It is likely that Charles's subsequent inability to face the disappointment of failure with the dignity that his father always displayed, was due in no small measure to the immature, unstable, behaviour of his mother, which, compared with the strength and wisdom of his grandmother, Mary of Modena, would account for this fundamental difference between father and son. The lack of healthy mother love may also have been responsible for Charles's inability in later life to form stable, lasting, relationships with women. His brother Henry's answer was to be the priesthood, celibacy and homosexuality.

Henry applied himself to his books more diligently than did Charles, thereby becoming James's favoured son. And James, although devoted to his Carluccio, was not beyond making unfavourable comparisons when trying to make Charles conform to his ideals. In their early life the brothers were apparently devoted to one another, but Charles's relationship with his father was always less than satisfactory. James could not help carping about things, with little in the way of light relief. He came to be the voice of authority that Charles resented in later life.

Charles could be incredibly stubborn and anyone telling him what he should do was likely to have a difficult time if he disagreed with them. Whether it came in reproving letters from his father, or advice from the vastly more experienced Lord George Murray, or obstructive tactics by the French government, his reaction, when he could not get his own way, tended to be the same: first, a stubborn, sulky resistance; then dislike, turning to downright hatred and paranoia, out of all proportion to the initial disagreement. This is not to say that Charles was always wrong; some of his ideas often revealed a degree of awareness greater than that of his advisers.

It has sometimes been said that Charles lacked intelligence; that he was a blockhead, schooled from birth for a task for which he was not mentally equipped. In many ways Charles's intelligence is central to the interpretation of the 'Forty-five. As will become clear, with many of the decisions taken in the course of the rising, Charles's reasoning was not always as rash as might at first appear. His poor spelling is sometimes cited as evidence of his lack of intelligence, but this is nonsense. Charles's badly spelt letters make much more lively reading than the perfectly composed epistles from his father; and it should be remembered that he was brought up in Italy, not England, and he also spoke French. One of Charles's letters, quoted by McLynn in his biography *Charles Edward Stuart* is reproduced here in full.[1] The spelling has been corrected.

The Jacobite army is retreating from Derby and, having crossed the border into Scotland a couple of weeks earlier, Charles is laid low with influenza and is being cared for by Clementina Walkinshaw in Brannockburn House. Since being thwarted at Derby the Prince has stubbornly refused to call any council meetings and the relationship between Lord George Murray and Charles has been cold and hostile. Lord George presents himself at Brannockburn House suggesting that, in emergencies, decisions should be taken by a committee of regimental commanders and, rubbing salt into the Prince's wounds, reminds him that it was the majority decision taken at Derby which saved the army from destruction, and that if Charles had called a council meeting at Lancaster they could have avoided spending an extra day there. He then went on to mention the loss of Carlisle. Charles penned the following reply to Lord George:

'When I came into Scotland I knew well enough what I was to expect from my enemies, but I little foresaw what I meet with from my friends. I came vested with all the authority the King could give me, one chief part of which is the command of his armies, and now I am required to give this up to fifteen or sixteen persons, who may afterwards depute five or six of their own number to exercise it, for fear if they were six or eight that I might myself pretend to the casting vote. By the majority of these all things are to be determined, and nothing left to me but the honour of being present at their debates. This I am told is the method of all armies and this I flatly deny, nor do I believe it to be the method of any one army in the world. I am often hit in the teeth that this is an army of volunteers, and consequently very different from one composed of mercenaries. What one would naturally expect from an army whose chief officers consist of gentlemen of rank and fortune, and who came into it merely from motives of duty and honour, is more zeal, more resolution and more good manners than in those that fight merely for pay: but it can be no army at all where there is no general, or which is the same thing no obedience or deference paid to him. Everyone knew before he engaged in the cause, what he was to expect in case it miscarried, and should have stayed at home if he could not face death in any shape: but can I myself hope for better usage? At least I am the only person upon whose head a price has been already set, and therefore I cannot indeed threaten at every other word to throw down my arms and make my peace with the government. I think I show every day that I do not pretend to act without taking advice, and yours oftener than any body's else, which I shall continue to do, and you know that upon more occasions than one, I have given up my own opinion to that of others. I stayed indeed a day at Lancaster without calling a Council, yet yourself proposed to stay another but I wonder to see myself reproached with the loss of Carlisle. Was there a possibility to carrying off the cannon and the baggage, or was there time to destroy them? And would not the doing it have been a greater dishonour to our arms? After all did not you yourself instead of proposing to abandon it, offer to stay with the Atholl Brigade to defend it?

I have insensibly made this answer much longer than I intended, and might yet add much more, but I choose to cut it short, and shall only tell you that my authority may be taken from me by violence, but I shall never resign it like an idiot.'

As McLynn says: 'Anyone who still clings to the canard that Charles Edward Stuart was an unintelligent Italian princeling should ponder that letter: concise, lucid and shrewd.'[2]

Perhaps what gives Charles Stuart the 'rash adventurer' image more than anything else is his arrival in Scotland in 1745 with a handful of companions. If this was not rash what on earth was? But his unannounced arrival in Scotland needs to be considered against the background of events following the collapse of the French invasion plans in March 1744.

Charles's arrival in Paris on 8 February 1744 caused consternation in the French government. Who had invited him? Would it not destroy their invasion plans? Indeed it is more than likely that it was Charles's presence in Paris which alerted the English to the imminence of the French invasion. When he moved to the coast and arrived at Gravelines there was no longer any doubt. Charles was soon at loggerheads with the French. When storms decimated the French invasion fleet and Marshal Saxe called off the expedition, the sparks began to fly. The French believed that Charles's premature arrival had scuttled their invasion plans, and Charles accused the French of cowardice and incompetence. Many in his position would have returned to Rome but not the Prince. He insisted that the French should mount another invasion. But Louis XV was not going to be told what he should or should not do and he asked Charles to retire, incognito, to Soissons. Charles refused. Repeated requests followed but the Prince was defiant. So began his lifelong mistrust and dislike of the French. His presence on their soil was an embarrassment to the French but this does not excuse their deplorable treatment of him during 1744-45. Louis made vague promises he had no intention of keeping, stringing the Jacobites along and passing their requests from one minister to another. Charles for his part continued to goad the French by making surprise public appearances when he was supposed to be incognito. James, alarmed at his son's behaviour, and not wanting to upset the French, preached patient diplomacy; not what Charles wanted to hear.

He set his mind on a landing in Scotland and with borrowed money began to store arms and ammunition. Through Antoine Walsh he gained the use of the *Du Teillay* and then the *Elisabeth*, without the French having any knowledge of his real intentions.

Charles knew that his father's patient diplomacy would get him nowhere. He was well aware that the French only wanted to use the Jacobites for their nuisance value and would never initiate a Stuart restoration; they would only act when they saw the Jacobites themselves making some headway. Charles had no intention of acknowledging defeat and returning to Rome. He was taking what to him seemed the only logical course of action: he was making the first move and gambling that the French would join in when they saw the opportunity he had created. It was a calculated decision; and, of course, he had no means of knowing that the *Elisabeth* would be forced to return to France with the arms he had gathered and the 700 men of the Irish brigade.

Of the 'Forty-five it has been said that, after the Battle of Prestonpans, the Jacobites made three crucial decisions which were all blunders, and that on each occasion Charles was in disagreement with his council. The first time he got his own way and was wrong; on the other two occasions he was right but was overruled by his council. The first two decisions were taken in Edinburgh. The Jacobites were in control of Scotland. The clan chiefs had promised Charles to regain the throne of Scotland for the Stuarts and, so far as Lord George Murray was concerned, they had achieved their objective. Lord George said they should consolidate their position and wait for the French to lend support. Charles said that he had promised his father to regain the English throne as well as that of Scotland, and he argued that they needed to maintain momentum; if the Highlanders stayed too long in Edinburgh they would lose interest and begin to drift away. Moreover, money supplies were low and if the army had to be maintained without pay the desertion rate would increase further. Charles wanted to advance into England and engage Marshal Wade at Newcastle; another victory, this time on English soil, was, he said, essential to persuade the clans that had not yet joined them to come over to their side, and also to rouse the English Jacobites. Murray had little faith in the English Jacobites but, if England was to be invaded, he favoured a route through the north-west of England, which was supposed to be strongly Jacobite. This route, he said, would also confuse the Hanoverians into believing that they might be heading for Wales to join up with Sir Watkin Williams Wynn.

Charles won the vote on the invasion of England but Lord George won on the north-west route. It is not possible to say whether Charles was right to insist on his 'forward momentum' strategy of invading England. If the Jacobites had remained in Edinburgh it would really have depended upon how quickly the French might have sent assistance. Louis XV was not known for decisive action and the Hanoverians would not have allowed the rebels to maintain a defensive position for long; they would soon have mounted a massive counter attack which the Jacobites might have been powerless to resist. Charles's strategy of engaging Wade and taking the shortest route to London had much to commend it. The Jacobite army would have been a good match for Wade and a victory on English soil would have been a tremendous psychological boost to the rebel campaign. Whatever the rights or wrongs of the arguments, they show that Charles was no madman; his reasoning was sound and displayed a flair for fast-moving military strategy. He saw the opportunities and was prepared to seize the moment. In this sense he was ahead of his time, for the eighteenth century was still the age of ponderous set battles with armies taking days and weeks to square up to one another.

The third crucial decision, the retreat from Derby, is one of history's great controversies. Murray argued that their situation was grave and the army in great danger; they should return while they still had the chance and build up their strength in Scotland. The clan leaders agreed with him and, on the face of it, this course of action seemed the only sensible one to adopt. They had penetrated to the very heart of England yet the response from the English Jacobites had been virtually non-existent, nor had there been any word from the French. They were threatened by three armies: Cumberland's, Wade's and the militia at Finchley. The Jacobite army consisted of about 5,500 men and Murray believed the opposing forces were probably four times this number. He argued that to continue the advance on London would be suicidal; their line of retreat would be severed and they would have to succeed or risk being totally annihilated.

But again, Charles's instinct that the advance on London should continue was probably, on balance, correct. Wade was coming down from the north but was still a long way off. The militia encamped on Finchley Common numbered some 4,000 but their disorderly departure from the Tottenham Court Road turnpike, as immortalized by William Hogarth in his *March to Finchley* (Plate 3), does little to encourage the belief that they would have been any match for a Highland army within sight of its goal. Cumberland's army had taken the bait that Lord George Murray had offered and was 30 miles to the west. His troops had been making forced marches and were exhausted while the Highlanders, like Charles, were in high spirits and eager either to face Cumberland or continue the advance on London. Nothing succeeds like success and London could easily have been Edinburgh all over again.

The situation in the capital was desperate. George II had at last been forced to admit that Charles Stuart posed a deadly threat. The mood of apprehension had been growing in London as the Jacobite army got nearer. News that the rebels were at Derby produced extreme alarm, turning to panic as rumours filtered through that the French were launching an invasion. There had also been stories, quite without foundation, that the Highlanders murdered, raped, and burnt anything in their path. There was confusion as some offered support to George II and London Jacobites exhibited posters openly welcoming the Pretender. The financial markets plunged and there was a run on the banks. The Jacobite, Chevalier de Johnstone, made the assertion the George II had his yachts ready for a rapid departure, but this is almost certainly untrue. George II was not without courage and he would not have deserted his throne on 'Black Friday'.

True, the English Jacobites had not risen but then neither had the Hanoverian supporters. The rebel army had come to within 120 miles of London without meeting any local resistance. George II's greatest fear was the intelligence that the French were massing an invasion force of some 15,000 men at the Picardy ports. They were set to invade England at the end of December and, of course, the Whigs believed that the French and Charles were acting in concert. The irony is that the Whigs' greatest fear was Charles's final undoing, because the Jacobites knew nothing of the French invasion plans. All along Charles had been giving the clan chiefs assurances that French assistance would be on the way but, at the council meeting at Derby, he was forced to admit that he was not in direct communication with the French, that he did not know when they would be mounting an invasion or even if they had any definite intention of doing so. This, together with the fact that he also had to admit that there had been no communication with any of the English or Welsh Jacobite leaders since he landed in Scotland, finally destroyed his credibility, and led to the Jacobite retreat from Derby on 6 December 1745.

Once the Jacobites started to retreat the Whigs knew that Charles and the French were acting independently of one another, and they were relieved of their greatest anxiety: that of being forced to fight defensive battles on two fronts. Derby was the high point of Charles's life; he was never the same again thereafter and believed to his dying day that he had been betrayed and a great opportunity had been missed. In one sense Lord George Murray's decision to retreat was the only realistic course of action; any field commander with regard for the welfare of his men would have done the same. And, it is true that to have continued the advance on London would have been a tremendous gamble. But what great enterprises in history have not involved risk? In another sense to press forward was the rebels' only hope. They were well past the point of no return and had they been going to retreat to Scotland they should have done so long before Derby. Once they turned back defeat became certain because they were going to be pursued to destruction. There was to be no question of them being allowed to build up their strength in Scotland. Their only hope had been to continue and conquer. The overall knowledge that comes with hindsight reveals that a

Jacobite victory would have been quite feasible. They had this brief advantage and had they grasped it they could have succeeded. Stranger things have happened. Charles had only limited knowledge but he could sense that what would, quite literally, have been a world-shattering victory was within his grasp; any hesitation and the moment would be lost. He was impulsive and he did not stop to consider the likely consequences if they failed but, on this occasion, his instincts were probably correct.

Derby was not the last shock to Charles's psyche. When he returned to France after his months in the heather he was a hero and his exploits were the talk of Europe. Everyone wanted to catch a glimpse of the prince who had almost toppled the Hanoverian dynasty and who, even in defeat, had managed to escape their vengeful clutches. A week after he got back to France there was a joyful reunion with his brother Henry, who had been in Paris trying to get French support for Charles during the rebellion. The brothers were treated to lavish dinners and an audience with Louis XV. Charles was the toast of Paris and a visit to the opera brought the ecstatic audience to their feet. He would have been less than human if some of this adulation had not gone to his head. Maybe his ideas about the French had been wrong. He had proved his worth; surely, now they would see the opportunity they had missed and mount another expedition. But no. Louis again started to distance himself and employ the same evasive tactics. The French had no intention of attempting another invasion or getting involved in any more Jacobite exploits.

Charles also began to be irritated by Henry. There were taunts that Henry had not done enough to galvanize the French into lending support earlier in the 'Forty-five campaign, and suggestions that he ought to marry, a thought which filled Henry with horror. Devoted as Henry had always been to his brother, he must have found Charles insufferable. Eventually the brothers took separate residences but Henry had to get further away from Charles and his machinations. Henry may have had the foresight to see that the Jacobite cause was lost or maybe he was just seeking refuge for his own tormented personality; whatever it was, when James suggested to Henry that he might consider becoming a cardinal in the Church of Rome he leapt at the idea (Colour Plate 17).

Knowing his brother's likely reaction, Henry had to conspire with his father to bring about his entry into the priesthood without Charles's knowledge. First, James asked Henry to return to Rome, explaining to Charles that he needed Henry with him for a few months. Even so, Henry for some reason felt the need for further subterfuge. He invited Charles to dinner at the end of April 1747. All was prepared when Charles arrived; the servants were ready to wait on table, but Henry was nowhere to be seen. He had already left Paris and was on his way to Rome. Charles waited, then left Henry's residence mystified and angry at his brother's discourtesy. He remained ignorant of Henry's departure for Rome until a letter from him arrived a few days later, apologizing for his absence and explaining that he had felt obliged to return to see his father as a matter of some urgency. Henry's journey took almost a month but arrangements were already in hand for the Pope to bestow the cardinal's hat in July. Louis XV had been informed but Charles was still in the dark until the fateful letter, dated 13 June, arrived from his father. Knowing full well what Charles's reaction would be on learning of his brother's decision to take holy orders, James squirms in his efforts to be placatory:

'I know not whether you will be surprised, My Dearest Carluccio, when I tell you that your Brother will be made a Cardinal the first Days of next month. Naturally speaking you should have been consulted about a resolution of that kind before it had been executed; but as the Duke and I were unalterably determined on the matter, and that we foresaw you might probably not approve of it We thought it would be showing you more regard, and that it would be even more agreeable to you, that the thing should be done before your answer could come here, and so have it in your power to say it was done without your knowledge or approbation.——'

To say this letter was a shock for Charles is to put it mildly; he could barely comprehend it. At a stroke James and Henry had destroyed all that for which he had been striving. James, as head of the Stuart dynasty, had placed his son, who was leading the Jacobite movement, in an impossible situation. The damage to the cause was irreparable. The Whig propaganda machine had been given enough ammunition to ensure the end of effective Jacobite resistance. It proved what they had been saying all along: the Stuarts were wedded to the Roman Catholic church. As a celibate, Henry had abandoned all responsibility for continuing the Stuart line; that now rested with his brother. Charles not only had to contend with the knowledge that all this had been brought about by his own father and brother, but also that Louis XV had been fully aware of Henry's intentions, while at the same time making vague promises to Charles of possible military assistance.

Charles's reply, on 10 July, was brief:

'Sir, I have received yrs of ye 13th and 20th June had I got a Dager throw my heart it would not have been more sensible to me than at ye Contents of yr first.

My Love for my Brother and concern for yr Ca[u]se being the occasion of it. I hope your Majesty will forgive me not entering any further on so disagreeable a subject the shock of which I am scarce out of, so shall take ye Liberty of refering to next Post anything in yours to be answered. I lay myself full of Respect and Duty at yr Majestys Feet, moste humbly asking Blessing. Your Most Dutifull Son, Charles.P.'

Charles had his faults and the cracks in his personality were beginning to appear but, reading this misspelt letter from 'the dutiful son', it is difficult not to feel desperately sorry for him at this time. The utter frustration, the weariness, and the yearning for a father who could understand him; it is all there. It was a blow more devastating than Derby or Culloden. He could not forgive his brother's disloyalty. Henry wrote to Charles beseeching him to reply but there was no response. Charles now hated the French, his brother and his father. He vowed never to return to Rome, a vow he was to keep until his father's death in 1766.

There were further traumas to come. After Henry's betrayal Charles seemed to adopt a devil-may-care attitude. He took every opportunity to snub the French and he had two tempestuous love affairs: first with his cousin, Louise de Montbazon, whose husband was with the army in Flanders, and then with Princesse de Talmont. The final confrontation with the French came in 1748 when they decided that Charles would have to leave their territory. The Treaty of Aix-la-Chapelle had been ratified and one condition, upon which the English were adamant, was that the Young Pretender should leave French territory for good. The Prince stubbornly refused. The French tried to persuade and cajole but he was simply defiant; he was determined to humiliate Louis XV. It must be remembered that Charles continued to be the talk of Europe, his personal public image had not changed and he was still regarded as one of the foremost romantic figures of his day. The battle of wills between Charles and Louis was followed throughout Europe becoming the Continent's greatest scandal for some years. Charles's standing with the Jacobites in England grew as he resisted every turn of the screw. As a last resort the French were obliged to have Charles arrested on the steps of the Opera on 10 December. It was a humiliation for all concerned. In a sense Charles had won the battle and lost the war. He had succeeded in forcing Louis's hand and bringing discredit upon France but, in so doing, he had sown the final seeds of his own destruction.

The remainder of Charles's life: his move to Avignon; his mysterious movements and disguises; his life with Clementina Walkinshaw and their illegitimate daughter, Charlotte; his brief, unhappy marriage to Princess Louise of Stolberg; his death in 1788; all of this is the province of the biographer. The 'cause' was dead. The sentiment remained, of course, and the scheming continued but, as a serious threat, the Jacobite movement was finished. In some respects the decline of the 'movement' emboldened the spirits of certain Jacobite sympathizers. Some county elections were accompanied by minor riots, and the wearing of plaid waistcoats and white cockades became common expressions of defiance.[3] Dr William King made his 'redeat' speech[4] and the Oak Society struck the Oak Medal (p.108). But, the Whigs could relax and Stuart supporters could, once again, raise their glasses to the 'King over the Water' in the certain knowledge that they would not be called upon to draw their swords.

Charles made a secret visit to London in 1750 where he pondered the possibility of using a petard to seize the Tower, and in 1752 the Elibank Plot was hatched: George II and his family were to be kidnapped from St James's Palace and taken to France; but it all came to nothing. Charles, who had never had much time for organized religion, relinquished his Roman Catholic faith, but it came too late to further his cause. He never saw his father alive again. When he returned to Rome on his father's death it was to claim James's title. The Pope refused to recognize Charles's claim and, when Henry interceded on his brother's behalf, the Pope reminded Henry that Charles had converted to Protestantism in 1750. Charles would often shed a tear when he thought of his gallant Highlanders and those who had died for his cause, but he never revealed that he felt in any way responsible for their deaths.

After his arrest in Paris, Charles's story is that of a crumbling personality. However, he should not be denied his brief period of fame. He really was a remarkable man, but he was born into a rôle which demanded greater strength of character than he possessed. His fragile childhood rendered him vulnerable. It is true that he could not cope with failure; he needed forward momentum and he needed to succeed. When events were in his favour his attributes shone: courage, generosity, compassion, charm and wit. But, faced with rejection and failure the darker side of his character was accentuated and he became disagreeable, stubborn and spiteful. This immaturity was his undoing; he clung to the impossible dream until his bitterness destroyed him. Yet he possessed qualities which almost crowned his endeavours with the glory he so desperately sought. He was a colourful individual and he should not be dismissed as a nonentity simply because his personality could not withstand the extraordinary stresses to which it was subjected. Charles was neither the knight in shining armour, as depicted in romantic mythology, nor was he the ogre he appeared to be in later life; he was, like most of us, a less than perfect human being. It is fitting that he is remembered for the brief time he spent in the country to which he rightly belonged.

CHAPTER 3
The Jacobite Clubs

History needs to do much more than simply chronicle events; more even than provide critical analysis of the events. These are the bare bones of the past and they need flesh. History should seek to tell us about society; about what life was really like for the people who lived at the time and how the events in history affected them and how they, the people, influenced the events.

What is meant by 'the Jacobites'? Who were they? The active participants in the rebellions are known; those who were executed or dispossessed are known, but who were the ordinary people who held Jacobite sympathies? The word 'Jacobite' comes from *Jacobus*, the Latin for James, and the original Jacobites were the supporters of James II. Later in the eighteenth century it referred to those who favoured a return of the Stuart dynasty. However, Jacobites often supported the Stuart cause for widely differing reasons. There were, of course, the genuine ideologists who believed in hereditary monarchy and Divine Right. That is they believed that the monarch ruled by the will of God. In a religious age such as the seventeenth and eighteenth centuries many people were happy to go along with the concept that the monarch ruled through the will of God. They also accepted the hereditary principle, which exists to this day, that the monarch's claim to the throne falls to his or her descendants in a strict line of succession. This at least tended to avoid the costly wars which had occurred in more feudal times when disputes arose over the succession. But, the absolute monarchs, ruling by Divine Right, encountered trouble over the word 'right' when it came to be interpreted as 'right or wrong'. Charles I at his trial repeatedly asserted that 'a king cannot be tried by any superior jurisdiction on earth. ... Princes are not bound to give an account of their actions but to God';[1] and he went to the executioner's block upholding this belief. The idea that a monarch could never be legally deprived of the throne no matter what he did, was asking too much. The old principle whereby parliament sat at the will of the monarch to serve the monarch, had to be abandoned. The Whigs insisted that the monarch must rule through the will of parliament.

To those who upheld Divine Right the Glorious Revolution of 1688, which deprived James II of his throne, was an offence against God; they were prepared to risk all and many paid with their lives. Mortally wounded on the battlefield at Killiecrankie, Dundee's last words are reputed to have been: 'How goes the day?' 'Well for King James', came the reply, 'but I am sorry for your Lordship.' To which Dundee whispered: 'If it is well for him it matters the less for me.'[2] Such devoted Jacobites were probably few in number.

The Whigs liked to maintain that Roman Catholics were Jacobites but there is no evidence for this. Although it is generally accepted that if the Stuarts had relinquished their Roman Catholic faith they would have been restored, the reverse, namely that a Roman Catholic was likely to be a Jacobite, did not apply. Anglican non-jurors, who had refused to take the Oath of Allegiance in 1689, and in Scotland the Episcopalians, were far more likely to be Jacobites than the Catholics.

If there was one group which could, by and large, be identified with Jacobitism, it was a political group – the Tories. This is because during the period of Whig supremacy under the first two Georges, a period of forty-five years after 1714, the Tories were proscribed. They were unable to achieve high office in the civil service, the church or the professions, or high ranks in the army or the navy. Tory officers lost their commissions, Tory lawyers could not become judges or K.Cs, Tory clergy could not become bishops, and government contracts went to Whig merchants. This proscription affected half the nation and consequently many Tories, seeing Whig dominance continuing from one generation to the next, turned to Jacobitism out of desperation rather than ideology. Eveline Cruickshanks has shown that at the time of the 1745 rising the Tories in parliament were 'a predominantly Jacobite party, engaged in attempts to restore the Stuarts by a rising with foreign assistance'.[3] However, they never managed to translate their Jacobitism into a cohesive military presence.

Then there were the malcontents, who simply opposed the government of the day for a whole variety of reasons and who were Jacobites because they bore a grudge. Some of these lived on the fringe of the law or beyond it, using the Jacobite cause as an excuse for their activities.

The truly dedicated Jacobites were few, but then so were the truly dedicated Hanoverians. Jacobite wine glasses are rare but not so rare as the glasses sporting the White Horse of Hanover. Under Walpole there was a period of peace and relative prosperity and, excluding politically active Tories and malcontents, most people were prepared to settle for the status quo.

A distinction should be made, however, between the Scottish Jacobites on the one hand and the English and Welsh Jacobites on the other, because they were motivated in different ways. The clan chiefs, as has been seen, had problems with inter-clan rivalry and the threat in the Highlands to the whole clan system. In addition many Scots, particularly in the Highlands, felt they had an axe to grind with the English over the Act of Union. In all these respects, Scottish Jacobites felt that they would fare better with the Stuarts. It must also be remembered that the clan structure provided the Scottish Jacobites with a built-in military call-up system which neither the English nor the Welsh Jacobites possessed. The predicament for the English Jacobites was that they needed military assistance from the French to make a rising effective, but the French were not prepared to commit themselves to an invasion before the English Jacobites had made the first move.

The extent to which Jacobite society was based on intrigue and danger is still unclear. It is known that drinking the Pretender's health early in the eighteenth century was a serious offence but, around the middle of the century, which is the period applicable to most Jacobite glasses, were you really taking your life in your hands or risking imprisonment if you raised your glass at a dinner party to toast 'The King over the Water'? And were the special glasses they used engraved in great secrecy by dedicated Jacobite craftsmen or, had the whole attitude to Jacobitism become more relaxed? Were Jacobite sympathies tolerated provided they did not get out of hand?

A more intimate view of the Jacobite movement can be glimpsed from the activities of the Jacobite clubs. Little has ever been written, or at least published, about these so-called secret societies. The important ones are well known but a debt is owed to an enthusiastic amateur, an early member of the Glass Circle, Muriel Steevenson, for unearthing many of the lesser known Jacobite clubs.

The Glass Circle, which today boasts several hundred members, in the U.K., Europe, and as far away as Australia and America, was inaugurated in 1937 with just nine founder members. Originally known as The Circle of Glass Collectors, members met in one another's houses and read papers on topics of interest related to glass. During the Second World War meetings were not possible and stencilled copies of papers were distributed amongst members. Muriel Steevenson produced several papers dealing with Jacobite clubs, but the fruits of her research were shared only by members of the Glass Circle. Just before the Second World War she was listing about fifty Jacobite societies[4] but, some years after the war she wrote a paper which included a map showing about one hundred and twenty clubs or centres of Jacobite activity.[5] F.P. Lole has now extended the list to over one hundred and forty[6] and he points out that the Jacobite club was largely an English phenomenon since of the total number of clubs only thirteen were Scottish and of these nine were in Edinburgh.[7]

These societies were the focal points of Jacobite discontent and they were most numerous in the north and west of the country. They were usually small, private gatherings of Stuart sympathizers. They met at regular intervals to drink toasts and talk politics, usually over a dinner. Some of the societies were very secret and little is known of them, while others, such as the Cycle Club, concealed their treasonable nature and posed as legitimate societies. Minutes were kept of meetings, as well as lists of members, and some of these records have survived to the present day. The clubs varied considerably in the type of membership and the extent of their political activities. Some, like the Beaufort Club, which met at Truby's in the Strand, were actively involved in anti-government plots; the Layer Plot of 1722 is said to have been the work of the Beaufort Club.[8] Other societies were little more than local community social clubs. As the Jacobite movement became a sentimental memory the more political clubs either went out of existence or changed character to become antiquarian societies, some of which remained in existence till late in the nineteenth century.

Prominent Jacobites were often members of more than one club but there is no evidence of any liaison between different clubs. The concept of a national network of Jacobite societies must have been an attractive one and, had one existed at the time of the 'Forty-five the response of the English Jacobites might have been better. In 1739 the Jacobite historian, Carte, wrote to James in Rome outlining a plan for just such a network of Jacobite clubs, but his idea did not find favour with the other Jacobite leaders.[9]

The older clubs, like the Gloucestershire Society, had their origins even earlier than the Jacobite movement, having started life as Cavalier clubs in Cromwell's Commonwealth.

One feature common to all Jacobite clubs and societies was the ritual of drinking the health of the King.

> Then all leap'd up, and joined their hands
> With hearty clasp and greeting.
> The brimming cups outstretched by all,
> Over the wide bowl meeting.
> 'A health,' they cried, 'to witching eyes
> Of Kate, the landlord's daughter!
> But don't forget the white, white rose
> That grows best over the water.'
>
> ---
>
> 'But never forget the white, white rose
> That grows best over the water.'
> Then hats flew up and swords sprang out,
> And lusty rang the chorus—
> 'Never,' they cried, 'while Scots are Scots,
> And the broad Firth's before us.'[10]

As a rule, drinking the health of the king was a very solemn act; the Cavaliers of Charles I's reign drank the toast on their knees, a custom which persisted into the eighteenth century. To drink the Pretender's health was a treasonable act and the penalties for being caught could be severe, especially around the time of the 1715 rising. In 1715 one Captain Silk was imprisoned for eighteen months for drinking King James's health on his knees and, about the same time, the Mayor of Nottingham was imprisoned for two years for drinking the same toast in the same manner in his own home.[11] The public flogging of soldiers who spoke for King James was a common occurence. In 1719 one unfortunate trooper, named Devenish, was stripped and tied to a tree in Hyde Park. He was flogged with savage cruelty then flung into a hospital to die.[12] More fortunate was Miss Clarke, a pretty girl in Sunderland. In 1718 she was brought before the court for having boldly drunk King James's health. She was discharged with a light fine and several of the justices kissed her as she passed before the bench on her way out of court.[13] In the London coffee houses the toast to 'Miss Clarke and her friend' became popular.

Jacobite clubs developed different ways of drinking the toast but it usually involved drinking the health of the King 'over water' to signify the King in exile (Colour Plates 18 and 19). For instance, members of the Cycle Club stood on chairs with one foot on the table. They passed their glasses over water bottles and drank 'The King'.[14] The Independent Electors of Westminster held a glass of water in their left hand and passed the wine glass, held in the right hand, over the water before drinking the toast. This club was informed against in 1746 for their custom of drinking the Pretender's health.[15]

The author has knowledge of a similar ceremony being conducted in the home of a Scottish laird to the present day. This occurs once a year on the anniversary of the Battle of Culloden. After dinner, glasses of water are set around the table and wine glasses are filled. Then, the blood-stained gauntlet of the ancestor who died in the battle is placed in the centre of the table. The toast to 'The King over the Water' is given and the guests pass their wine glasses over the water before drinking. The laird, of course, is loyal to the present monarch and, with the passage of time, this little annual ceremony has become an innocent after-dinner ritual, but for his forbears in the eighteenth century, it would have had a much more solemn significance.

If a Jacobite wanted to toast 'The King' in a more public place, any water that happened to be on the table would suffice and, until late in the nineteenth century, finger bowls were not permitted on the dining tables at any official function until after the loyal toast had been given. In a public place the so-called Lord Duff's toast is said to have been used. This was an alphabetical list of abbreviations familiar to those in the know. G.H.J— God Help James, Q.R.S.— Quickly Resolve Stuart and T.U.V.W.— Truss Up Vile Whigs, are examples. Other concealed toasts were the 'Health of Sorrel', William III's horse which stumbled on the mole hill, leading indirectly to the monarch's death, and 'Confusion to the White Horse', referring to the White Horse of Hanover. 'Job' was another toast, standing for: James, Ormonde and Bolingbroke. In Douglas, Isle of Man, there are records of a trial in 1716 brought on suspicion of drinking to 'Job'.[16]

There were many different types of Jacobite club catering for all classes of society. In the country there were the numerous Hunts which were known to be Jacobite. These were in existence mainly in the middle and latter half of the eighteenth century. The Fraternity of the True Blue Hunt, founded in 1750, met at the Raven in Shrewsbury. The Friendly Hunt was a Worcestershire meet, probably connected with a Jacobite society in Worcester known as the Friendly Association. Founded in 1747, the Association met annually in rotation in the neighbouring towns of Droitwich, Bromsgrove, Dudley, Kidderminster and Stourbridge.[17]

The Newton Hunt, which met at John Ellams Inn at Newton-le-Willows, was founded in 1748. They petitioned the French king when Charles was arrested in Paris. Some other Jacobite Hunts were: the Mervyn Hunt, 1749; the Stafford Hunt, 1750; the Congleton Hunt, 1760; the Anglesey Hunt, 1761; the Tarpoley Hunt, 1762; the Whitechurch True Blue Hunt, 1760; the Barnhill Hunt, 1763.[18]

Where better than the open air to talk treason? Thus the Loyal Brotherhood of Badminton is said to have met on a bowling green. In the same way the race meetings at Lichfield, Oxford, and in Scotland at Loch Maben, were known to be centres of Jacobite intrigue.[19] In 1747 there were riots at the Staffordshire County elections. The Tories put up against all the Whig candidates, and at Lichfield races they turned out in force, many wearing plaid waistcoats and white cockades. The Pretender's health was drunk in the streets, and treasonable songs were sung. About this time many Englishmen were beginning to feel sympathy for the plight of the Scots and had taken to wearing the plaid as a sign of their support.[20]

In towns and cities Whigs and Tories tended to frequent their own inns and coffee houses. In London the Mourning Bush was a Jacobite tavern as also was the Blew Posts in Dukes Court, where meetings were held in a small room behind the kitchen. The Cocoa Tree in St. James's Street was a well-known Jacobite coffee house. Jacobites would sometimes attack Whig mug houses. One notorious mug house was Mr Read's, in Salisbury Court, Fleet Street. In 1716 Mr Read's was attacked by the 'Jacks' who smashed windows and forced an entry. They broke furniture and opened casks of wine and spirits. Then, having drunk their fill, attempted to set fire to the building before escaping in triumph with the sign of the house. The escapade was not without cost however, because the Whigs discharged their pistols into the mob killing one man and wounding several others. The dead man was a weaver called Vaughan and Read was charged with his murder. The coroner referred the case to the Old Bailey and Read narrowly escaped the gallows.[21]

On 4 November 1715, the anniversary of William III's birthday, a group of London Jacobites built a bonfire in Old Jewry and prepared to burn an effigy of the monarch. Members of a Williamite club at the Roebuck in Cheapside, hearing of this, rushed out with cudgels and set about the 'Jacks'. They succeeded in carrying off the effigy and installed it in their own club room.[22]

The Oak Society, which was one of the more secret Jacobite clubs, met in the Crown and Anchor in the Strand. They were responsible for the Oak Medal being struck in 1750. This depicts the head of Prince Charles and on the reverse a severed oak and the motto *revirescit* (Plate 74).

Another club, which met at various London taverns was the Board of Brothers.[23] Founded in 1709, the president of the club was the Duke of Beaufort, a leading Jacobite who was also a member of the Loyal Brotherhood of Badminton in the west of the country. Members, who were all prominent Jacobites, wore specially embroidered hats and drank from a 'Great Glass'. It was a different club to the Brothers Club founded by Bolingbroke in 1710.

In the towns another form of Jacobite society was the Mock Mayor and Corporation. These clubs existed in the North of England. The Mock Corporation of Walton-le-Dale, the Mayor and Loyal Corporation of Cheadle and the Corporation of Rochdale are examples. The Mayor and Corporation of Walton-le-Dale was a famous Jacobite club and was in existence from 1701 until the middle of the nineteenth century. The Earl of Derwentwater was its 'Mayor' in 1711. The club met at the Unicorn Inn at Walton and was composed of Catholic and Jacobite nobility and gentry.[24]

The Ancient and Loyal Corporation of Ardwick, which was founded in 1714, maintained one of its old customs until 1938. This was at the annual banquet when an empty chair was always placed to the right of the Mayor. This remained empty until after the first course when the Mayor would ask the Recorder, 'Will he come?' To which the Recorder replied, 'No, he will not come I fear.' The chair and place setting were then removed. The absent guest was Prince Charles who may have visited the Corporation at the time of the 'Forty-five.[25]

John Shaw's Club in Manchester was founded in 1738. It was a punch club and was known to be a favourite Jacobite haunt. The founder member, John Shaw, was an expert at making punch and at closing time he is said to have cleared his customers by cracking a whip. John Shaw died in 1798 but the club was in existence until 1892, the same punch bowl having been used for the whole of the club's existence.[26]

Some of the Masonic Lodges were Jacobite and were among the most secret of their societies. The Canongate Kilwiming Lodge at Edinburgh was one to which many of the leading Scottish Jacobites belonged. Murray of Broughton was a member but his name was removed from the membership after he turned King's evidence against Lord Lovat in 1747.

Some Jacobite societies were exclusive clubs for prominent citizens rather than hotbeds of treachery. Such was a club founded in Preston in the second half of the eighteenth century. It went by the strange name of the Oyster and Parched Pea Club and was in existence until 1841. The club was exclusively Tory and membership was originally limited to twelve prominent citizens. Meetings were held at the houses of its members and for each meeting a barrel of oysters was sent up from London.[27]

For the glass collector the Jacobite clubs of greatest interest are those, like the Oak Society, which are thought to have had associations with certain engraved glasses. Many of these clubs were in the country houses of prominent Jacobites and probably the oldest known Jacobite club of this type was the Gloucestershire Society.[28] This was founded in 1657 as a Cavalier club and it remained in existence until the early part of Queen Victoria's reign, by which time it had become an antiquarian society. It is probable that Chastleton Manor was a centre for this society's activities during part of the eighteenth century. The manor house, lying deep in the countryside of the Oxfordshire-Gloucestershire border, retains many of its original features. A Royalist household during the Civil War, it had known the tread of Cromwell's Roundheads, and in the eighteenth century, Henry Jones, the owner of Chastleton until his death in 1761, was a zealous Jacobite. He was responsible for planting the Scotch firs at the Manor. These were known as 'Charlie's Trees', and were said to have acted as a guide to Jacobite fugitives.[29] Two decanters (Plates 4 & 61) and eleven wine glasses engraved with Jacobite emblems were discovered at Chastleton.

A similar find of Jacobite glass was made at Oxburgh Hall in Norfolk in 1907.[30] It

b

c

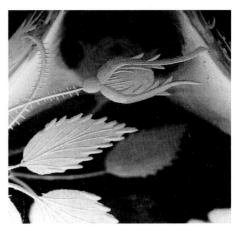

d

Plate 4 a, b, c, d. Chastleton Manor Decanter. H. 25.5cm. [A] See also Plate 62

Plate 5 a, b, c, d, e, f, g.
Oxburgh Hall glass.
H. 17.6cm. [B]

a

was in 1482 that Edward IV gave the founder, Sir Edmund Bedingfeld, permission to crenellate his manor house in the lonely Fenland marshes, and the Bedingfelds have occupied the house in unbroken descent ever since. The family still live there but the property is now owned by the National Trust. Although there is no known connection with any Jacobite society the find itself is interesting. In 1907 Oxburgh Hall was the seat of Sir Henry Bedingfeld and on the day in question Sir Henry was having a discussion about Jacobite relics with a visiting journalist, C.E.Jernyngham. The journalist happened to be an enthusiastic glass collector and the discussion came round to Jacobite glass, whereupon Sir Henry recalled that in his youth there had been mention of some curious glasses in the house. The contents of the china cupboard were put out onto a table and there, amidst hundreds of pieces of modern glass, Sir Henry and his guest discovered eleven Jacobite glasses, thick with dust (Plate 5). The Bedingfelds retained their Roman Catholic faith through 500 years and the presence of Jacobite glasses in the house suggests that in the eighteenth century they were one of the Catholic families with Jacobite sympathies.

The best known of all Jacobite clubs is the Cycle Club or, to give it its full title, the Cycle of the White Rose.[31] Founded on the 10th June 1710, the anniversary of the Old Pretender's birthday, White Rose Day, this North Wales club had an unbroken existence of nearly one hundred and fifty years. A good deal is known about the Cycle of the White Rose: its rules of membership, the lists of members, the songs they sang, and the records of meetings and dinners throughout its unbroken history.

The founder, Sir Watkin Williams Wynn of Wynnstay, was a well-known Jacobite. The meetings were held at Wrexham and, initially, the members all lived within a radius of seven miles of the town. In 1724 the club was reconstituted and new rules, carefully disguising the true nature of the club, were drawn up. Rule '2' increased the radius of membership to 'within the Compass of 15 miles from the place of Meeting', and stated that : 'Every Member that cannot come shall be obliged to send Notice of his Non appearance by 12 of the Clock at Noon together with his Reasons in Writing, otherwise his Plea shall not excuse him.' Meetings were held at three-weekly intervals and a new member could be admitted on each occasion. Between 21 May 1723 and 24 April 1724 seventeen new members had signed. Rule '6' stated: 'It is agreed that a General Meeting shall be held of all the Subscribers at the house of Daniel Porter, Innholder in Wrexham on the 1st day of May 1724 by 11 of the clock in the forenoon and there to dine and to determine upon all Points relating to and according to the sense and meaning of these Articles.'

It was the custom to dine at the house of each member in turn – hence the name 'Cycle'– and a general meeting was held when necessary. Members presumably provided suitable glasses for these dinners and, during the period when engraved glasses were available, these would have been engraved with Jacobite emblems. However, the old theory that *Fiat* was the 'word' of the Cycle Club is now no longer accepted; this motto occurs too frequently on Jacobite glasses for it to have been confined to any one club.

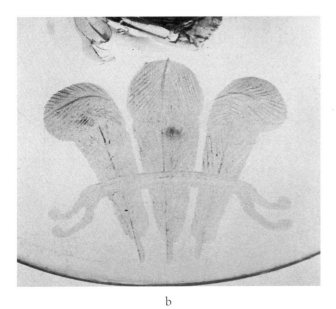

b

c

d

e

f

g

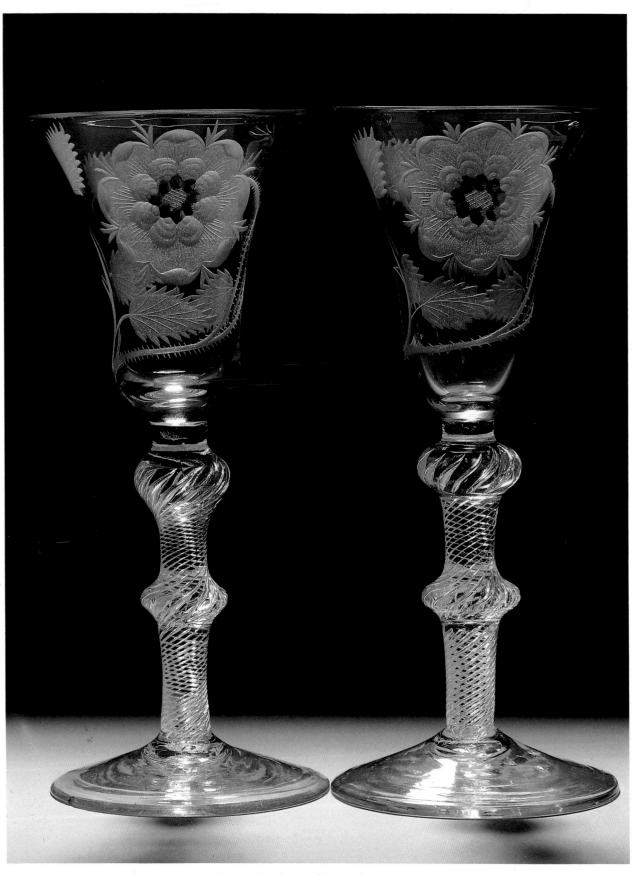

Colour Plate 18. Pair of Jacobite wine glasses, each engraved with a rose and a single bud. H. 18.3cm. [D]. (COURTESY DRAMBUIE LIQUEUR CO.)

Colour Plate 19. Jacobite water glass, engraved with a rose and a single bud. H. 11.6cm. [C]. (COURTESY DRAMBUIE LIQUEUR CO.)

CYCLE SONG

I hope there's no soul,
That over his Bowl,
But means honest Ends to pursue,
With the Voice goes the Heart,
And let's never depart,
From the Faith of an honest True Blue.
(chorus)
True Blue! From the Faith of the honest True Blue.

For Country and Friends,
Let us damn private Ends,
And keep old British Virtue in View,
Despising the Tribe,
Who are bought by a Bribe,
Let's be Honest and ever True Blue.
True Blue! etc.

Here's a Health to all those,
Who Slavery oppose,
And our Trade both defend and renew,
And to each honest Voice,
That concurs in the Choice,
And Support of an honest True Blue.
True Blue! etc.

For the Days we've misspent,
Let us truly repent,
And render to Caesar his due,
Here's a Health to the Lad,
With his Bonnet and Plaid,
For the World cannot stain his True Blue.
True Blue! etc.
(The last verse of the Cycle Song was added in 1745.)

The Cycle was probably on the march in 1745, but the Jacobite army had already started the retreat from Derby. Having failed to make contact with the Highland army

Plate 6 a, b. The Cycle Jewel

a   b

the incriminating papers were destroyed and the Cycle Club survived. Sir Watkin Williams Wynn, like many other Welsh and English Jacobites, but unlike their unfortunate Scottish counterparts, was left unmolested after the 'Forty-five; he died in 1749.

In 1770, when there were about fifty members of the Cycle, the club met at the Eagle in Wrexham and was again reconstituted. It became non-political and in 1780 a lady patroness was elected. Afterwards meetings were always held at Wynstay, the Williams Wynn of the day being the patron and his wife the lady patroness. The Cycle Jewel (Plate 6), a gold and enamel badge, was made for the lady patroness and she was the only lady ever admitted to the dinners. The Cycle Club was dissolved in 1869 and the Jewel was given to Lady Williams Wynn. The last lady patroness was known personally to Albert Hartshorne who published the first authoritative book on antique glass, *Old English Glasses,* in 1897, in which he gives a detailed account of the Cycle Club.[32]

Another club known to have used Jacobite glasses is the Cheshire Club.[33] This was founded about 1689 by Peter Legh of Lyme. The first meeting was in the Stag Parlour at Lyme Hall, and thereafter at monthly intervals in the houses of the members. Peter Legh was arrested for his Jacobite activities in 1694 and again in 1696, but was released on both occasions. The Cheshire Club voted against joining the 1715 rising by one vote and about 1720 the club was dissolved. It reformed later because a meeting was held in 1745 when again there was a casting vote against joining the 1745 rising. It is said this vote was given by the nephew of the club's original founder.

There were at least two maritime clubs of which the best known is the Society of Sea-Sergeants. This South Wales society is usually regarded as a Jacobite club and it has been said that it was to South Wales what the Cycle Club was to the North. Being a maritime club, it has been suggested that it may have assisted in smuggling Jacobite agents in and out of the country. There is no evidence that it ever acted in this way and although in its lifetime it was openly accused of 'disaffection to the government and of trafficking with the exiled royal family',[34] the Sea-Sergeants themselves always strongly denied this.

It was certainly a secret society and its members were all well-to-do gentry. They had a president, a secretary, an examiner and two stewards. New members were asked a number of searching questions, the first two being: 'Do you bear true allegiance to His Majesty?' and 'Are you a member of the Church of England as by law established?', which hardly reflect a strong Jacobite influence. Members had to be probationers for at least a year before being admitted to full membership. An annual meeting was held at a seaport town and during the week of the meeting every member had to wear the badge of the Society in his coat. This was a silver star with the figure of a dolphin in the centre, the same emblem that is engraved on their wine glasses (Plate 7).

In 1749 a lady patroness, who had to be an unmarried lady of the neighbourhood, was elected. Members were allowed to introduce a lady to attend the lady patroness and to dine with the Society on one of the days. On this occasion there was a penalty of five guineas for any member caught swearing or throwing dice.

The origin of the Society of Sea-Sergeants is obscure, but it is known to have been revived in 1726. Its end is equally obscure but there was certainly a meeting of the Society in 1762 and the last recorded president was the Rt. Hon. Sir John Philipps who died in 1764.[35]

There were also Jacobite clubs for exiles abroad. The Sun Inn at Rotterdam and Gordon's in Boulogne were the names of Jacobite meeting places.

A letter written on 5 July 1759 by Duncan Robertson of Struan to James Edgar, the Old Pretender's secretary in Rome, is interesting and refers to a 'club' near to Paris:

'On June 10th (the Old Pretender's birthday) Gask's family and mine as usual joined at Carbeil with our best clothes and white roses. We had no other person of the three kingdoms in the place, but two honest Irish gentlemen who were of the party. I forgot to mention your old acquaintance Balhaldy is a member of the club. We drank the health of the day, with the Prince, the Duke and the restoration. All that we can do, in the present situation of things, is to wish and to hope.'[36]

These Jacobites were meeting 'as usual' at the 'club' and were wearing their white roses. The reference to 'honest' Irishmen meant that they too were Jacobites; it was a common Jacobite custom to use the word 'honest' in this way. It is also worth noting that they were drinking, not only to James's birthday and Prince Charles, but also to Prince Henry, Duke of York, twelve years after he had supposedly fallen from favour among Jacobites by becoming a cardinal in the Church of Rome.

Many Jacobite clubs have not been mentioned, and many have probably disappeared without trace, while others remain to be discovered. In Scotland the sentiment died hard and as late as 1772 the Royal Oak Club was founded in Edinburgh. However, after the death of Charles Edward in 1788 there were few who relished the prospect of a Roman Catholic cardinal as king, and there were other issues of concern, for the French Revolution did not go unnoticed on this side of the Channel. The Highlands had been drained of opposition with large numbers of Scots leaving their homeland; some 50,000 Scots emigrated to America. The English were even less inclined than they had been in 1745 to risk losing the prosperity which had been gained, in order to restore a Stuart dynasty that was fast receding into history.

Samuel Johnson, himself a Jacobite, had already experienced this difficulty. He had accepted a pension from King George and when questioned about this by Boswell in 1763 he replied: 'I retain the same principles. It is true I cannot curse the House of Hanover, nor would it be decent to drink King James's health in wine that King George gives me the money to pay for, but I think the pleasure of cursing the House of Hanover and drinking King James's health are amply overbalanced by three hundred pounds a year.'

Thus it was that Jacobitism sank even further into sentimental memory.

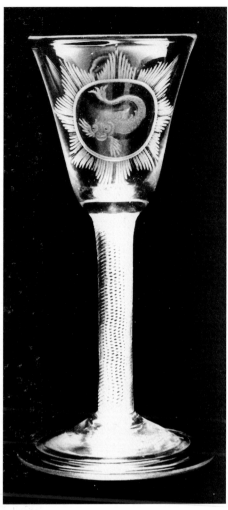

Plate 7. Society of Sea-Sergeants glass. H. 16.1cm.

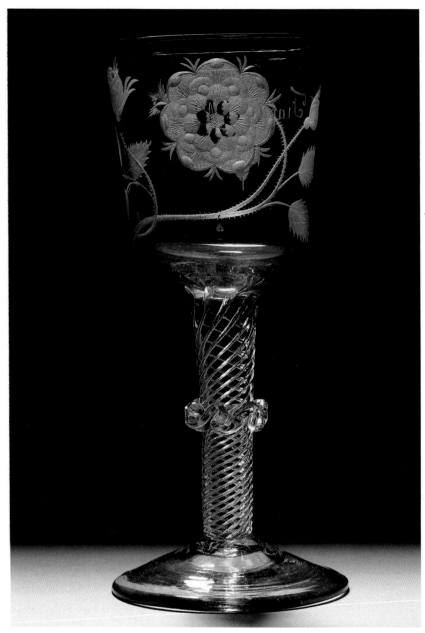

Colour Plate 20. Large Jacobite wine glass, engraved with a rose, two buds, an oak leaf, a star and 'fiat'. The foot is engraved with the fleur-de-lis within a crown. H. 20cm. [A]. (COURTESY DRAMBUIE LIQUEUR CO.)

CHAPTER 4
English Glass in the Eighteenth Century

Glass, one of the oldest of all man-made substances, is a strange and fascinating material. In the present scientific age, when its manifold applications extend far beyond window panes and domestic wares, it becomes difficult to imagine a world without glass and it is perhaps small wonder that the material itself is sometimes taken

Colour Plate 21. Jacobite firing glass, engraved with a rose, two buds, an oak leaf and 'fiat'. H. 10.5cm. [C]. (Courtesy Drambuie Liqueur Co.)

for granted. But this has not always been so. Although glass is made from the most commonplace ingredients … sand, ash and lime … and although it has a history going back at least thirty-five centuries, glass-making in the past was always surrounded by mystery; the conversion of humble sand and ash into a transparent, colourless solid resembling quartz crystal being akin to alchemy. Glass was regarded as a valuable material, sometimes rivalling silver and gold on the dining table, and glass-makers enjoyed a high standing among other craftsmen. During the Renaissance, when Venetian glass was supreme throughout Europe, the Venetian glass-makers were confined to Murano, a small island some five kilometres from the city of Venice. There, they ranked with the nobility, having a prosperous lifestyle. A nobleman could marry a glass-maker's daughter without any loss of status. However, if a glass-maker tried to leave the island to disclose his secrets elsewhere the Grand Council of the Venetian Republic could impose severe punishments ranging from a term as a galley slave to death at the hands of a hired assassin.

Glass is composed of silica which is widespread in nature as quartz, flints and sand. Very high temperatures are required to reduce silica to the molten state but the addition of a flux reduces the melting point of the silica to a temperature that can be achieved in a wood-fired furnace. Two alkaline fluxing agents, or 'salts' as they were called, were in general use: soda, or sodium carbonate, producing soda glass, and potash, or potassium carbonate, producing potash glass. In the Mediterranean regions a soda flux was used and this 'salt' was obtained from the ash of a marine plant, *Salicornia herbacea* or *Glasswort*, growing in the salt marshes around the coast. Alicante in Spain became the centre for the production of this fluxing agent, known in Spanish as *barilla*. In Northern Europe potash glass was produced using the ash from burnt forest vegetation, notably ferns, beech-wood and oak. The other essential ingredient for making glass was lime; this gave stability and produced a tougher, clearer glass.

The quality of the glass depended upon the purity of the silica. Ordinary golden sand contains substances, such as iron oxide, which discolour the glass giving it a dark green tint. Some of these impurities can be neutralized by the addition of magnesia but it is better to start with clear white sand. Today some of the purest silica sand is found in Scotland but in the seventeenth and eighteenth centuries the English glass-makers obtained white sand from Maidstone in Kent and King's Lynn in Norfolk. The Venetians made their clear *cristallo* glass by crushing the white quartz pebbles found in the alpine rivers, the finest glass being made from the pebbles in the river Tricino.

The art of glass-blowing to produce hollow vessels was developed by the Syrians in about 50BC. Prior to this the core technique had been used. Molten glass was poured to cover a core modelled in mud and straw; the core was then picked and washed away when the glass had cooled. The techniques of hand glass-blowing, and the tools used, are much the same now as they were two thousand years ago.

The Romans became skilled glass-makers and, due to the pagan custom of burying the dead with some of their worldly goods, a number of fine examples of Roman glass have survived. With the coming of Christianity these burial customs gradually ceased and this, together with the stifling of culture as the Dark Age spread across Europe, accounts for the rarity of Anglo-Saxon glass. It is likely that the Romans made glass in England and one or two probable sites have been discovered, but much of the Roman glass found in Britain may have been brought over from the Continent. Likewise, the specimens of Anglo-Saxon glass that have been discovered closely resemble glasses found on the Continent and it cannot be shown that they were produced in this country. The earliest glass known to have been made in England is attributed to Lawrence Vitrearius who is thought to have come here from Normandy and who established a small glass furnace on a twenty acre wooded site at Chiddingfold, Surrey in 1226. He made mainly window-glass and by 1240 was making windows for Westminster Abbey.

This was the pattern of glassmaking in England until the latter part of the sixteenth century. Each glasshouse consisted of a single furnace housed in an open-sided shelter, with just a roof to protect the furnace and the workmen from the elements. The furnace was fuelled by wood, so was always positioned in or near to a forest. They were small concerns with a master and three or four assistants, the master paying the landowner for the use of the surrounding timber as fuel. A supply of suitable sand was required and also clay for making the pots in which the glass was made. The flux was potash derived from burning bracken. When the surrounding timber was used up the whole furnace would be dismantled and moved to a new location. Their staple product was window-glass, principally for churches, but they also made simple domestic wares.

Meanwhile in Europe the Renaissance saw the skill of the Venetian glass-makers reaching extraordinary heights. Using their clear *cristallo* soda glass they fashioned thin, delicate glassware of astonishing intricacy, and luxurious items, keenly sought by the wealthy, came to grace the tables of noble families across Europe. Henry VIII was one of the first in England to acquire Venetian glass to replace the silver and gold plate at the royal dining table. Some of his Venetian wine glasses had gold mounts which testifies to the value which was accorded them.

In 1549 eight Venetian glass-makers tried to settle in London but they were ordered to return to Murano by the Grand Council of Venice. However it was becoming easier for Venetian glass-makers to leave and in 1570 a further group appeared in London. They were introduced by a French merchant named Jean Carré. Carré had arrived in England from Antwerp in 1567 and had established the Crutched Friars glass furnace in London. He petitioned Elizabeth I and was granted a licence to produce Venetian-style glass. One of the Venetians brought to London by Carré was a man called Giacomo Verzelini who had been working as a glass-maker in Antwerp for several years. When Carré died in 1572 Verzelini took over the Crutched Friars glasshouse and in 1574 he was granted a twenty-one year monopoly to be the sole producer of Venetian-style glass. The following year disaster struck and the Crutched Friars glasshouse burnt down. Verzelini suspected that the fire had been caused deliberately by glass merchants who made their living by importing glass from abroad and were jealous of his monopoly. He promptly applied to become an English citizen, which entitled him to own property, and set about restoring the glasshouse. He also built another furnace in Broad Street. Verzelini was soon established in London and the Venetian style was to dominate the English glass industry for the next century. He prospered and bought property in Kent, retiring in 1592 a wealthy man. He lived at Downe in Kent until he died in 1606 at the age of 84. He and his wife were commemorated by brasses in Downe parish church.

A few glasses attributable to Verzelini have survived and these valuable relics are now safely housed in the major museums. His monopoly was taken over by Sir Jerome Bowes who was a soldier and had been Elizabeth I's ambassador to Russia. However Bowes had little or no knowledge of making glass.

By the turn of the sixteenth century the government was becoming increasingly concerned by the loss of woodlands. It was not only the wandering glassmakers who were denuding large areas of forest, but the iron smelters who also used timber as fuel. In 1611 a company headed by Sir Edward Zouch had taken control of the glass industry and obtained a twenty-one year privilege to make glass using coal as fuel. There was opposition from the wood-burning glass-makers and also from the landowners who sold them the timber. There were also practical problems. In the wood-burning furnaces the clay crucibles which contained the molten glass were open at the top, but when coal was used as a fuel the fumes discoloured the glass. The pots had to be enclosed and higher temperatures were required. This meant that the furnace itself had to be redesigned. Thomas Percival, one of Zouch's partners, is believed to have been responsible for designing the coal-fired glass furnace which was to have a dramatic effect upon the English glass industry as glass-making gradually concentrated around coal producing centres. In 1615 a Royal Proclamation forbade the use of wood as a fuel in the manufacture of glass and iron. In that same year another member of Zouch's company, Sir Robert Mansell, bought out his partners and gained control of the industry.

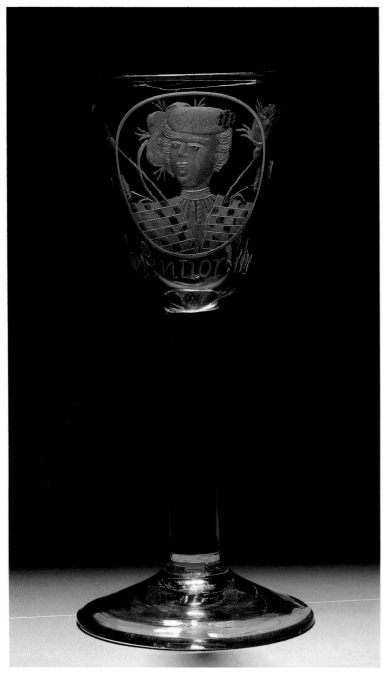

Colour Plate 22. Jacobite portrait glass with a round funnel bowl, plain stem and plain foot. H. 15.5cm. [A]. (COURTESY DRAMBUIE LIQUEUR CO.)

Mansell was a Vice-Admiral with a distinguished naval career. He too had little knowledge of glass-making but he was a man with considerable business acumen and he was to shape the structure of the English glass industry for the next forty years. As a naval man he had a vested interest in the preservation of woodlands for shipbuilding and he promoted the coal-fired furnaces against the continuing opposition from the woodland glass-makers. There may well be surviving examples of Mansell glass but it is not possible to distinguish them from other *façon de Venise* glasses of the period. There is no record to suggest that his glass was of any great artistic merit but it was utilitarian and it put the English glass industry on its feet.

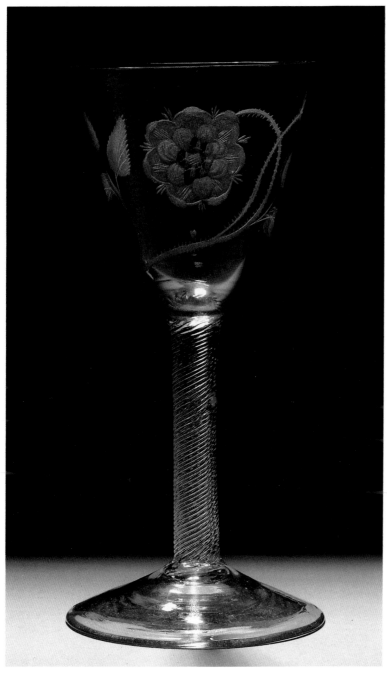

Colour Plate 23. Jacobite wine glass with a round funnel bowl, incised-twist stem and plain foot. H. 16.5cm. (COURTESY DRAMBUIE LIQUEUR CO.)

It was during Mansell's period that English glass-makers first started to produce bottles in thick, dark glass. Hitherto bottles, like other vessels, had been made in fairly clear glass. It is impossible to store wine in such bottles for any length of time, and it was the custom to drink wine 'new' after a short maturing process in a wooden cask. Bottles were only used for carrying the wine from the cask and for serving it at the table. It was found that the dark glass protected the wine from deterioration and, properly corked, the wine could be left to mature in the bottle for long periods. The wine-growing countries were quick to appreciate the value of this discovery and the dark English bottle was to become England's first glass export.

When Sir Robert Mansell died in 1656 he was succeeded by George Villiers, second Duke of Buckingham. The Commonwealth was drawing to a close; Cromwell's high ideals of government of the people, by the people, for the people, had foundered due to his inability to achieve his aims without repression and the need to maintain a large standing army. 1660 saw the restoration of Charles II. On Tuesday 29 May, ever after known as 'Oak-apple Day', the King entered London while John Evelyn, 'stood in the Strand and beheld it and blessed God'.[1] The ending of the long years of oppression released vital new energy into English life. It was the dawning of an age of extravagance and enterprise which was to affect both the arts and the sciences. The Royal Society, of which Charles II was himself a member, was founded in 1662 and the spirit of exploration and experimentation came to influence the manufacture of glass. The London Company of Glass-Sellers was at last granted a Royal Charter in 1664. They had attempted to organize themselves into an official governing body as early as 1635 and had obtained a charter from Charles I but the City of London had refused to enrol the Company as a Guild. The Glass-Sellers' Charter of 1664 empowered the Company to set standards and impose penalties on those who did not comply. Their control extended for a radius of seven miles around the City of London.

England still imported considerable quantities of Italian glass. The surviving letters and drawings of one prominent member of the Glass-Sellers' Company, John Greene, to his Italian counterpart, testify to this fact. However, there was a constant quest to produce glass of equal quality to the Venetian *cristallo* and in 1673 a London merchant, named George Ravenscroft, established a glass furnace in the Savoy. Ravenscroft had traded with Venice and had an interest in glass-making. In 1674 he petitioned Charles II for a patent for the making of 'a Perticuler sort of Chrystaline Glasse resembling Rock Christall'. The patent was granted for a period of seven years. A few weeks before the granting of the patent Ravenscroft had reached an agreement with the Glass-Sellers' Company that they would sell the glass he produced and they would also allow him to use another glasshouse at Henley-on-Thames.

Doctor Plot, a Fellow of the Royal Society, visited Ravenscroft's furnace and recorded that he was using: 'the blackest flints calcined'. In calcining, the stones, in this case flints, were heated then plunged into water causing them to fragment. Further crushing reduced them to a fine powder. Ravenscroft also used white quartz pebbles from the river Po in Italy. However, a few months after manufacture the new glasses developed a fault called crizzling. This is a fine network of cracks in the glass, obscuring the clarity of the metal, caused by decay in the chemical structure. At some point in his efforts to overcome the problem of crizzling Ravenscroft replaced some of the potash with lead oxide and this was the birth of what is known today as English lead-glass.[2] The term flint glass has also persisted and is synonymous. In 1676 the Glass-Sellers' Company announced that the crizzling defect had been overcome and Ravenscroft was allowed to mark his products with his seal — a raven's head.

The concept of using lead in glass was not entirely new. An Italian, Antonio Neri, had published a book on glassmaking, *L'Arte Vetraria*, in 1612. Doctor Christopher Merret, a Fellow of the Royal Society, translated Neri's book into English in 1662. Neri refers to, 'glass of lead, known to few', and it is likely that Ravenscroft had read Merret's translation and may have based his experiments on information in Neri's book.

The new lead-glass was to transform the English glass industry. It had a limpid clarity and refractive properties hitherto unseen in any glassware. Moreover, it was heavy and being softer and less brittle than other glasses it was to prove ideal for cutting and engraving. It was also durable and able to stand up to domestic use. By the eighteenth century good quality glassware was becoming generally available. English lead-glass was no cheaper then than it is today and the prices paid, when related to average earnings, were about the same as those paid now for quality lead-crystal. Good glass was still beyond the reach of the lower classes but the emerging middle classes were able to afford it. England started to export domestic glassware and during the eighteenth century came to dominate the world glass markets. By the end of the century English lead-glass was the finest glass available anywhere in the World.

Glass-blowing is a spectator craft. Being a product of fire, it never fails to fascinate. The making of a wine glass is a study in teamwork and precision; success depends upon skill, timing, and co-operation between the glass-blower and his assistants. The team is known as a 'chair' and consists of the glass-blower or gaffer and, usually, two or three assistants. A gather of metal is taken from the furnace pot onto the end of the blowing iron. This is rolled or marvered on a polished metal plate. The gaffer then blows the gather of molten glass into a bulb shape before sitting in the chair which has long extending arms. The blowing iron is placed across the arms of the chair and rolled back and forth to keep the bulb, which is to be the bowl of the wine glass, a regular shape. An assistant then attaches a small lump of molten glass to the end of the bulb and this is shaped into the stem. A further lump of metal is applied to the end of the stem and the gaffer forms the foot of the glass using a pair of wooden clappers. Throughout, the blowing iron is being rolled along the arms of the chair to keep the glass in line and prevent it sagging out of shape. Then an assistant applies a solid pontil iron, with a small blob of molten glass, to the underside of the foot and the gaffer marks the rim of the bowl with wet pincers. A crack spreads around the bowl and a sharp tap separates it from the blowing iron. The wine glass is now supported by the pontil iron attached to the foot. The gaffer reheats the bowl at the mouth of the furnace and finishes the final shaping using pincers and shears. After being detached from the pontil iron the glass is transferred to the annealing oven where it is allowed to cool gradually over the next day or two. This is a wine glass made in three parts: bowl, stem and foot. An alternative is the two-part wine glass in which the bowl and stem are made from one gather of metal, the stem being drawn from the base of the bowl and the foot added in the usual way.

The rough pontil mark is a feature of the eighteenth century wine glass and it is also the reason why the foot of the glass had to be conical in shape. The early eighteenth century glass can have a pontil over an eighth of an inch long and these glasses tend to have high conical or domed feet. Later in the century the pontils became neater and the feet flatter. By the end of the century many of the better glasses had the pontil mark ground and polished.

The early lead-glasses of the last quarter of the seventeenth century show that, initially, the English glass-makers tried to continue with the Venetian styles. But, it soon became apparent that this new, thicker metal needed different treatment. By the eighteenth century simpler, less frivolous, designs were in use and it was then that English glass-making really came into its own.

Colour Plate 24. The engraving on Jacobite glasses is not always of high quality. This finely engraved glass is an exception. H. 22cm. [E]. (COURTESY DRAMBUIE LIQUEUR CO.)

Jacobite glass is concerned with glass from the middle of the eighteenth century but, for the sake of completeness it is appropriate to give a brief description of the principal styles encountered throughout the century. *Figs. 1,2 & 4* illustrate some of the descriptive terms applied to the bowl, stem and foot formations, and *Fig. 3* shows the main stem formations available during the Jacobite period. These illustrations are a guide and do not represent a complete classification; for more details the reader should consult one of the textbooks on English glass.

Colour Plate 25. A pair of Jacobite wine glasses, each with a six-petal rose, two buds, an oak leaf and a star. H. 15.8cm. [B]. (Courtesy Drambuie Liqueur Co.)

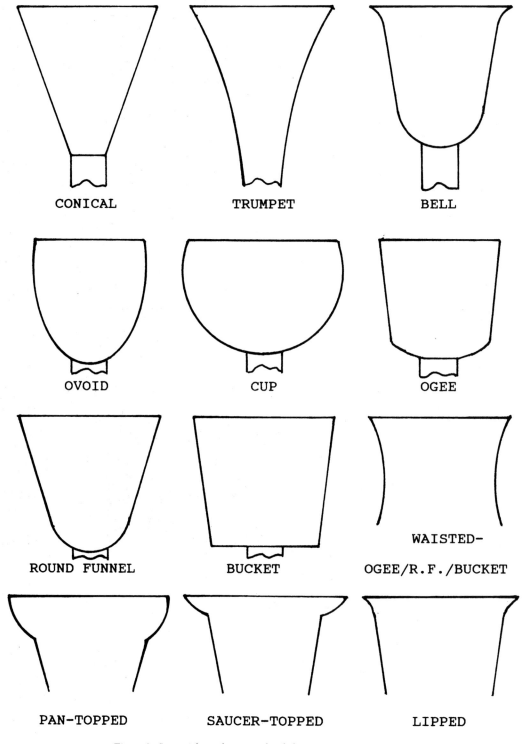

CONICAL TRUMPET BELL

OVOID CUP OGEE

ROUND FUNNEL BUCKET WAISTED-
OGEE/R.F./BUCKET

PAN-TOPPED SAUCER-TOPPED LIPPED

Figure 1. Some eighteenth century bowl shapes

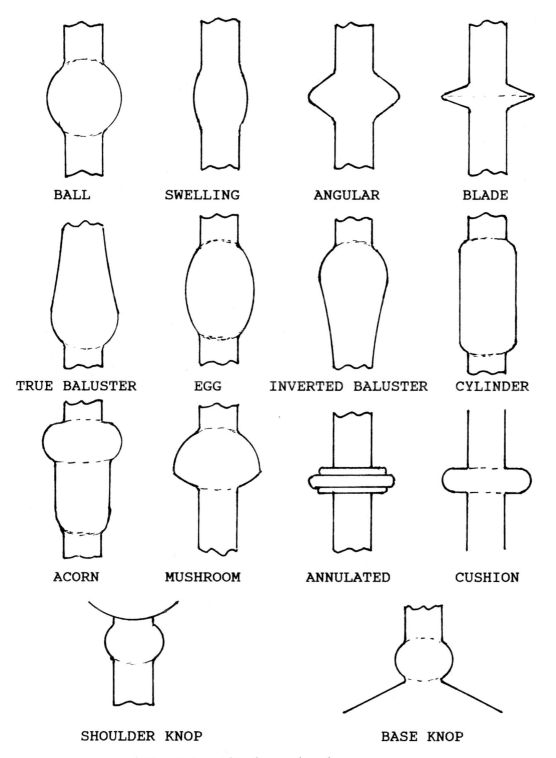

BALL SWELLING ANGULAR BLADE

TRUE BALUSTER EGG INVERTED BALUSTER CYLINDER

ACORN MUSHROOM ANNULATED CUSHION

SHOULDER KNOP BASE KNOP

Figure 2. Some eighteenth century knop shapes

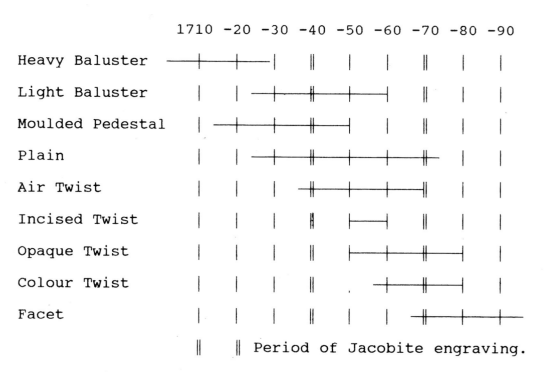

Figure 3. Some eighteenth century stem periods

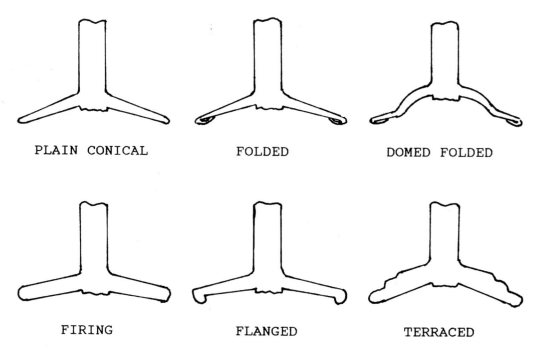

Figure 4. Main eighteenth century foot forms

Plate 8. (Far left) Wine glass with round funnel bowl, inverted baluster stem and a folded foot. H. 18cm.

Plate 9. (Left) Wine glass with bell bowl, 'Newcastle' light baluster stem and a domed folded foot. H. 17.4cm. [A]

Baluster Stems

These are usually subdivided into heavy and light balusters. The heavy baluster period is from about 1690 to 1725. As the name implies, these are heavy, solid glasses with simple shaped bowls and knopped stems (Plate 8). They invariably have a folded foot, the edge of the foot being folded under for added strength, rather like the hem on a piece of cloth. The heavy balusters are regarded by many as some of the finest English glasses ever produced.

About 1725 the heavy baluster gave way to the light baluster or balustroid glass (Plate 9). These have a more varied bowl form and lighter stems with knops that are more elaborate than on the heavier glasses. The light balusters persisted until about 1760. Around 1740, when balusters generally were declining, a distinctly elegant type of light baluster appeared, known as the Newcastle baluster. W.A.Thorpe first attributed these glasses to Newcastle-on-Tyne and the name has persisted.[3] Many of them are Dutch engraved and it is known that there was a trade in English glass between Newcastle and Holland. However, there is no definite evidence that this particular type of light baluster was ever a feature of that trade or that they were ever made in Newcastle.

Moulded Stems

Another stem which is thought to have arrived in England about the time of the accession of George I, in 1714, is the moulded pedestal or, so-called, 'Silesian' stem.

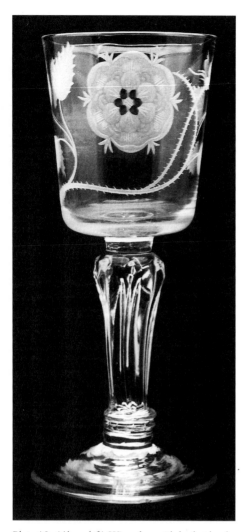

Plate 10. (Above left) Wine glass with bucket bowl, moulded pedestal stem and plain foot. H. 17.6cm. [E]

Plate 11. (Above right) Wine glass with trumpet bowl, plain drawn stem and plain foot. H. 14.4cm. [C]

This tapering, shouldered stem was made in a four-, six- or eight-sided mould. Initially a heavy glass in line with the heavy balusters, it too became lighter and modified in form (Plate 10). While not achieving the popularity of some of the other eighteenth century styles it nevertheless remained in existence until about 1750.

Plain Stems

Between about 1725 and 1775 glasses with simple plain stems were in common use. The majority are two-piece glasses with trumpet bowls and drawn stems. The plainness of the stem is frequently relieved by the presence of an enclosed tear of air, which was produced by pricking the molten glass with a blunt tool before drawing the stem (Plate 11).

Air-Twist Stems

From the tear in the plain stem it was but a small step to the air-twist stem which is thought to date from about 1735. A pricking tool was employed which introduced a number of beads of air into the molten glass, which was then drawn and twisted. Two beads of air produced a paired corkscrew twist (Plate 24), and a ring of beads of air

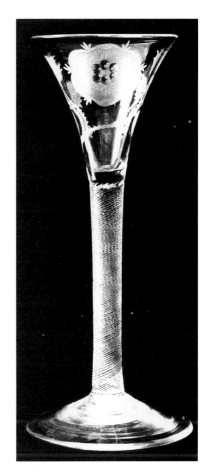

Plate 12. (Above left) Wine glass with waisted ogee bowl, composite stem and plain domed foot. H. 15.3cm. [C]

Plate 13. (Above centre) Wine glass with trumpet bowl, composite stem and plain foot. H. 17.7cm. [B]

Plate 14. (Above right) Wine glass with trumpet bowl, incised twist stem and plain foot. H. 15.8cm. [C]

the familiar multiple-spiral air-twist (MSAT) (Plates 15,16,17,18 and 19). If the pricking tool was equipped with two flat blades the bright, reflecting corkscrew twist which resulted became known as a 'mercury' twist (Plate 22). Yet another kind of air-twist stem is the spiral gauze or cable (Plate 20). These are all examples of single-series air-twist (SSAT) stems. The more complicated double-series air-twist (DSAT) has a central twisted column surrounded by an outer spiral of threads (Plate 23).

The MSAT is the most common variety and, as with its plain stemmed forebear, the two-piece glass with the trumpet bowl and drawn stem is the style most frequently encountered. However, there are many variations and knopped air-twist stems are often found (Plate 21). Some composite stems have plain and air-twist sections (Plates 12 and 13).

Another stem which is usually related to the air-twist is the incised twist (Plate 14). These enjoyed short popularity about the middle of the century and were really an imitation of the air-twist. The stem has fine twisted ribbing on its outer surface with no enclosed air.

Although air-twists continued into the 1770s their period of greatest popularity was probably from about 1740 to 1755 and therefore they naturally figure prominently amongst glasses with Jacobite engravings. The air-twist stems were gradually overtaken in popularity by the opaque-twists.

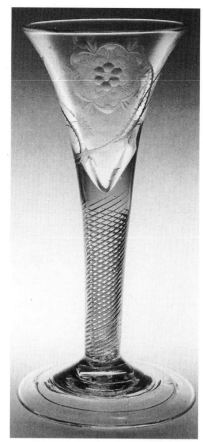

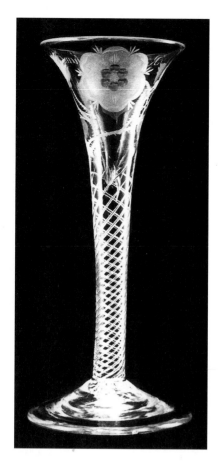

Plate 15. (Above left) Wine glass with round funnel bowl, M.S.A.T. stem and plain foot. H. 16cm. [A]

Plate 16. (Above centre) Wine glass with large trumpet bowl, drawn M.S.A.T. stem and folded foot. H. 14.3cm. [A]

Plate 17. (Above right) Wine glass with small trumpet bowl, drawn M.S.A.T. stem and plain foot. H. 16.5cm. [C]

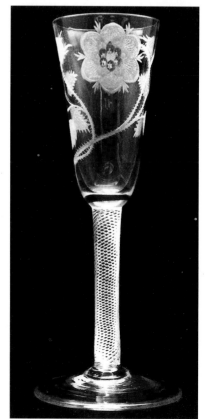

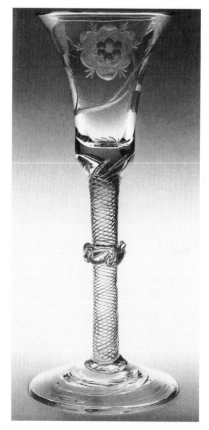

Plate 18. (Far left) Ale glass with round funnel bowl, M.S.A.T. stem and plain foot. H. 20.2cm. [D]

Plate 19. (Left) Wine glass with bell bowl, drawn M.S.A.T. stem with applied vermicular collar and plain foot. H. 17.5cm. [A]

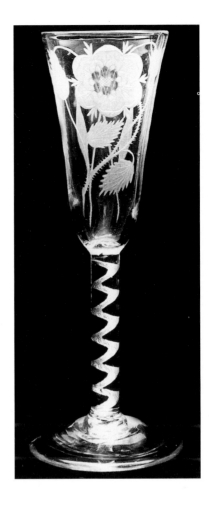

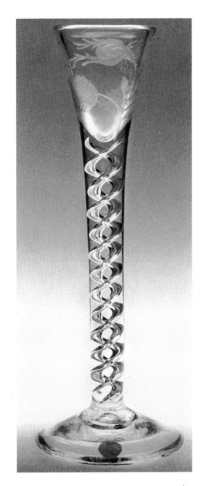

Plate 20. (Above left) Ale glass with round funnel bowl, S.S.A.T. – spiral cable – stem and plain foot. H. 20.4cm. [D]

Plate 21. (Above centre) Wine glass with bucket bowl, double knopped M.S.A.T. stem and plain foot. H. 14.5cm. [E]

Plate 22. (Above right) Cordial with drawn trumpet bowl, mercury-twist stem and plain foot. H. 17.2cm.

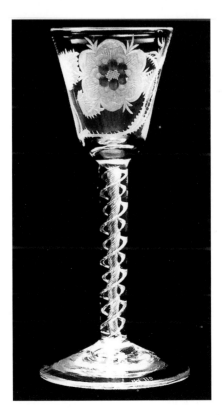

Plate 23. (Right) Wine glass with round funnel bowl, D.S.A.T. stem and plain foot. H. 15.2cm. [D]

Plate 24. (Far right) Wine glass with ogee bowl, S.S.A.T. – paired corkscrew stem and plain foot. H. 14.6cm. [E]

Opaque-Twist Stems

This is a large and varied group of eighteenth century wine glasses. The stems, sometimes called 'cotton-twists', contain spiral threads of white enamel glass. The use of white enamel in glass was nothing new; the Venetians had used it to great effect in their *latticinio* glass of the sixteenth century. The English glassmakers of the early eighteenth century knew about it and Charleston illustrates an early eighteenth century seal or pipe-stopper containing a white enamel corkscrew twist.[5] However, the use of enamel in wine glasses arose from the need to produce ever more decorative stems and was a natural progression from the air-twist design. It occurred around the middle of the eighteenth century and was to last until about 1780.

Like the air-twists there are multi-spiral opaque-twist (MSOT) stems (Plate 28) but these are nowhere near as common as the MSAT stems. There are single-series stems (SSOT) (Plate 25), and double-series stems (DSOT) (Plates 26 and 27), in which an outer twist encloses an inner spiral; but here the similarity ends because opaque-twist stems were made in a completely different way. Canes of white enamel glass were arranged in a mould and clear molten glass was poured around them. The whole was then drawn out while being twisted. A long opaque-twist cane resulted and short lengths of this cane were then used to form the stems of these attractive glasses. Using this method it was possible to produce patterns which were much more complex than any that could be achieved with an air-twist, and there are even some triple-series opaque-twist stems. Wine glasses with opaque-twist stems always have a three-part construction because the stem had to be made as a separate entity. The drawn stem does not occur and therefore the trumpet bowl is far less common on opaque twist glasses.

Colour-Twist and Mixed Twist Stems

These are collectors' rarities. The colour-twists have stems with twists of coloured enamels. The colours are most frequently red, blue or green; the rarest colour of all being yellow. Mixed twists are, as the name implies, glasses with stems containing a mixture of air and enamel twists.

Facet Stems

During the last quarter of the eighteenth century the fashion for wine glasses with cut stems completely dominated the market. Glass-cutting was, again, nothing new; the technique had been used on larger pieces of glass, such as mirrors, since early in the century, but it was an applied decorative technique which added considerably to the cost of the article. Cutting facets on the stems of better quality wine glasses probably started in the late 1760s and gradually replaced the opaque twist as a decorative technique (Plate 29).

It can be seen from the foregoing brief description of stem forms that, throughout the eighteenth century, there was a gradual change of style from the heavy knopped balusters with large bowls and folded feet, to the lighter glasses with small bowls and delicate stems. This transition from heavy baroque to the more decorative rococo affected all the arts in the eighteenth century. The natural change in style of wine glasses was also influenced by a series of Glass Excise Acts imposed to help raise

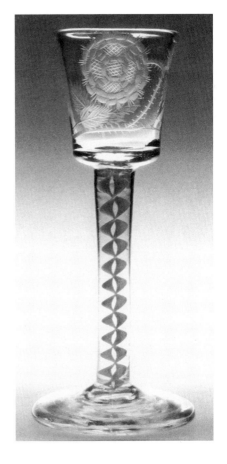

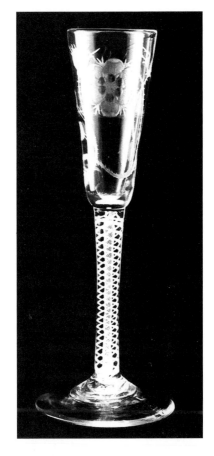

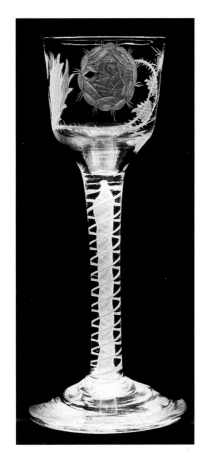

Plate 25. (Above left) Wine glass with bucket bowl, S.S.O.T. stem and plain foot. H. 15.5cm.

Plate 26. (Above centre) Ratafia glass with round funnel bowl, D.S.O.T. stem and plain foot. H. 18.3cm. [F]

Plate 27. (Above right) Wine glass with ogee bowl, D.S.O.T. stem and plain foot. H. 14.6cm. [G]

Plate 28. (Right) Wine glass with round funnel bowl and enamel decoration, M.S.O.T. stem with swelling knop, plain foot. H. 14cm.

Plate 29. (Far right) Wine glass with round funnel bowl, hexagonal-faceted stem and plain foot. H. 14.9cm.

Plate 30. Firing glass with trumpet bowl and short plain stem. H. 8.6cm. [A]

Plate 31. Firing glass with bell bowl and rudimentary stem. H. 9.5cm. [C[

revenue for the wars in Europe. The first was the Excise Act of 1745, which came into operation in 1746 and which levied a tax on the weight of metal in the glass pot. It was therefore in the glass-maker's interest to get as many glasses as possible out of a given quantity of metal. This tax was doubled by a further Act in 1777 and increased again in 1787. The Glass Excise imposed considerable hardship on the glass-makers and was one of the reasons for the rise of the glass industry in Ireland where there was no such duty. The Excise remained in force until 1845 when it was repealed.

The 1745 Excise Act is sometimes viewed as a watershed in the changing styles of eighteenth century wine glasses, as though the tax itself was responsible for dramatic alterations in style. It has been said that small-bowled wine glasses (Plate 17) must be post-1745 and a glass with a folded foot (Plate 16) must be pre-1745, but these rigid criteria cannot be applied to eighteenth century glasses; the smaller bowl had been developing before 1745, and a folded foot can occur, albeit rarely, on an opaque-twist glass. It is important to realize that the transition from heavy to lighter styles was the result of a gradual change in fashion which coincided with, and was influenced by, the Excise Act, but the tax was not the sole cause of the changes.[6]

A relatively heavy glass in existence throughout the Georgian period was the 'firing glass' (Plates 30 and 31). These stubby little glasses have thick feet, the usual form being the firing foot *(Fig 4)* which is a flattish disc, sometimes up to half an inch in thickness. Less common are the terraced foot and the flanged foot. These glasses had to stand up to being rapped on the table after a toast had been drunk; the noise so produced was said to resemble musketry fire.

The accurate dating of a glass can be an intriguing problem. Unlike silver or porcelain, there are no hallmarks or maker's marks to help pin-point the date of manufacture, only the overall style of the glass. It is necessary to study each part of the glass: the foot, the stem and the bowl, and in this way it may be possible to date a glass within five or ten years.

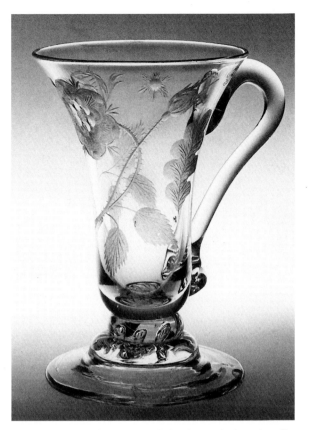

Plate 32. Jelly glass with bell bowl, single loop handle, rudimentary beaded stem and plain foot. H. 11.4cm. [A]

Wine glasses have been engraved to commemorate all manner of events and a date is sometimes included in the engraving. Dates of this kind can be helpful in dating the glass itself but they have to be viewed with caution. Such a date is unlikely to be referring to some event in the future but it could be commemorating some event several years prior to the date of manufacture of the glass. Conversely a contemporary date could have been engraved on an old glass, and a date can sometimes be a later addition to an existing engraving. However, having said this, the most likely probability is that the glass was engraved shortly after it was made, any date corresponding with the time of manufacture, but engraved dates have to be taken in conjunction with all the other evidence. Some glasses have a small coin enclosed in a hollow knop (Plate 105). Here all that one can say is that the glass could not have been made before the date on the coin.

The whole question of dating glasses is central to the problems surrounding Jacobite engravings and, for reasons which will become clear in a later chapter, the date when the opaque-twist glasses first appeared is of special importance. Indeed it may be that the Jacobite engravings can help to establish this date. Most authorities agree that opaque-twist glasses became freely available across the country between 1750 and 1755. The trade cards of the glass sellers, and advertisements in the newspapers of the time, are probably the best indicators of the glasses that were on sale in any particular period. Francis Buckley made a study of eighteenth century newspapers from London and a number of major provincial towns. He was looking for glass sellers' advertisements and items of news relating to glass. Difficulties arise over terminology used in the advertisements. 'Flint glass' usually refers to clear, lead table glass. However, when flint glass is being grouped with 'crown' window-glass and plate glass for comparison with bottle glass, the group is referred to as 'white glass', as opposed

Plate 33. Finger bowl and stand. H. of bowl 8.9cm. Diameter of stand 15.8cm. [C]

to the bottle, 'green glass'. Sometimes the phrase 'white and flint glass' appears and here 'white' could well be referring to enamel glass. Although Bristol ultimately became the main centre for the making of enamel glass, Buckley came to the conclusion that opaque-twist glasses first appeared in London.[7]

Norwich glass-sellers bought glasses made in London and, in February 1757, one such glass-seller, Jonas Phillips, makes specific reference to enamelled glass in his advertisement: 'The Goods are entirely new, and of the neatest Patterns now made in England, either cut, flower'd, enamel'd, moulded, worm,d or plain.'[8] The term 'worm'd' referred to air-twists and 'enamel'd' undoubtedly referred to opaque-twists. Buckley was of the opinion that earlier advertisements, in 1753 and 1754, referring to 'Glasses made of the best metal and from the newest patterns now in England', also probably related to opaque-twists.[9] Charleston's observation that: 'a phenomenon normally finds its way into print only some time after it has occurred',[10] should also be taken into account when trying to establish the date when a certain style appeared.

The Glass Excise Act of 1745 makes no mention of enamel glass, so it seems safe to assume that opaque-twists were not a regular product of English glasshouses prior to this date. It has even been suggested that the opaque-twist glasses were introduced because the enamel canes were exempt from duty, but the saving in weight would have been minimal and their development is more likely to have been part of the general trend towards a more decorative style. Even so, it may be noted that the decline of the opaque-twist stem coincided with the introduction of the Excise Act of 1777 which did impose a duty on enamel glass.

Thorpe believed that enamelled twists came into use in the 1740s and records that as early as 1744 some 'composition glass' was stolen from a warehouse in Southwark, and in 1747 the White Glass-house advertised 'a quantity of glass cane for making beads of various colours' and 'also about 56lb of white enamel'.[11] The earliest recorded opaque-twist glass is engraved with the date 1747,[12] and white enamel canes were advertised for sale at 10p per pound in 1748;[13] so, the date on the 1747 glass may well be a valid contemporary date. Another recorded glass is dated 1748,[14] which again lends support to the date on the 1747 glass and two others are dated 1754 and 1755.[15] To this will be added the evidence of the Jacobite engravings. Buckley's conclusion was: 'Taking the evidence as a whole, it is probable that the glasses with opaque-twisted stems were first made in London rather before 1750, and in Bristol a few years later'.[16]

Glass Engraving

With the exception of a few opaque-twist glasses with enamel decoration, all the decoration on Jacobite glasses is by glass engraving. There are three glass engraving techniques: diamond-point, wheel and stipple. Of these only the first two are found on Jacobite glasses; the third, more artistic technique of stipple engraving, does not occur.

The diamond-point technique consists of scratching the surface of the glass with a diamond-pointed tool. It was used in Roman times and re-emerged among the Venetian glass artists in the sixteenth century. The technique was practised in England long before the eighteenth century and most of the surviving Verzelini glasses were engraved in this way. The artist responsible for these glasses is thought to have been a French engraver, Anthony de Lysle, who was living in London at the same time as Verzelini. Good diamond-point engraving requires great skill but the equipment required is minimal and any enthusiast, however inexperienced, can attempt an engraving. With the notable exception of the 'Amen' glasses, most of which show considerable expertise, many of the diamond-point engraved Jacobite glasses fall into this 'amateur' category.

Wheel-engraving, which was the technique used for the great majority of Jacobite glasses, is quite different. A bench tool is required and a long training needed to acquire the skill necessary to produce work of an acceptable standard. The engraver sits in front of a revolving horizontal spindle which, in the eighteenth century, was worked by a foot-treadle. Copper discs, varying in diameter from one eighth of an inch to four inches and in thickness from paper-thin to one quarter of an inch, can be attached to the end of the spindle. A complete set of discs can number over one hundred. A pointed leather strap trails on the top of the revolving disc conveying an abrasive, such as fine emery, suspended in an oily medium. The engraver presents the glass to the underside of the wheel, the shape of the cut being determined by the diameter and thickness of the disc, and the texture of the cut by the fineness of the abrasive. If desired, part of the cut can be polished to highlight certain areas. This is done using softer discs, made, for example, of lead or wood, and a polishing agent such as tripoli powder or pumice.

The development of wheel-engraving in England needs to be examined in some detail. The technique was practised in Bohemia in the sixteenth century and was well established on the Continent in the second half of the seventeenth century. The Germans used wheel-engraving to great effect on their thick potash glass, developing a high degree of skill. The English craftsmen, however, were slow to embrace the art, due probably to the fact that, prior to the development of lead-glass, they had not really had suitable glass upon which to work. Consequently wheel-engraving by English craftsmen did not become established until the second quarter of the eighteenth century. Some wheel-engraved glasses with heraldic inscriptions relating to King William III and Queen Anne, dating from the end of the seventeenth century and the first quarter of the eighteenth century, were almost certainly engraved in this country but are likely to have been the work of foreign engravers. In 1699 the marriage of one Alexander Nichols, an 'engraver in glass and living near the Star in Nightingale Lane, Wapping', was recorded in the church register,[17] but 'engraver' could well refer to diamond-point engraving. The first wheel-engravers in England were German or Bohemian craftsmen. Charleston mentions the Nuremberg engraver Anton Wilhelm Mäuerl being in England between 1699 and 1710,[18] and also George Franz Kreybich a Bohemian merchant and engraver.[19] Kreybich visited London in 1688 and admired English lead-crystal. He often travelled with a portable wheel-engraving tool and may well have practised his craft in this country. The early German engravers were employed in the mirror grinding workshops cutting the glass frames which often surrounded the better quality mirrors. These frames were strips of glass set around the edge of the mirror and they were frequently cut and decorated with wheel-engraving.

Some glasses from the first quarter of the eighteenth century, displaying what Thorpe calls 'decorative formalism',[20] are almost certainly the work of highly skilled German engravers. The engraving is usually around the rim of the bowl and takes the form of intricate formal borders of arabesques with detailed scrollwork. This precise baroque ornament is typical of styles in a number of German pattern books published in the early eighteenth century and the engraving is often of a high quality.

The earliest English engraved glasses probably date from about 1730. On 12 June 1735 one London glass seller, Benjamin Payne, advertised 'the Arms of all the Royal Family finely engraved on glasses',[21] and on the 30 August in the same year he placed the following advertisement in the *Daily Journal*: 'The Glass Sellers Arms. Where are to be had the best Double Flint Glass, Diamond-Cut and Plain, with several curiosities engraved on glass. The lowest price is marked on each glass.'[22] It is thought likely that Payne himself was a glass-engraver.

In the hands of the English wheel-engravers the baroque borders of complex, almost architectural, symmetry gradually became less formal and eventually gave way to the period of 'decorative naturalism'.[23] Glasses were engraved displaying large natural flowers, moths, butterflies, and insects; indeed, anything natural from the garden. These designs were probably better suited to the English temperament and they had the added advantage of not requiring the same meticulous skill as the heraldic inscriptions and the German baroque designs, a degree of skill which, for the most part, eluded the early English craftsmen. 'Flowered Glasses' were first referred to in an advertisement placed in the *Daily Advertiser* on 21 December 1742 by a glass seller named Jerome Johnson, of the Entire Glass Shop on the Strand, at the corner of St Martin's Lane.[24] Johnson later describes himself as 'the Maker and Glass Engraver'.[25]

It can be seen that wheel-engraving in England by the middle of the eighteenth century was a relatively new craft. It was also a craft requiring considerable expertise and competent wheel-engravers at this time were few in number. London was, undoubtedly, the centre for this expertise and again we have to look at the newspaper advertisements to plot the early spread of wheel-engraving. All the evidence suggests that in the early years the craft was confined to London and did not spread to the provinces until after 1750.[26]

'Decorative naturalism' was the fashion of English engraving from about 1740 to 1760 and it was this period which gave rise to the wheel-engraved Jacobite glasses.

CHAPTER 5
Some Jacobite Glasses

The typical Jacobite engraving is a rose with six outer petals and six inner petals around a seeded centre. Three pointed sepals appear between each of the outer petals and the base of each outer petal, adjacent to the seeded centre, is highlighted as a polished circular concavity. A thorned stem branches to support one or two buds. If there is a single bud (Plate 34), it is always a closed bud on the sinister side of the rose (that is, to the right of the rose as viewed from the front) and there are five leaves. If there are two buds (Plate 35), one is a closed bud on the sinister side of the rose and the other is an open bud on the dexter side (that is, to the left of the rose as viewed from the front). When two buds are present there are four leaves.

This pattern is remarkably constant although there are variations: the rose may have seven or eight petals (Plates 36 and 37) and can sometimes be multi–petalled (Plate 38).

a

b

Plate 34 a, b, c. Wine glass engraved with a single-bud rose. [D]

c

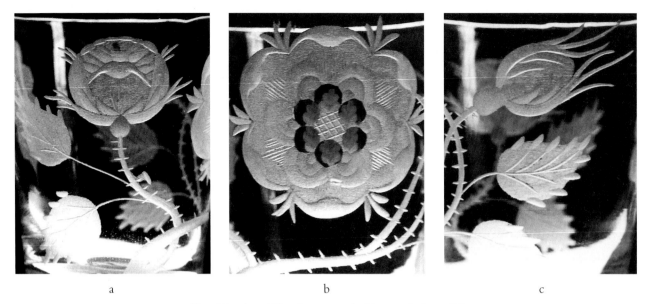

a   b   c

Plate 35 a, b, c. Wine glass engraved with a two-bud rose [E]

Plate 36. Seven-petal rose [A]

Plate 37. Eight-petal rose [C]

Plate 38. Multi-petal rose [G]

Plate 39. The arms granted by Charles II to Colonel Carlos

Plate 40. Wine glass engraved with an oak tree, three crowns and a bust of Charles II

The five-petal rose, like the heraldic Tudor rose, is so uncommon on Jacobite glasses that, when it occurs, it can almost be regarded as an engraving error. However, it does appear on the Cycle Jewel and Grant Francis claimed that the five-petal rose was the emblem of the White Rose Society.[1]

The significance of the rose is the subject of a later chapter but it seems likely that the idea of engraving Jacobite emblems on drinking glasses came about during the period of decorative naturalism when flowers of all kinds were being engraved. The earliest Jacobite glasses usually display a simple engraving with just a single-bud rose. Later glasses are more elaborate with additional emblems and mottoes.

The Oak

Trees have featured in royal badges since Plantagenet times. After the execution of Charles I, Cavaliers would often top, or behead, an oak-tree as a symbol of mourning for their dead king. The oak came to be of particular significance to the Stuarts after Charles II's escape from the Battle of Worcester in 1651 when he hid in the Boscobel oak and watched Cromwell's men searching for him below. The original tree was destroyed by souvenir hunters after the Restoration; the present Boscobel oak is said to have been grown from one of the old tree's acorns. When Charles returned to London on his restoration in 1660 (Oak-apple Day, 29 May), he was wearing a sprig of oak leaves on his coat.

Colonel William Careless (later Carlos), who shared the hiding place in the 'royal oak' with Charles, was granted a coat of arms featuring an oak-tree and three crowns (Plate 39). A rare group of glasses display a similar tree with the three crowns and the head of Charles II (Plate 40).

The oak leaf was a Tory emblem in the 1710 election and it was also an emblem of the Stuart clan. In battle clansmen often wore a flower or a sprig of green in their bonnets; for the Stuarts it was an oak leaf. Thus the oak is not solely of English significance. After the death of Queen Anne, oak leaves were offensive to the Hanoverians and on Oak-apple Day 1716, some soldiers were severely beaten in Hyde Park for wearing oak leaves in their hats.

When represented on a Jacobite glass the oak usually takes the form of a single leaf

Plate 41. (Left) Wine glass with an oak leaf engraved on the bowl [C]

Plate 42. (Above) Wine glass with oak leaves engraved on the foot [C]

Plate 43. Wine glass engraved with the stricken oak [B]

on the reverse side of the bowl to the rose (Plate 41), or a pair of leaves on the foot of the glass (Plate 42).

A few finely engraved glasses display what is known as the 'stricken oak'. This shows the stock of a dead oak-tree with a vigorous young sapling springing from the roots (Plate 43). The new sapling presumably represents the anticipated second restoration of the Stuarts.

The Star

On the night Prince Charles was born, in December 1720, a new star was said to have been observed for the first time. This was seen as an omen of good fortune and the star appears on a silver medal (Plate 44a) of 1729. This is the 'Micat Inter Omnes' medal (He shines amongst all) and the six-pointed star is before the face of the young Prince Charles. On the reverse is Prince Henry.

On drinking glasses the six-pointed star is engraved on the reverse side of the bowl to the rose. It sometimes appears alone (Plate 45) but, more usually, with the oak leaf (Plate 46) and rarely with the thistle (Plate 47). Jacobites would often kiss the star on their glass after drinking the loyal toast.

Plate 44 a, b. Jacobite medal showing: a. Prince Charles with a six-pointed star before his face and b. on the reverse, Prince Henry

Plate 45. Bowl of a wine glass engraved with a six-pointed star [C]

Plate 47. Wine glass engraved with a thistle and a star. [D] See also Plate 97

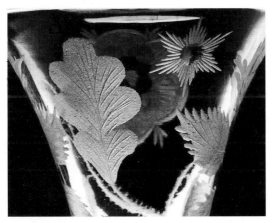

Plate 46. Wine glass engraved with an oak leaf and a star [A]

a

b

Plate 48 a, b. Wine glass engraved with an oak leaf and a thistle [C]

Plate 49. (Left) Wine glass with a thistle engraved on the reverse side of the bowl to the rose [E]

Plate 50. (Above) Wine glass with a thistle engraved on the foot [E]

Plate 51. (Right) Royal badge of Scotland

Plate 52. (Far right) Wine glass engraved with a thistle and crown [D]

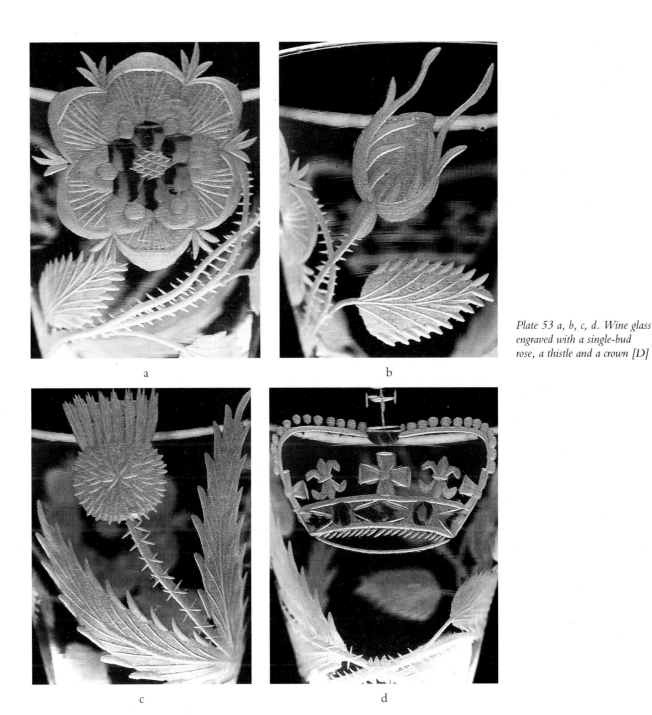

a

b

c

d

Plate 53 a, b, c, d. Wine glass engraved with a single-bud rose, a thistle and a crown [D]

The Thistle

The Scottish floral emblem was first used as a royal badge in the fourteenth century by James III of Scotland. The Most Ancient and Most Noble Order of the Thistle is second only to the Most Noble Order of the Garter. It is probable that a Scottish Order of Chivalry existed in the fifteenth century but the Order of the Thistle was instituted in its present form by James II in 1687.

On wine glasses the thistle usually appears alone on the reverse side of the bowl to the rose (Plate 49), but is sometimes found on the foot of the glass (Plate 50) and can also occur in conjunction with an oak leaf (Plate 48). The royal badge of Scotland is a thistle surmounted by a crown (Plate 51), as represented on the wine glass (Plate 52). Plate 53 is of a glass where the thistle is on the reverse side of the bowl to a six-petal rose which has a crown on the dexter side and a single bud on the sinister side.

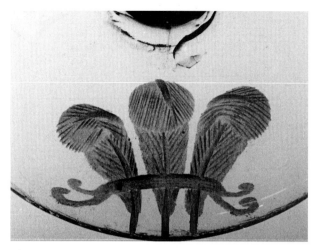

Plate 54. Wine glass with the fleur-de-lis engraved on the foot [C]

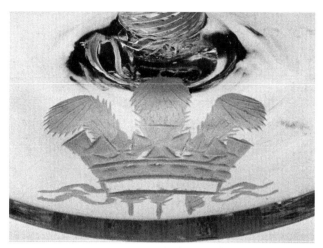

Plate 55. Wine glass with feathers and crown engraved on the foot [B]

Plate 56. Badge of the heir apparent

Plate 57. Wine glass engraved with the badge of the heir apparent [D]

Feathers

These are the fleur-de-lis, the ancient cognizance of France. They can occur on the bowl of the glass (Plate 78) but are usually engraved on the foot (Plate 54). The reference is to the Prince of Wales and the fleur-de-lis sometimes arises from a crown (Plate 55). Rarely the complete badge of the Heir Apparent (Plate 56) is displayed as a plume of three ostrich feathers arising from a crown above the motto *'Ich Dien'* (Plate 57).

Butterflies

Butterflies, moths and bees are less easy to explain. They could simply be part of the floral theme which typified the period of decorative naturalism but, where Jacobite engravings are concerned, there seems to be a need to find some hidden meaning. Insects and grubs, when they appear on Jacobite glasses, are said to represent the 'return of the soul' in the form of Prince Charles Edward. This stems from the belief that if a Scot dies away from his or her native land the soul returns home instantaneously by a subterranean route.

These emblems are sometimes said to represent the decay of the Jacobite movement

Plate 58. Wine glass engraved with a butterfly [D]

Plate 59. Ale glass engraved with a butterfly [F]

Plate 60. Decanter engraved with a bird [D]

and it is true that they do tend to occur on later glasses, when the Jacobite cause was lost, but it is interesting to note that the butterfly or moth also appears on some very early single-bud glasses when, one would imagine, Jacobite hopes were high.

Butterflies and moths belong to the order *lepidoptera*, the butterfly having knobbed antennae (e.g. Plates 108j and 112n) unlike the moth (e.g. Plate 113i). Whether the engravers really intended to distinguish between them, however, may be doubtful.

Birds

The bird, sometimes said to be a jay, is an uncommon feature on Jacobite glasses (Plate 60). It is found more frequently on the later glasses.

The Compass

When this device occurs it is usually on a decanter (Plate 61). It could represent a nautical compass alluding to the 'King over the Water', although this is, perhaps, not a very convincing explanation. The compass points North East and usually points in the direction of the star (Plate 62).

Plate 62. The other Chastleton Manor decanter (Plate 4) showing detail of the compass point [A]

Plate 61. Chastleton Manor decanter engraved with a compass. H. 30.1cm. [C]

Crests and Shields

Occasionally family crests are, rather boldly, incorporated in the engraving (Plates 63 and 64). One wine glass (Plate 65) displays a finely engraved shield with the arms of England quartered with those of Scotland; on the reverse side of the bowl is the fleur-de-lis and the motto *'Radiat'* (Plate 78).

Mottoes

The custom of drinking toasts in wine must go back to the beginning of recorded history. And, what better than the wine glass for commemorating all manner of events and personalities? The sentiment is usually expressed by the use of an emblem accompanied by some words in the form of a name or a motto. What is rather odd about Jacobite glasses is the extent to which Latin is used in the wording of the mottoes. With the exception of some club glasses such as: *'The Friendly Hunt'*, *'Success to the Society'* and a *'Health to all our Fast Friends'*, the majority of Jacobite mottoes are in Latin. The language is unlikely to have been used as a means of disguising the

Plate 63. (Right) Jacobite finger bowl engraved with a crest – a griffin's head erased, gorged with a ducal coronet [C]

Plate 64. (Below left) Jacobite wine glass engraved with a crest – a lion statant guardant. The crest is probably that of Fairfax. [A]. See also Colour Plate 41

Plate 65. (Below right) Wine glass engraved with a shield divided quarterly with the arms of England in the first and fourth quarters and those of Scotland in the second and third quarters. The reverse side of the bowl is engraved with the fleur-de-lis and the motto 'Radiat' [B]. See also Plate 78

message because the classics were probably more widely understood in the eighteenth century than they are today. It will be shown in a later chapter that the rose emblems on Jacobite glasses follow certain heraldic principles and, since Latin is the language of heraldry, this could well be the reason why it was used so extensively for the Jacobite mottoes.

For an interpretation of the Jacobite mottoes the present author draws heavily upon a paper read to the Glass Circle in 1983 by F.J.Lelièvre.[2]

Fiat

This is the motto most commonly encountered on Jacobite glasses (Plate 66). At one time it was thought to be the 'word' of the Cycle Club and, in a Jacobite context, it could have started life in this way, but it clearly became far more widespread for it occurs too frequently to be the 'word' of any one society.

'Fiat' has dual significance because it means 'may it come to pass', but it is also the equivalent of the word 'Amen', which is derived through Greek from Hebrew and means 'may it be so'.

The following may illustrate the reciprocal use of 'Amen' and 'Fiat': On 30 July 1746 nine Jacobites were executed on Kennington Common. It had started to rain as

a   b

c   d

Plate 66 a, b, c, d. A few examples of Jacobite glasses engraved with 'Fiat'. a [A]. b [B]. c [C]. d [E]

the three sledges, lined with straw, were drawn-up in the prison yard to convey the condemned men to the gallows. Their fetters were removed as they climbed on to the sledges and they were drawn, three to a sledge, through the waiting crowds. On the scaffold there was no priest to comfort them but they made their final speeches. Below the scaffold was the quartering block and the fire. The condemned men were unrepentant. After praying they threw papers into the crowd; these were later discovered to be printed documents of a treasonable nature, stating that they died willingly for their king and his cause, regretting that the attempt had failed and asserting that they would make the same attempt again were the opportunity to arise. One or two threw their gold-laced hats into the crowd and others, it is said, threw their prayer-books. The pages were found to be turned down at the 89th Psalm, from the 21st verse to the end.[3] This psalm, which is appropriate in times of national distress, is a mixture of joy and grief but concludes with a prayer for deliverance. David is the Lord's annointed servant. He has been promised the Lord's mercy, and protection against his adversaries. Verse 29: 'His seed also will I make to endure for ever, and his throne as the days of heaven'. But David has been defeated in battle and his enemies are triumphant. The similarity between the plight of the Old Pretender, James, and that of David is obvious. There is the temptation to reproach the Lord but the psalm concludes: Verse 52: 'Blessed be the Lord for evermore. Amen and Amen.'

In the Vulgate the same psalm ends 'Benedictus Dominus in aeternum. Fiat. Fiat.'[4]

Reddite

'Restore', 'give back' (imperative, plural).
The word occurs on a Jacobite medal (Plate 67) engraved at the time of the failed '1708' attempt. The medal shows a bust of James III with the motto '*Cuius Est*', 'Whose is this image'. The reverse shows Great Britain and Ireland with the motto '*Reddite*'.

a   b

Plate 67 a, b. (Above) James III and VIII and the 'Restoration of the Kingdom' medal. 1708

Plate 68. Prince Charles and the 'Redeat Magnus Ille' medal. 1752

Redeat

'May he return'.

This motto appears on a Jacobite medal with a bust of Prince Charles (Plate 68). The medal was struck in 1752 for the Oak Society and this society may also be connected with some of the wine glasses engraved with this motto. '*Redeat*' usually occurs on the bowl of the glass (Plate 69) but glasses engraved with '*Turno Tempus Erit*' on the bowl sometimes also have '*Redeat*' on the foot (Plate 70).

Plate 69. Wine glass with 'Redeat' engraved on the bowl [A]

Plate 70. Wine glass with 'Redeat' engraved on the foot [A]

Plate 71. *(Left) Wine glass with oak leaves and 'Redi' engraved on the foot [A]*

Plate 72. *(Above) Wine glass with 'Revirescit' engraved on the bowl [B]*

a

b

Plate 74. *The Prince Charles 'Oak Medal' of 1750*

Plate 73 a, b. *Charles II medal with oak-tree, crowns and 'Revirescet'*

Plate 75. *Wine glass engraved with the misspelt motto 'Reverescit' [E]*

Redi

'Return', 'come back' (imperative form of '*Redeat*').

This motto usually appears on the foot of the glass between a pair of oak leaves (Plate 71), the bowl of the glass being engraved with a rose and buds in the usual manner. Some authors have regarded '*Redi*' as a contraction of '*Redii*', meaning 'I have returned', because it was thought that '*Redi*' and '*Redeat*' were mottoes to commemorate clandestine visits to London by Prince Charles after the 'Forty-five. The '*Redeat*' medal may have been struck for this reason but it does not follow that this also applies to the glasses and more will be said about this in the next chapter.

Revirescit

'It grows green again', 'it shoots again'.

This motto (Plate 72) occurs in conjunction with the 'stricken oak' (Plates 43 and

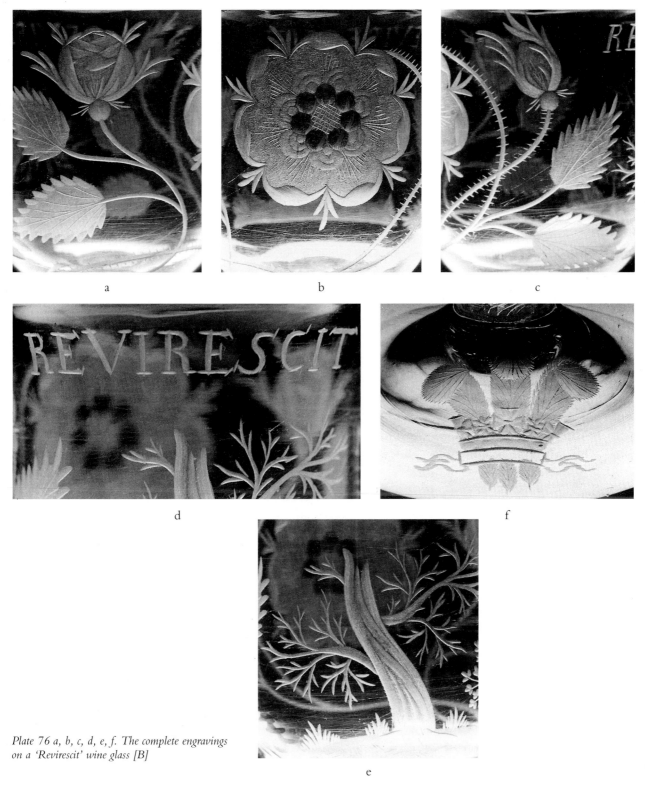

a   b   c

d   f

Plate 76 a, b, c, d, e, f. The complete engravings on a 'Revirescit' wine glass [B]

e

76e). It is said to have been a word first used in this context by Charles II before his restoration. A medal with a bust of Charles II on one side has, on the reverse, an oak tree with three crowns and '*Revirescet*' (Plate 73). The Oak Medal (Plate 74), which is known to have been struck for the Oak Society in 1750, has on one side a bust of Prince Charles and on the other the 'stricken oak' and '*Revirescit*'. The motto '*Reverescit*', when it occurs on a glass, is a misspelling (Plate 75).

a   b

Plate 77 a, b. Wine glass engraved with 'Reddas Incolumem' [C]

Plate 78. Wine glass engraved with the fleur-de-lis and 'Radiat'. [B]. See also Plate 65

Reddas Incolumem

'(May you) restore unharmed'.

This is derived from Latin poetry. It occurs in an ode by Horace addressed to a ship conveying his friend Virgil across the sea. This 'across the water' sentiment is, of course, particularly apt in the Jacobite context (Plate 77).

Radiat

'It shines'.

An uncommon motto on Jacobite glasses (Plate 78).

Turno Tempus Erit

'For Turnus there shall be a time'.

These glasses also usually bear the motto '*Fiat*' and Grant Francis believed that they too belonged to the Cycle Club, a view which is difficult to sustain since some of the glasses also carry the motto '*Redeat*' which Francis had already ascribed to the Oak Society (Plate 79).[5]

'*Turno Tempus Erit*' comes from Virgil's *Aeneid* and the temptation is to equate Turnus with Charles Edward. Lelièvre, however, suggests a more likely interpretation.[6] Turnus and Aeneas are in conflict for mastery of Italy. A young ally of Aeneas has been slain. In their final struggle Aeneas defeats Turnus but is inclined to spare his life. However, when he sees that Turnus is wearing the sword-belt belonging to his young friend, Aeneas kills his adversary. Turnus, therefore, is probably meant to represent the Duke of Cumberland, the message being that the Hanoverian victory might be short-lived.

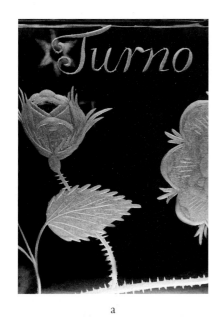

a

b

c

d

e

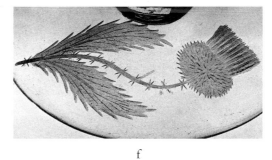

f

Plate 79 a, b, c, d, e, f. Wine glass engraved with 'Turno Tempus Erit' and 'Fiat' on the bowl and 'Redeat' on the foot [A]

Floreat

'May it flower (flourish)'.

Ab Obice Major

'Greater from the check'.

Cognoscunt Me Mei

'My own recognize me'.
This is known to occur on a portrait glass.[7]

Premium Virtutis

'Reward of valour'.
This is on the same portrait glass as *'Cognoscunt Me Mei'*.

Plate 80 a, b, c. Wine glasses engraved with 'Audentior Ibo'. a [A]. b [C]. c [E]

a

b

c

Pro Patria

'For the sake of the Country'.

Caelum Non Animum Mutant Qui Trans Mare Currunt

'They change clime, not heart, who speed across the sea'.

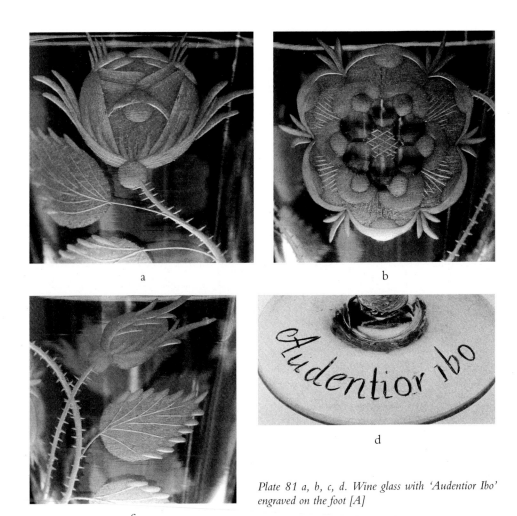

a

b

c

Plate 81 a, b, c, d. Wine glass with 'Audentior Ibo' engraved on the foot [A]

d

This motto, which is derived from Horace's *Epistles,* is engraved in diamond-point on a glass belonging to a group known as 'Old Pretender' glasses (pp. 187 and 236). These wine glasses also carry the reversed cypher 'JR' (Jacobus Rex) with a crown above and the figure '8' below. They are similar to the *'Amen'* glasses and will be discussed with them in a later chapter. The 'Old Pretender' glass bearing this inscription is now believed to be fake engraved (p. 233).

Tempora Mutantur Et Nos Mutamur In Illis

'The times change and we change in them'.
One glass is known with this inscription.[8] The glass is engraved with the Jacobite rose and two buds but the engraver has mistakenly engraved *'Mudantur'* for both *'Mutantur'* and *'Mutamur'*.

Audentior Ibo

'I shall go with greater daring'.
This motto is almost invariably in association with a wheel-engraved portrait of Charles Edward (Plate 80). An exception is the glass (Plate 81) which has the motto engraved on the foot and a rose and two buds on the bowl.

Lelièvre has some interesting theories about the derivation of this motto but concludes that it probably comes from the sixth book of *Aeneid.*[9] In this Aeneas consults a mystic who tells of grim fighting to come but says to Aeneas 'sed contra audentior ito', 'but go forth against it with greater daring'. In the Jacobite inscription the imperative 'ito'–'go' is changed to 'ibo', future, – 'I shall go'.

Colour Plate 26. This Jacobite wine glass has a rose and two buds engraved on the bowl. The foot is engraved with oak leaves and the motto 'Redi'. H. 15.5cm. [C] (COURTESY DRAMBUIE LIQUEUR CO.)

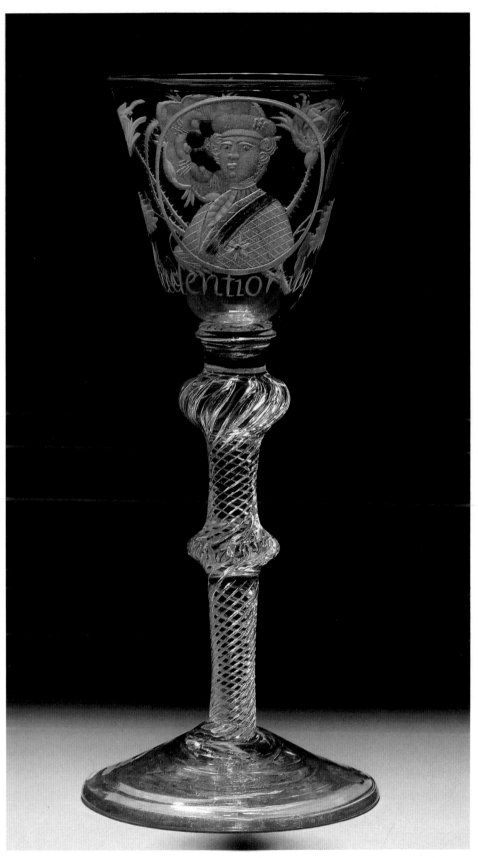

Colour Plate 27. Jacobite portrait glass engraved with a rose, two buds and 'Audentior Ibo'. H. 15cm.
[A]. (COURTESY DRAMBUIE LIQUEUR CO.)

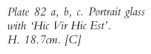

Plate 82 a, b, c. Portrait glass with 'Hic Vir Hic Est'. H. 18.7cm. [C]

a

b

c

Plate 83. James III medal with 'Hic Vir Hic Est'

Plate 84. Portrait tumbler engraved 'Everso Missus Succerrere Seclo. C.P.R.' H. 9.5cm.

a

b

c

d

Plate 85 a, b, c, d, e. Wine glass engraved 'Sir Watkin Williams Wynn'. H. 21.7cm. [B]

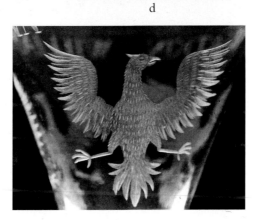

e

Hic Vir Hic Est

'This is the man (or hero), this is he'.
This extremely rare motto also occurs with a portrait of Prince Charles (Plate 82). Again the words come from Virgil's sixth book of *Aeneid*. After the fall of Troy, Aeneas escapes to Italy where he is permitted, for a while, to descend into the underworld to glimpse the future. This foretells the forthcoming foundation and glory of Rome. He meets the figures who are to be part of Rome's greatness and, with the introduction of Augustus Caesar who will found a golden age in Italy, comes the quotation '*Hic Vir Hic Est*'.

A medal struck to commemorate Prince Charles's landing in Scotland (Plate 83) has the same motto and, like the Virgilian quotation, refers to the restoration of a golden age for the Scots.

Everso Missus Succurrere Seclo C.P.R.

'*C.P.R.*' represents '*Carolus Princeps Redeat*', and the whole inscription reads 'Sent to help a ruined age, may Prince Charles come back'.

This is another rare inscription occurring in conjunction with a portrait of Prince Charles engraved on a tumbler (Plate 84). The phrase comes from the first book of Virgil's *Georgics* and fits perfectly into the Jacobite picture. Again the reference is to Caesar. Civil war follows the loss of the older Julius Caesar (the Old Pretender, James) and the gods are asked to favour the young Augustus (Prince Charles) in his efforts to restore a ruined age.

Other inscriptions in English are self-explanatory. '*Sir Watkin Williams Wynn*' glasses (Plate 85) reflect Jacobite sympathies as probably do club glasses like '*The*

Colour Plate 28. Jacobite portrait glass engraved with a rose, two buds and 'Audentior Ibo'. The foot is engraved with a thistle. H. 14.8cm. [E] (COURTESY DRAMBUIE LIQUEUR CO.)

Colour Plate 29. Colour portrait of Prince Charles. By unknown artist. (NATIONAL GALLERIES OF SCOTLAND)

Colour Plate 30. Colour portrait of Prince Charles. By Antonio David. (NATIONAL GALLERIES OF SCOTLAND)

a

b

c

d

e

Plate 86 a, b, c, d, e. Dram glass engraved 'The Friendly Hunt'.
H. 9.2cm.

Plate 87 a, b, c, d, e. Cordial glass engraved with 'Health to all our Fast Friends'. H. 17.4cm.

Friendly Hunt' (Plate 86), *'Health to all our Fast Friends'* (Plate 87) and *'Health to all True Blues'*. *'Success to the Society'* glasses (Plate 88) are usually opaque twists; they all appear to be by the same engraver and probably have a Scottish connection, being

Colour Plate 31. Jacobite portrait glass depicting Prince Charles with the star and riband of the Garter on the wrong side. The bowl of the glass is also engraved with a rose, a single bud, a thistle and a star. H. 16cm. [D] (COURTESY DRAMBUIE LIQUEUR CO.)

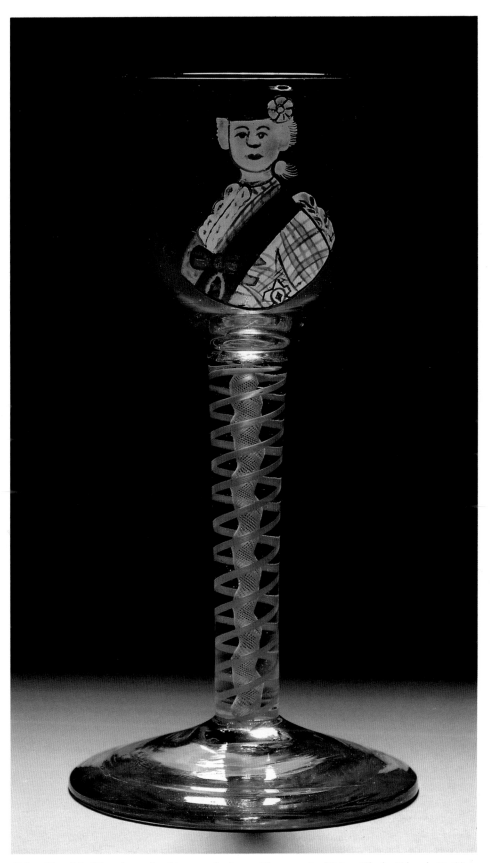

Colour Plate 32. Wine glass painted in enamel colours with a portrait of Prince Charles Edward. H. 12cm. (COURTESY DRAMBUIE LIQUEUR CO.)

a

b

c

d

Plate 88 a, b, c, d. Wine glass engraved 'Success to the Society'. H. 15cm. [H]

engraved with a thistle as well as a rose and two buds. The society in question is thought to be the Society of Jesus.[10]

Portrait Glass

The portrait glasses provide fertile ground for speculation. They should be able, one feels, to provide valuable evidence for the dating of Jacobite glasses and attempts have been made to identify the portraits used by the engravers and to study the type of dress portrayed in the engravings but the results are inconclusive. Grant Francis was of the opinion that any portrait glass depicting Charles in court dress must be pre-Culloden and any portrait in tartan post-Culloden.[11] Muriel Steevenson, however, pointed out that there are, at least, two portraits of Charles, one as a young boy and

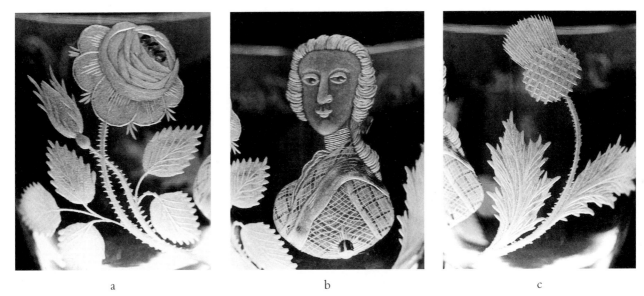

a   b   c

Plate 89 a, b, c. Portrait on the 'Hic Vir Hic Est' wine glass. [C]. See also plate 82

Plate 90. Portrait of Prince Charles Edward. By Robert Strange, during the Prince's stay in Edinburgh. Note the motto, the oak bough and the helm with the fleur-de-lis. (NATIONAL GALLERIES OF SCOTLAND)

one as a very young man, depicting him wearing tartan.[12]

All the portrait glasses relate to Charles Edward and they fall into three categories:

1. Usually Prince Charles is depicted in tartan dress but the wheel-engraved portraits seem to be derived from more than one source. Although it is not possible to be certain of the original source of many of the portraits, one has to agree with Grant Francis's assertion, that the portrait on the *'Hic Vir Hic Est'* glass (Plate 89) closely resembles a portrait of Prince Charles (Plate 90) undertaken when he was in

Colour Plate 33. A pair of Jacobite wine glasses, each engraved with a six-petal rose and a variety of other flowers: carnation, honeysuckle etc. With a little imagination the initial letters of the flowers can sometimes be made to spell 'Charles'. (See Chapter note 17). (COURTESY DRAMBUIE LIQUEUR CO.)

Colour Plate 34. Jacobite wine glass engraved with a sunflower, the stem of which also gives rise to a rose bud. On the reverse is a butterfly. H. 18.4cm. (COURTESY DRAMBUIE LIQUEUR CO.)

Colour Plate 35. Jacobite tankard engraved with a rose, two buds, a butterfly and a bee feeding off the open bud of the rose. H. 10cm. [E]. (COURTESY DRAMBUIE LIQUEUR CO.)

Plate 91. (Left) Wine glass with the familiar wheel-engraved portrait of Prince Charles wearing tartan and bonnet with cockade. H. 14.9cm. [B]

Plate 92. (Above) Portrait of Prince Charles engraved on a tumbler. [?B]

Edinburgh after the Battle of Prestonpans in 1745. This portrait was the work of Robert Strange who was living in Stewart's Close, Edinburgh while Charles was occupying Holyrood House.[15] The only difference between the two is that in Strange's portrait the Prince is in court dress and on the glass he is in tartan.

Strange's portrait also depicts an oak bough and a helm with the Prince of Wales feathers, as well as the motto *'Everso Missus Succerrere Seclo'* (p. 117). The portrait on the tumbler with this motto (Plate 84) shows Charles wearing the familiar bonnet and cockade. Indeed most of the portrait glasses depict Charles in tartan wearing a bonnet with cockade, and this is similar to the description of him when he was in Manchester (p. 38). This is how he is shown in a well-known portrait by an unknown artist (Colour plate 29). If this portrait is meant to represent the Prince at the time when his army was in Manchester, one wonders how it was compiled. It seems unlikely that Charles would have been able to sit for a portrait in the short time he was there, and he certainly does not look like a man of twenty-five. Indeed, he looks no older than in the portrait by Antonio David which was painted when he was about eleven (Colour plate 30). It may well be that the unknown artist derived his inspiration from an earlier representation of the Prince, dressing him in tartan and

a   b

c   d

Plate 93 a, b, c, d. Some other examples of wine glasses with wheel-engraved portraits of Prince Charles Edward. a [E], b [A], c [A], d [C]

placing the famous blue velvet bonnet with white cockade on his head. In the same way many of the portrait glasses could have been gleaned from a number of sources and dressed accordingly. Some of the glasses depict the Prince with the saltire of St. Andrew on the riband. This is derived from the Order of the Thistle, which he is wearing in the David portrait beneath the riband.

Another small portrait has also been attributed to Robert Strange (Plate 98a) and could well be the source of some of the portrait glasses. It seems likely that the group of glasses with portraits in coloured enamels is based upon it (Plate 98c), as also is a miniature painting (Plate 98b) by another unknown artist.

Plate 94. (Above) Bronze medal of Prince Charles as Prince of Wales, 1745

Plate 95. (Right) Wine glass engraved with bust of Prince Charles. [E]

a

b

Plate 96 a, b. Examples of portrait wine glasses showing Prince Charles with the star and riband of the garter on the wrong breast. a [D]. b [A]

2. Augustan portraits of Charles's head in profile (Plate 95). The head is the same as that depicted on the bronze medal of 1745 showing Charles as Prince of Wales (Plate 94), and the 'Redeat Magnus Ille' medal of 1752 (Plate 68).

3. An interesting group of glasses show Charles in profile, without a bonnet, but with the star and riband of the Garter on the wrong breast (Plate 96). Much ingenuity has been employed to explain these reversed portraits. Bles believed that they conformed to the principle that, on coinage, the ruling monarch faces the opposite direction to his or her predecessor. Grant Francis, who believed that they were simply engraved this way in error by foreign engravers, refuted Bles's theory in a complicated numismatic argument.[14] As is so often the case, the simplest explanation is probably the correct one. The glasses never have the *'Audentior Ibo'* motto above or

b

a

below the portrait. The absence of any motto lends support to the possibility that the portrait was intended to be viewed from the opposite side of the bowl, that is the 'King over the Wine' when, of course, the portrait would appear correct. The *'Everso Missus Succerrere Seclo'* tumbler, which depicts the conventional portrait with bonnet and cockade, is an oddity because it too shows the riband and Garter on the wrong breast. However, it has not been possible to attribute this finely engraved tumbler to any of the engravers responsible for the other portrait glasses.

A unique wine glass is the erect portrait (Plate 97) showing Prince Charles in tartan with a crown on his head and carrying a sword. On the reverse is the thistle and star (Plate 47).

The Enamel Portraits

Eight of these rare glasses are known to exist and they are all opaque-twist stem glasses. Three of the glasses have portraits in red, blue and white enamels and five have

a

b

c

Plate 98 a, b, c. Three portraits of Prince Charles Edward, each in a different medium but all similar in appearance:
a. An engraving which has been attributed to Robert Strange, although this is not certain
b. A portrait in oils. Artist unknown
c. Wine glass decorated with coloured enamels

Plate 99 a, b. Disguised Jacobite wine glass with the misspelt Williamite motto, 'The Imortal Memory' [B]

a

b

red, blue, white, green and yellow enamels (Colour plate 32). As already mentioned, they resemble the small portrait of Prince Charles which has been attributed to Robert Strange (Plate 98a). Of the five glasses in full polychrome enamel, three are by the same artist and two appear to be by another hand. Although the enamelling is quite competent it does not compare in quality with the work of the Beilbys.

It is recorded in the book of the Old Edinburgh Club, an antiquarian society founded in 1908 to promote interest in the history of Edinburgh, that a group of Jacobite sympathizers met annually in the house of one of their number to dine and to celebrate the birthday of Prince Charles.[15] This was the Steuart Club,[16] which was founded in 1757. The house in Edinburgh where they met was in Saint James's Square (Clelands Gardens) and belonged to Mr James Steuart. The last recorded

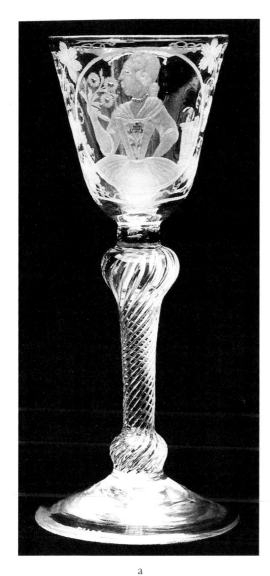

b

Plate 100 a, b. Wine glass engraved with a disguised portrait of Prince Charles Edward. H. 15.3cm. [?E]

a

annual celebration was in December 1787 and took place a few weeks before the death of Prince Charles. This dinner was also attended by Robert Burns. At one of their dinners, probably between 1770 and 1775, a Mr Thomas Erskine, who later became the 9th Earl of Kellie, produced six glasses 'having upon them a coloured representation of the Prince for drinking his health'. One of these glasses has passed down in the Steuart family to the present day. This glass is one of the three identical polychrome enamel glasses and is now in the National Museums of Scotland, Edinburgh. It is likely that the glasses Mr Erskine had made would all be the same design and that three of the glasses with five colours have been lost. The simpler tri-coloured glasses probably pre-date the more elaborate multi-coloured ones and it is probable that some of these have also failed to survive to the present day.

Disguised Jacobite Glasses

Jacobite glasses are described as disguised when the sentiment is hidden amongst other symbols. They are often disguised behind a Williamite motto such as *'The Immortal Memory'*. The glass (Plate 99) is such an example. 'Immortal' is misspelt but the rose, single bud and Prince of Wales feathers make it likely that the sentiments are Jacobite.

The wine glass, (Plate 100), is interesting. It closely resembles a portrait glass

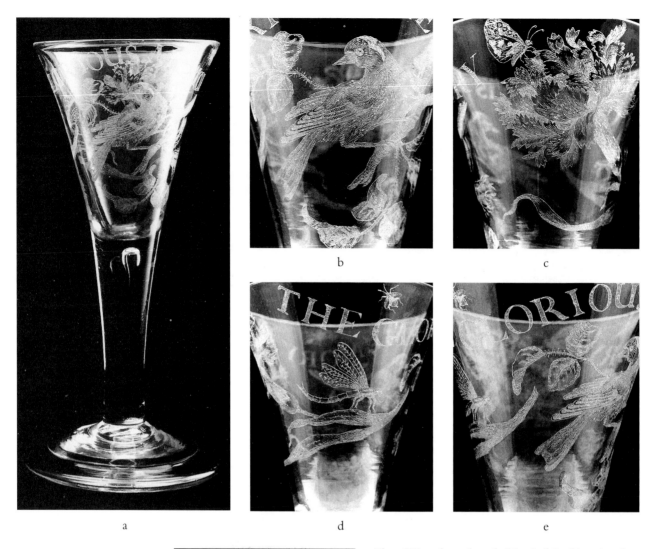

a

b

c

d

e

Plate 101 a, b, c, d, e, f. Disguised Jacobite wine glass, diamond-point engraved with a blackbird, a rose branch, a dragonfly and the Williamite motto, 'The Glorious Memory'. H. 21.8cm.

f

illustrated by Grant Francis which he describes as 'the only known representation of Flora Macdonald on a glass'.[17] The portrait which he illustrates certainly appears to be that of a female figure but the one shown here, which may be the partner to the Flora Macdonald glass and which is probably by the same engraver, is masculine in

Plate 102. Matching set of eight Jacobite wine glasses and a decanter. H. of glasses 15.5cm. H. of decanter 27.8cm. [D]

appearance. This could literally be described as a disguised portrait of Prince Charles because, at one point during his escape, he was obliged to disguise himself as Flora Macdonald's maidservant, Betty Burke.

Another disguised Jacobite glass is the diamond-point engraved wine glass (Plate 101). The sentiments are again hidden beneath the Williamite motto, *'The Glorious Memory'*. A blackbird ('Blackbird' was a favourite nickname for the Old Pretender), sitting on a rose branch displaying a single bud, casts a devouring backward glance at a dragon-fly (King George – a play on George and the Dragon).

Occasionally one encounters a matching set of Jacobite glasses and this is always a delight. The decanter and eight wine glasses (Plate 102) is one such set. The double-knopped MSAT stem was probably one of the most elegant glasses produced in the eighteenth century and a set such as this does, indeed, look very handsome. No less attractive, is the set of six Jacobite wine glasses (Plate 103) with trumpet bowls and drawn MSAT stems.

The foregoing factual account covers most of the Jacobite glasses likely to be encountered, with the notable exception of the *'Amen'* glasses. There are a few recorded examples which the author has not come across and there is a large group of glasses, usually described in sale catalogues as 'of possible Jacobite significance', which has been omitted deliberately. These are glasses engraved with flowers other than the rose. It sometimes seems that there is scarcely a flower which has not been accorded some Jacobite significance. The ingenuity engaged to establish a Jacobite connection has, at

Plate 103. Matching set of six Jacobite wine glasses, originally from Chastleton Manor. H. 14.4cm. [A]

times, been of a very high order. It is quite conceivable that some flowers, other than the rose, could convey some Jacobite sentiments, but it is equally likely that sunflowers, carnations, honeysuckle, forget-me-nots and beehives were simply part of the period of decorative naturalism which derived its inspiration from the garden, with no thoughts of treason. These glasses are probably better regarded in this light unless, as occasionally occurs, (Colour plates 34 and 35), the flower is combined with some other Jacobite symbol. Even then it is not always possible to attribute Jacobite significance. The ale glass (Plate 104) is, unquestionably, Jacobite but it would be wrong to assume that barley is a Jacobite emblem.

Coin glasses, such as the one illustrated (Plate 105) with a Charles II coin, are sometimes said to be Jacobite and, it has been suggested, that the very first Jacobite wine glass was the acorn knop baluster. Soaring even higher in the realms of fantasy, it

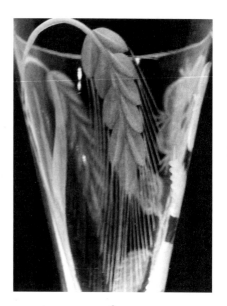
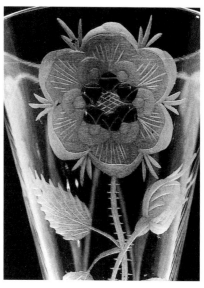
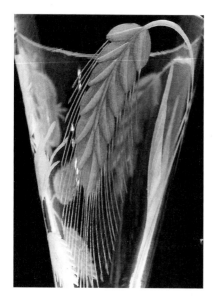

a　　　　　　　　　　　　　b　　　　　　　　　　　　　c

Plate 104 a, b, c. Jacobite ale glass. [D]

136

a   b

Plate 105 a, b. Coin glass with Charles II coin. H. 21cm.

has been intimated that the tear in the stem of a humble plain-stemmed glass is a symbol of Jacobite sorrow. All that can be said is that if such thoughts add a little spice to some cherished possession, so be it.

One might be forgiven, therefore, for thinking that, but for a brief description of the 'Amen' glasses such as appears in any number of good textbooks, this is the end of the story. So it would be if one was not tempted to ask a few questions. For example: this book is based on nearly five hundred glasses, generally considered to be Jacobite, which the author has personally photographed. This probably represents a fraction of those still in existence so, bearing in mind the likely wastage through loss and breakages, the number of Jacobite engraved glasses in the eighteenth century could run into thousands. It has to be remembered that in the middle of the eighteenth century English wheel-engraving was still in its infancy, and also that the possession, let alone the making, of a Jacobite glass is said to have been treasonable. So, where were these glasses engraved and by whom? Perhaps even more intriguing, when were these glasses engraved?

CHAPTER 6
The Jacobite Engravers

Just as handwriting is unique to the individual, so no two wheel-engravers will engrave the same subject in exactly the same way; each develops a recognizable style. With Jacobite emblems, where the same stylized motifs are repeated, there is a unique opportunity to identify the 'handwriting' of different engravers. It is necessary to compare like with like: unopened bud with unopened bud, thistle with thistle and so forth. It is not possible to identify the engraver of a sunflower on one glass by comparing it with a rose on another glass, unless there happens to be some other identical feature, which is common to both glasses.

Another difficulty is that, over a period of time, an engraver may vary his style and change certain features of an engraving. The period of active Jacobite engraving could have been five or more years during which time an engraver could introduce many variations. However, it is usually possible to plot these changes and, when considering the work of an individual engraver, the end result is a series of engravings with interconnecting features attributable to the same hand. By considering the style of the glasses themselves, and the complexity of the engraving, it is usually possible to say which were the earliest and which were the latest engravings of any individual engraver. The bulk of the engravings in the middle of a series will show readily recognizable features and sometimes two engravings will be so alike that one can surmise that they could almost have been engraved on the same day. However, the engravings at the beginning of a series are not always readily identifiable with those at the very end.

In employing these comparative techniques certain engravings fall quickly into easily discernible groups and it becomes apparent that a remarkably large proportion of Jacobite wheel-engravings were the work of a surprisingly small number of engravers. Indeed, over 60 per cent of wheel-engraved Jacobite glasses were produced by five engravers. Furthermore, this 60 per cent includes virtually all the important glasses: most of the portrait glasses and most of the glasses with mottoes; certainly all the rarer mottoes such as: *'Redi'*, *'Redeat'*, *'Revirescit'*, *'Radiat'*, *'Reddas Incolumem'*, *'Hic Vir Hic Est'*, and *'Turno Tempus Erit'*. It seems reasonable, therefore, to describe these five engravers as the 'major engravers' of Jacobite glasses and, for convenience, to refer to them here as Engravers A, B, C, D and E.

Statistics, even simple ones, can sometimes repel but it is worth examining the work of the five major engravers in a little more detail. The glasses in the series which have been photographed by the author total 487. A few of these glasses the author would not consider to be Jacobite; these are often glasses with flowers other than roses, but they are described in sale catalogues as being of Jacobite significance and are generally regarded as such, so they have been included to make the series truly representative.

Glasses Photographed

Wheel-engraved 459
Diamond-point engraved 19
Enamel decoration 5
Coin glasses 3
Plain glass with engraved silver foot 1

Total **487**

The Major Jacobite Engravers

	No. of glasses attributed	% of wheel-engraved glasses
Engraver A	72	15.7
" B	59	12.8
" C	51	11.1
" D	47	10.2
" E	53	11.5
Total	**282**	**61.3**

Subjects Engraved

	Oak leaf	Thistle	Star	Portrait	Butterfly	Crown	Compass
A	38	14	31	9	1	1	1
B	30	4	16	4	4	3	3
C	31	11	11	8	1	0	1
D	8	13	15	11	11	4	0
E	12	14	6	11	12	0	0

Mottoes

	Fiat	Redi	Redeat	Revirescit	Reddas Incolumem
Engraver A	28	2	7	0	0
" B	24	2	0	8	0
" C	24	2	0	0	2
" D	1	0	0	0	0
" E	8	0	0	1	0

	Audentior Ibo	Radiat	Turno Tempus Erit	Hic Vir Hic Est	Sir Watkin Williams Wynn
Engraver A	6	0	4	0	0
" B	1	1	0	0	2
" C	4	0	0	1	0
" D	1	0	0	0	0
" E	1	0	0	0	0

See Appendix for more details.

ENGRAVER **A**

Engraver A is responsible for a significantly larger percentage of the wheel-engraved glasses than any of the other four engravers, which leads one to suppose that he may have been the *primum mobile* of Jacobite engraving. With one or two exceptions Engraver A's work covers the whole field of Jacobite wheel-engraved subjects. One decanter (Plate 4) and six wine glasses (Plate 103) from Chastleton Manor are the work of this craftsman.

The rose is engraved with two loops to the inner petals and there is a scooped-out edge to the outer petals (Plate 106b). The open bud, which is always a good guide to an engraver's identity, is a distinctive design (Plate 106a).

a

b

c

d

e

*Plate 106 a to t. Wheel-engravings typical of Engraver **A***

f

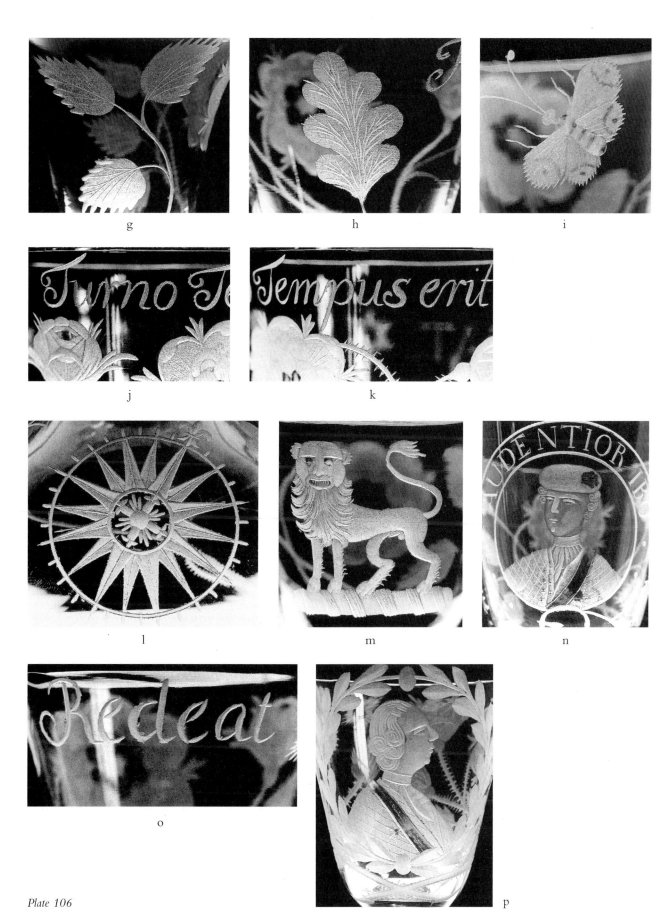

g

h

i

j

k

l

m

n

o

p

Plate 106

141

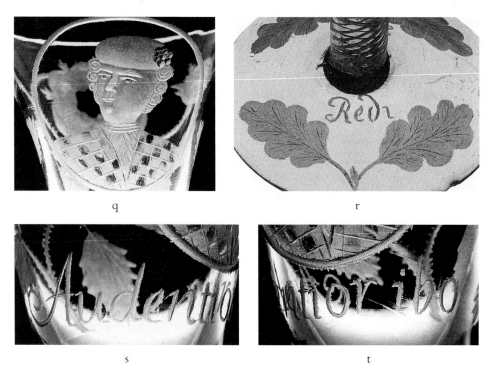

q

r

s

t

*Plate 106. For further illustrations attributed to Engraver **A** see Appendix*

Nine portrait glasses are attributed to Engraver A and these include three in profile with the star and riband of the Garter on the wrong breast (Plate 106p).

When it comes to mottoes Engraver A is well represented with a large number of '*Fiat*'s (Plates 66a, 106f, 107d and j) and a variety of other mottoes including two glasses with '*Redi*' (Plates 71 and 106r) and six with '*Audentior Ibo*' (Plates 80a, 81, 106n, s and t). The four '*Turno Tempus Erit*' glasses (Plates 79, 106j and k) in this series were all the work of Engraver A, as were all seven of the '*Redeat*' mottoes (Plates 69, 70 and 106o).

a

b

c

*Plate 107 a to k. Engraver **A** – variations in style*

d

e

f

g

h

i

j

k

Plate 107

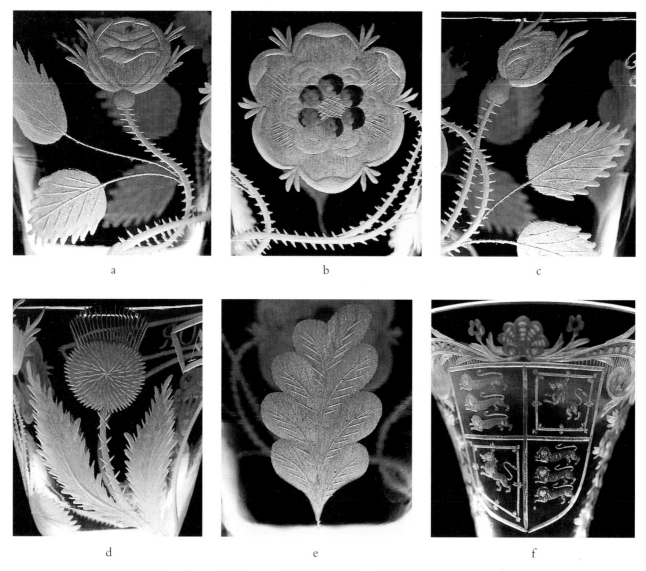

a

b

c

d

e

f

*Plate 108 a to w. Wheel-engravings typical of Engraver **B***

ENGRAVER **B**

A skilled engraver covering the same subjects as Engraver A but with different emphasis. The rose of Engraver B has three loops to the inner petals (Plate 108b) and the open bud has a characteristic wavy engraving stroke across the centre (Plate 108a).

This engraver did not engrave many thistles and only four portrait glasses can be attributed to him. A wine glass from Oxburgh Hall (Plate 5) is by Engraver B.

He engraved a considerable number of *'Fiat'* glasses (Plates 66b, 108l, 109d and 116c) and there are two glasses with the motto *'Redi'* (Plate 108p). All the *'Revirescit'* glasses (Plates 72, 76, 108h and i) with one exception, are the work of Engraver B. The one *'Radiat'* glass (Plate 78), with the beautifully engraved shield (Plate 65), testifies to his ability. The two *'Sir Watkin Williams Wynn'* glasses (Plates 85, 108r, s, t and u) and one disguised Jacobite glass (Plate 99) are attributed to Engraver B.

g

h

i

j

k

l

m

n

Plate 108

145

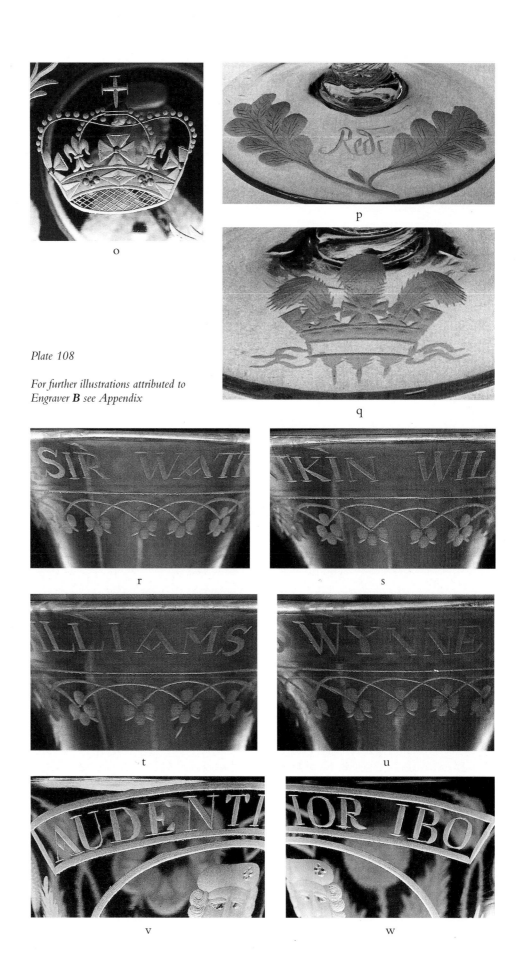

o

p

q

Plate 108

*For further illustrations attributed to Engraver **B** see Appendix*

r

s

t

u

v

w

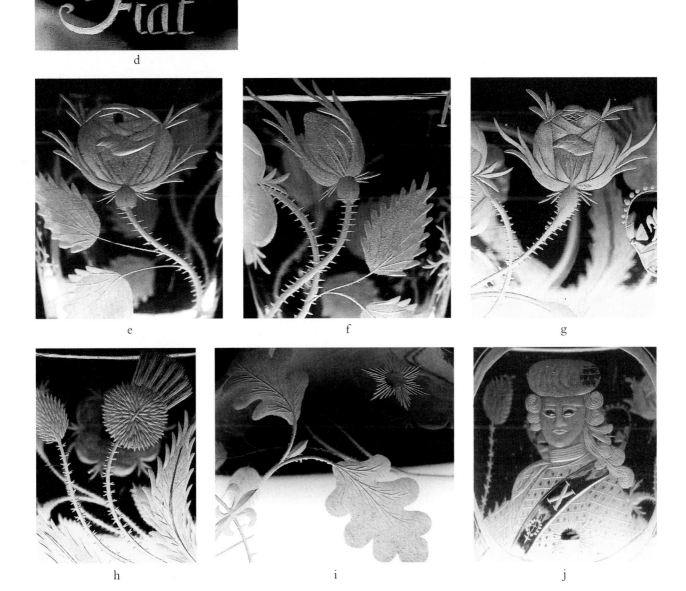

Plate 109 a to j. Engraver **B** – variations in style

147

ENGRAVER C

Engraver C's rose is similar to that of Engraver B and these two engravers will be discussed later. This craftsman engraved more thistles and more portrait glasses than Engraver B, including the very rare *'Hic Vir Hic Est'* portrait glass (Plates 82 and 89). The same number of *'Fiat'* glasses (Plates 66c, 110g, h, 111f and 116f) are attributed to Engraver C as to Engraver B; also two *'Redi'* glasses (Plate 110i), four *'Audentior Ibo'* mottoes (Plates 80b, 110n, o, 111g, h and i) and two *'Reddas Incolumem'* glasses (Plates 77, 110j and k). One of the decanters from Chastleton Manor (Plate 61) is by this craftsman.

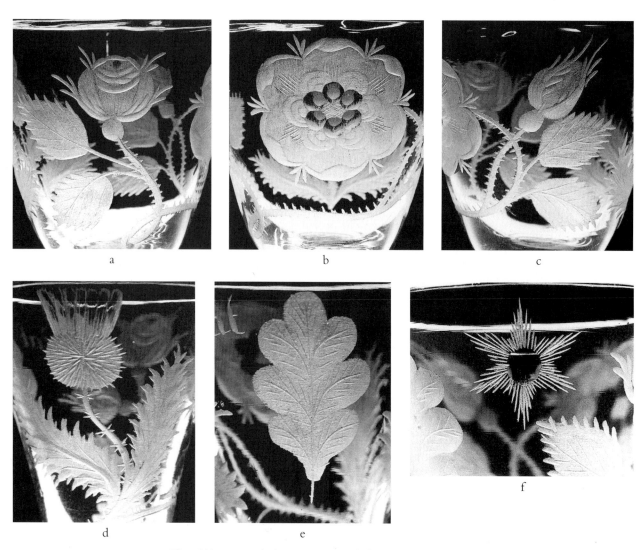

a   b   c

d   e   f

Plate 110 a to o. Wheel-engravings typical of Engraver C

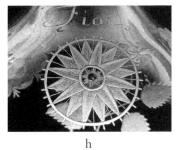

g

h

i

j

k

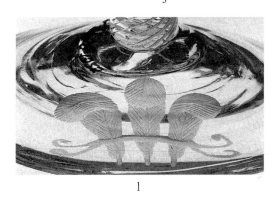

l

Plate 110

*For further illustrations attributed to Engraver **C** see
Appendix*

m

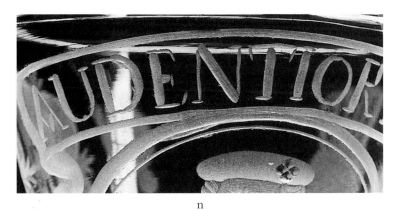

n

o

a   b   c

d   e   f

g   h   i

*Plate 111 a to i. Engraver **C** – variations in style*

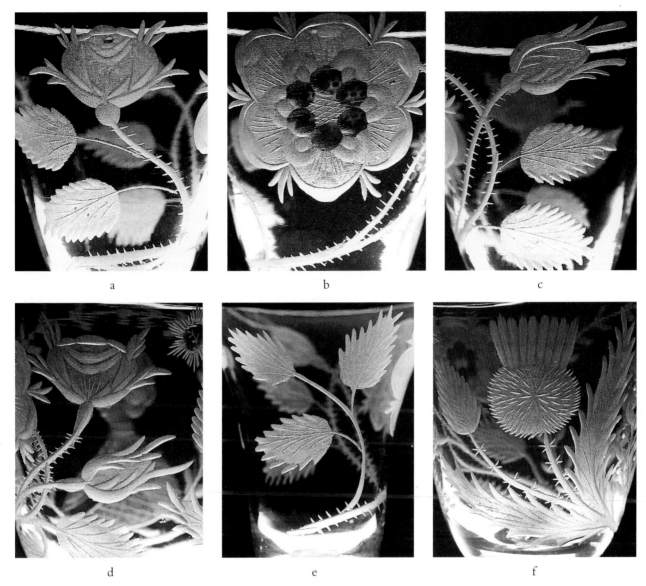

a   b   c

d   e   f

*Plate 112 a to n. Wheel engravings typical of Engraver **D***

ENGRAVER D

The number of glasses attributed to this engraver is the lowest of the five major engravers. Engraver D has a distinctive style with an easily recognizable rose which has two loops to the inner petals (Plates 34b and 112b).

His work differs from the other engravers in a number of respects. With the exception of Engraver E, who engraved approximately the same number of oak leaves as thistles, the other engravers, Engravers A, B and C, engraved many more oak leaves than thistles. With Engraver D this is reversed and he engraved more thistles than oak leaves. He is also unusual in that he engraved hardly any mottoes; only one *'Fiat'* (Plate 112j) and one *'Audentior Ibo'* (Plate 112l and m) can be attributed to him. Also about a quarter of his glasses are portrait glasses. Of the eleven portrait glasses by Engraver D, eight are portraits of the Prince in profile with the star and riband of the Garter on the wrong breast (Plate 112k and 113b) and one is the unique full-length portrait (Plate 97).

Plate 112

g

h

j

i

k

l

m

n

a   b   c

d   e   f

g   h   i

*Plate 113 a to i. Engraver **D** – variations in style*

153

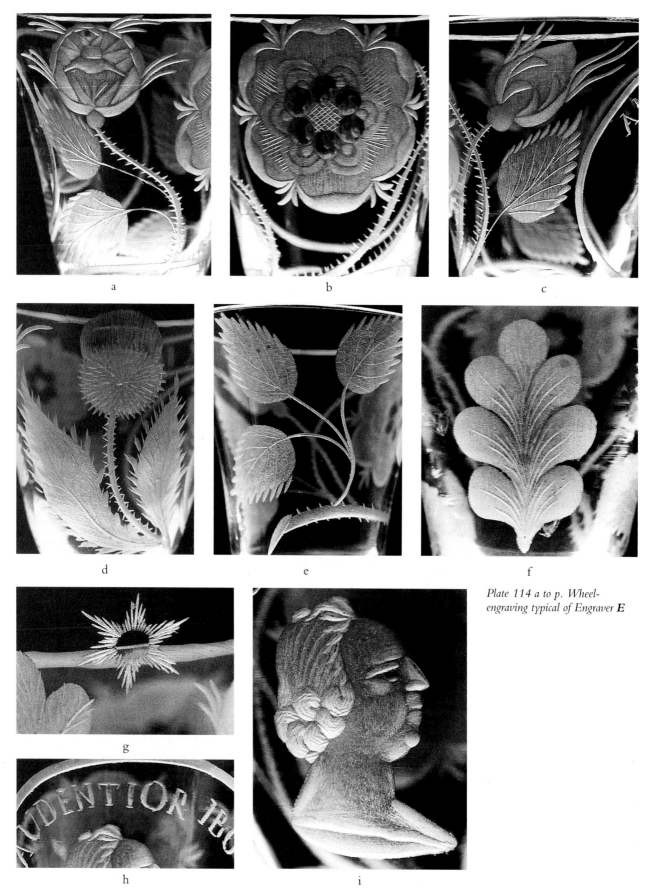

a

b

c

d

e

f

*Plate 114 a to p. Wheel-engraving typical of Engraver **E***

g

h

i

j

k

l

m

n

o

p

Plate 114

*For further illustrations attributed to Engraver **E** see Appendix*

ENGRAVER E

Engraver E is another fine craftsman with considerable versatility. The rose has three loops to the inner petals (Plate 114b) and the design of the closed bud is distinctive (Plate 114c).

Engraver E engraved approximately the same number of thistles as oak leaves and a relatively small number of *'Fiat'* mottoes (Plate 66d). He also engraved more portrait glasses than Engravers A, B or C. Two of his portrait glasses are Augustan portraits of the Prince's head in profile (Plates 114h and i). One *'Revirescit'* glass with the 'stricken oak' is attributable to Engraver E but the motto is misspelt, *'Reverescit'* (Plates 75 and 114k).

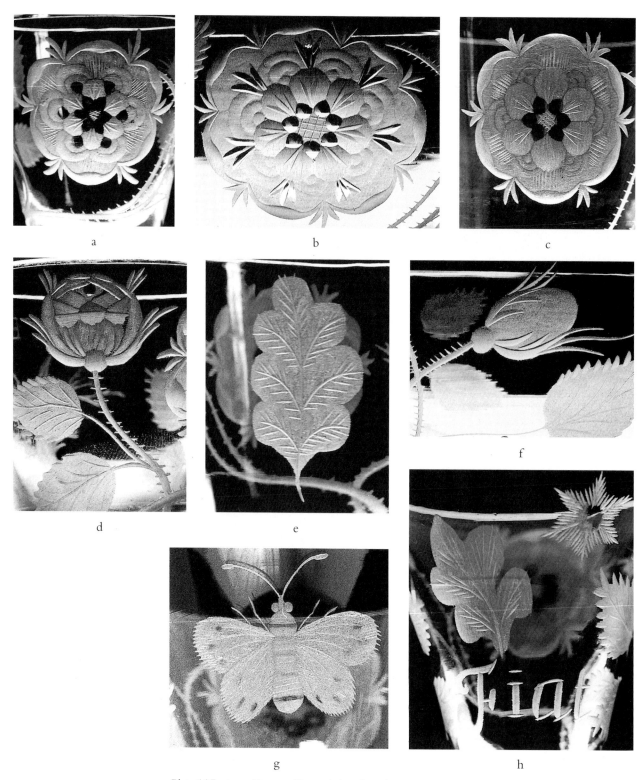

*Plate 115 a to m. Engraver **E** − variations in style*

ENGRAVERS **B** AND **C**

Engravers B and C are something of a puzzle. Certain features of their engravings are quite different while others are very similar and almost identical. Some of the differences occur in small details. Conceivably, they could be regarded as one and the same engraver

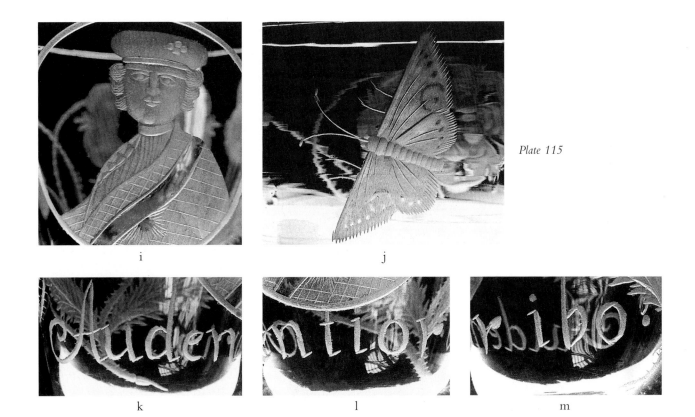

i
j

Plate 115

k
l
m

but the differences, although often small, occur together and are consistent which indicates that the work emanated from two separate engravers. It seems likely that at some stage they worked together in the same workshop, possibly sharing work, or maybe one was trained by the other. Of the two, Engraver C is probably the more experienced and was responsible for more portrait glasses than Engraver B but, on the other hand, some of Engraver B's engraving is of a high quality (Plate 65).

The roses of the two engravers are very similar and it is difficult to distinguish between them (Plates 108b and 110b); likewise, the closed buds. But, the open buds are quite different (Plates 108a and 110a). The leaves differ in small details: Engraver B usually uses a narrow wheel for the stem of the leaf and continues with the same wheel to form the central vein, while Engraver C tends to use a thicker wheel for the stem and changes to a thinner wheel for the central vein of the leaf (Plates 116a and d).

Some of their *'Fiat's* are very similar: Engraver B's *'Fiat's* are very consistent with an upturned scroll at the end of the 't', while Engraver C may do an upturned or a down-turned scroll at the end of the 't'. The capital 'F's differ with Engraver B forming a scroll on the down-stroke which is usually level with, the scroll on the cross-stroke, while with Engraver C the scroll on the down-stroke usually lies inside that of the cross-stroke (Plates 116c and f).

The *'Redi's* are similar but slightly different as also are certain letters like capital 'A'. The fleur-de-lis feathers seem to be identical.

It can be seen that these five engravers were responsible for most of the important wheel-engraved Jacobite glasses. They were not the only engravers of Jacobite glass; there were others with equally recognizable styles and some of these will be mentioned presently. However, the output of these other engravers was much smaller, the quality of the engraving is inferior and they must have come after the five major engravers because they worked on later styles of glasses.

If the five major engravers were indeed responsible for over 60 per cent of wheel-engraved Jacobite glasses then their total output of these glasses over their working period must have been considerable, bearing in mind the glasses which must have

*Plate 116 a to f. Engravers **B** – a, b, c and **C** – d, e, f*

been broken or lost since the eighteenth century.

Leaving behind the rather tedious minutiae of different engravers' styles, it now becomes necessary to try to answer a few questions such as: who were these craftsmen, where were they working and when?

When were the majority of Jacobite glasses engraved?

Any Jacobite glass appearing in a sales catalogue today is invariably dated circa 1750. This is because it has always been the considered opinion of experts on glass that, while a few Jacobite glasses may have been engraved around 1745, the majority were engraved after 1750. The implication of this is that most Jacobite glasses were really sentimental glasses engraved five or ten years after the last rebellion when any hope of a Stuart restoration had all but disappeared. This is contrary to what one would expect: pamphlets, mottoes, artifacts and slogans in support of any cause usually appear when the success or failure of the cause is in the balance, rather than years later when the cause is already lost.

The reason for the belief that most Jacobite glasses were engraved in the 1750s and not the 1740s is twofold. Firstly the style of the glasses. A large proportion of Jacobite glasses have drawn trumpet bowls and many of these are of the small-bowl variety (Plate 17). The 1745 Excise Act has been seen as a dividing line which dictated the style of glasses and any glass with a small bowl was considered to be post-1746 when the Act came into operation. As already pointed out (p. 90) it is now generally recognized that the Excise Act was merely one factor contributing to changes in style which were already taking place across the whole spectrum of the decorative arts, and small-bowled wine glasses were available several years prior to 1746.

The second reason may be described as 'the evidence of the medals'. Grant Francis was mainly responsible for bringing this evidence to bear on Jacobite glasses. The chapter on 'Glasses Devoted to the Jacobite Cause' in his book *Old English Drinking Glasses*, published in 1926, was the first serious attempt to correlate the various engraved Jacobite emblems since Hartshorne's pioneering work, *Old English Glasses*, in 1897. Grant Francis's chapter was based upon a paper he had contributed to the journal of the British Numismatic Society. Although he had a wide knowledge of English glass, his approach to Jacobite glass was always that of a numismatist. Certain Jacobite medals carry mottoes and emblems which also appear on Jacobite glasses, and the dates when these medals were struck are known. The 'Oak Medal' (Plate 74), made to the order of the Oak Society, was struck in 1750 and depicts the 'stricken oak' with the motto '*Revirescit*'. The '*Redeat Magnus Ille*' medal (Plate 68) was struck in 1752. Grant Francis always made the assumption, for no apparent reason, that the mottoes and emblems on the '*Revirescit*' and '*Redeat*' drinking glasses were copied from the medals and not *vice versa*. There is certainly no reason why the glasses should not pre-date the medals because mottoes such as '*Revirescit*' and '*Redeat*' were in use long before 1750. Dr King made his famous '*Redeat, Redeat, Redeat*' speech in Oxford in 1747, and the Charles II medal (Plate 73) is an even earlier example of the use of '*Revirescet*'.

Returning to the five major engravers, can anything further be gleaned from the glasses they engraved? If the glasses they used are classified it soon becomes clear that their work was confined to certain types of drinking glasses. They used a few light balusters, a few incised-twist glasses, a considerable number of plain stem glasses and a large number of air-twist stem glasses. They did not use opaque-twist or facet stem glasses. The absence of facet stems is understandable but, if they had been working in the 1750s they would certainly have had opaque-twists at their disposal. The implications for the interpretation of Jacobite engravings could be important because, not only does it explode the theory that the majority of these glasses were engraved in the 1750s, it alters the whole thinking about Jacobite glasses. This being so it is worth repeating. In the present series of 487 glasses there is not a single opaque-twist stem drinking glass which can be attributed to any one of the five major Jacobite engravers. This is not to say there are none in existence but, if so, they must be very few in number. It seems inconceivable that these craftsmen would not have used the opaque-twists had they been freely available, and this is why the date when the opaque-twist stems first appeared is so important. If Francis Buckley's evidence is accepted, namely, that the opaque-twists first appeared in London some time before 1750 (p. 93), and if the dates 1747 and 1748 on the earliest opaque-twist glasses are taken as genuine, then the picture of Jacobite glass changes. If the opaque-twist glasses first appeared in 1747-48 this means that most of the important Jacobite glasses had already been engraved. In other words these glasses were not sentimental glasses engraved years after the 'Forty-five rebellion but highly political glasses engraved before, during and just after the rebellion.

It seems that Jacobite engraving came to an abrupt end before, or at about the same time the opaque-twists started to appear. This introduces another intriguing question. What would cause five independent craftsmen, who had been responsible for most of the important Jacobite glasses, to suddenly and simultaneously stop producing these engravings? There may well have been a decline in demand after the rebellion but this

a   b   c

d   e   f

*Plate 117 a to f. Wheel-engravings typical of Engraver **F**. For further engravings attributed to Engraver **F** see Appendix*

a   b

*Plate 118 a, b. Engraver **F** – variations in style*

Colour Plate 36. Jacobite wine glass engraved with a rose, two buds, an oak leaf and 'Fiat'. H. 17.4cm. [B].
(COURTESY DRAMBUIE LIQUEUR CO.)

would not account for a complete standstill. The most likely answer is that the abrupt halt was due to some clamp-down by the government in the aftermath of the rebellion. There is no documentary evidence to support this but it seems the only logical explanation.

Jacobite engravings are found on opaque-twist glasses but, as can be seen from the photographs, these are the work of different, and usually less skilled, engravers. With these engravers the opaque-twist stems predominate accounting for 75 per cent of the glasses attributed to Engravers F, G, H and I. These glasses are the ones which can truly be said to be sentimental glasses, because they represent a resurgence of Jacobite engraving in the 1750s and 1760s when wheel-engraving had spread beyond the capital, and when it was again considered safe to produce them.

OTHER ENGRAVERS

Engraver F (Plates 117 and 118)
Thirteen glasses in the series are by Engraver F and of these five have opaque-twist stems and three have colour-twist stems. Twelve of the glasses are engraved with a butterfly or moth in addition to the rose emblems.

*Plate 119 (a), (b), (c). Wheel-engravings typical of Engraver **G**. For further illustrations attributed to this engraver see Appendix*

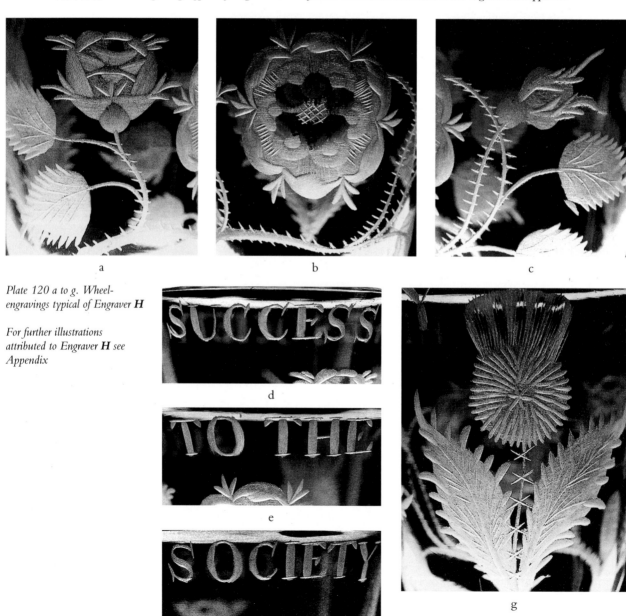

*Plate 120 a to g. Wheel-engravings typical of Engraver **H***

*For further illustrations attributed to Engraver **H** see Appendix*

162

*Plate 121 a to e. Wheel-engravings typical of Engraver **I***

Engraver G (Plate 119)

Five glasses are attributed to this engraver. All have DSOT stems and all have the same engraving with a single-bud rose and a thistle.

Engraver H (Plate 120)

Five glasses are by this engraver, four of which have DSOT stems and are engraved with a rose, two buds, a thistle and *'Success to the Society'*.

Engraver I (Plate 121)

Five glasses are by Engraver I and four of these have opaque-twist stems.

Engravers F, G, H and I together account for twenty-eight glasses in the series or 6.1 per cent of all the wheel engraved glasses. Of their twenty-eight glasses, twenty-one have enamel-twist stems.

Where were the major engravers working?

This is answered more easily. If the major engravers were working in the mid-1740s then all five of them must have been working in London. This can be deduced from Francis Buckley's evidence from newspaper advertisements which show that wheel-engraving did not spread to the provinces until after 1750 (p. 94). It has previously been assumed that the engravers may have been working in different parts of the country but if they were all working in London it could explain a good deal. In the first place, since skilled wheel-engravers were still few in number, they would probably all have known one another which would explain why they all acted simultaneously when Jacobite engraving came to a sudden halt. It would also account for the similarity in the designs of certain glasses they produced, such as the portrait glasses; knowing one another they would probably have exchanged ideas and seen one

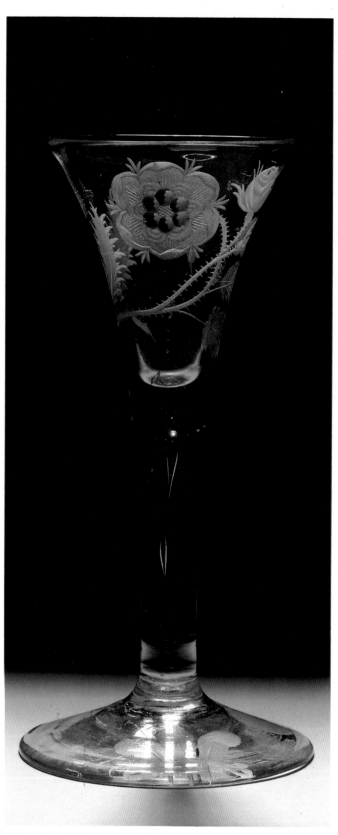

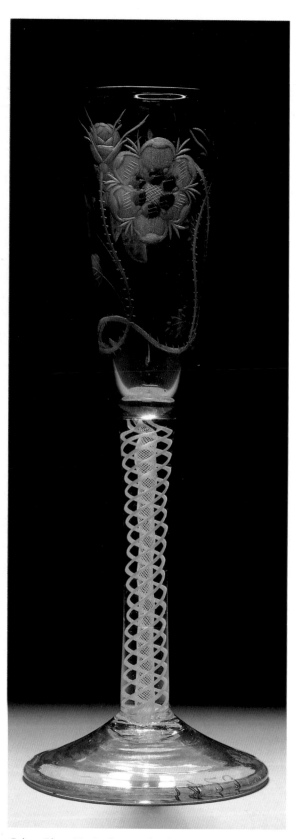

Colour Plate 37. Jacobite wine glass engraved with a rose, two buds on the sinister side of the rose, a thistle on the dexter side, an oak leaf and 'Fiat'. The foot is engraved with the fleur-de-lis. H. 14.5cm. [C].
(Courtesy Drambuie Liqueur Co.)

Colour Plate 38. Jacobite ratafia glass engraved with a rose, two buds and a butterfly. H. 18.5cm. [F].
(Courtesy Drambuie Liqueur Co.)

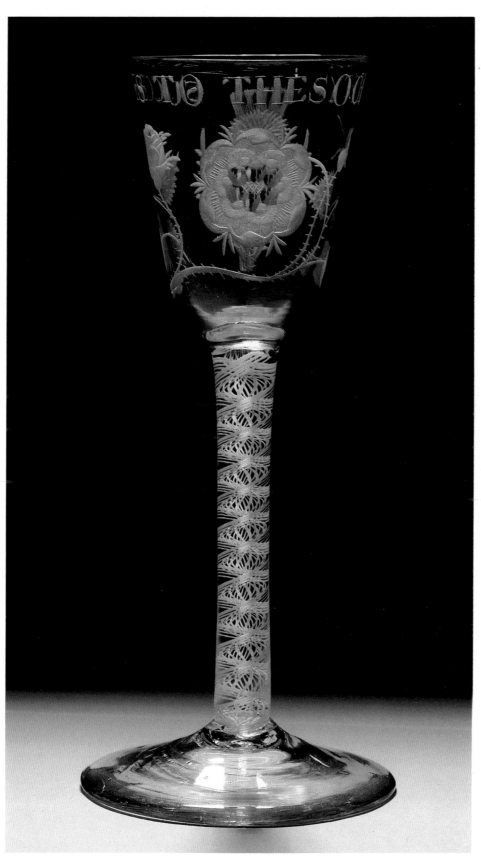

Colour Plate 39. Jacobite wine glass engraved with a rose, two buds, a thistle and 'Success to the Society'. H. 15.2cm. [H]. (Courtesy Drambuie Liqueur Co.)

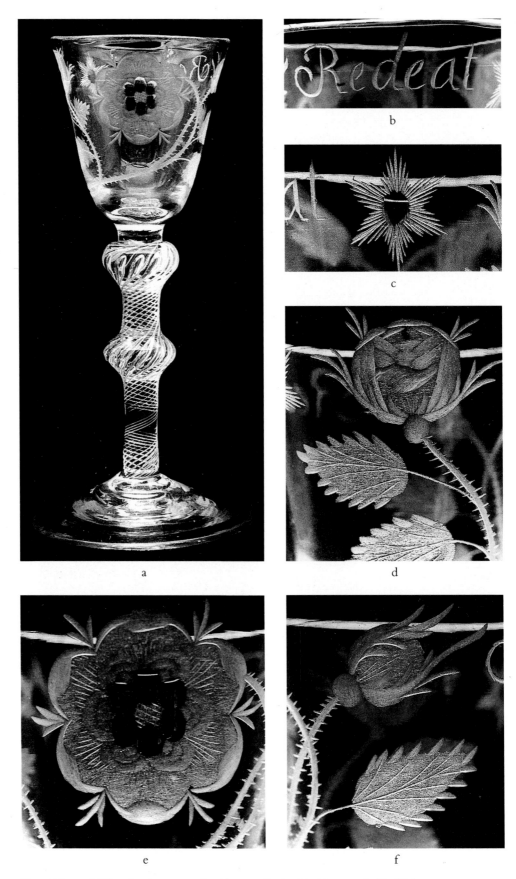

*Plate 122 a to f. Wine glass by engraver **B** with motto 'Redeat' by Engraver **A**. H. 15.2cm.*

another's work. Co-operation and proximity of this kind might also account for oddities such as the glass illustrated (Plate 122), where the rose is the work of Engraver B and the motto, *'Redeat'*, is clearly that of Engraver A, and might, therefore, have been added at a later date.

Who were the major engravers?

It may never be possible to identify the engravers by name but it is possible to make a number of reasonable deductions. In London at this time there were many shops which sold glass but the principal glass-sellers were distinguished by the scale of their business and by the fact that they incorporated workshops on their premises for the cutting and engraving of glass. They would receive glass direct from the glasshouses some of which they would cut and engrave. They would advertise in the newspapers and they would sell direct to the public as well as supplying smaller shops on a wholesale basis. Again, Francis Buckley, through his study of eighteenth century newspapers and journals has been responsible for most of the information about the London glass-sellers:

Plate 123. Trade card of Thomas Betts, c.1738-48

John Akerman has been described as the father of English glass-cutting. In April 1719 *The Weekly Journal* records the earliest published reference to cut glass in England and cites Akerman's premises as the West Walk of the Royal Exchange, Cornhill. The firm was John Akerman and Son and later the same year another notice, also referring to cut glass, gave his address as the Rose and Crown, Cornhill.[1] Although there is no evidence to suggest that Akerman himself was a glass-cutter or engraver, he clearly played a very important role in the development of English glass-cutting and in 1741 he was made Master of the Glass-Sellers' Company. In 1746 he moved his premises to Fenchurch Street and in 1756 his son, Issac, became Master of the Glass-Sellers' Company.

It is likely that Akerman employed a German glass-cutter called Haedy who advertised himself as being the 'German who was the first that brought the art of Cutting and Engraving Glass from Germany'.[2] Charleston believes Haedy's boast was probably unfounded and he envisages a more gradual development of cutting and engraving through the mirror-grinding industry.[3] Haedy later tried to set up in business on his own but was unsuccessful and by 1766 was bankrupt. His son, Christopher Haedy, took over and became a very successful glass-seller. He had premises at St. Clement's Inn, Foregate and developed extensive business in the south-west of England, particularly in Bath and Bristol.

Thomas Betts was a younger contemporary of Akerman and he started his business in about 1730. He is first mentioned in 1738 when he was in Bloomsbury. Shortly afterwards he moved to Cockspur Street or, as his trade card describes 'At ye King's Arms Glass-Shop, Opposite Pall-Mall, Charring Cross.'(Plate 123). This was a fashionable London shopping district and indicated that Betts was a prominent glass-seller. Even so, he never held office with the Glass-Sellers' Company. Unlike

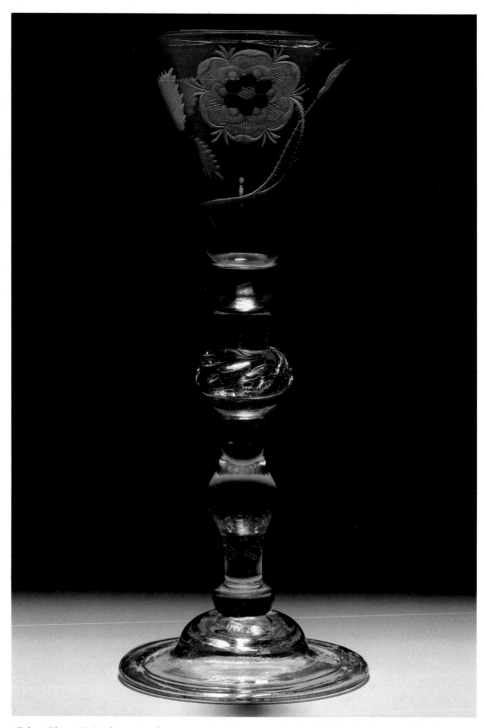

Colour Plate 40. Jacobite wine glass engraved with a rose and a single bud. H. 17.2cm. [A]. (COURTESY DRAMBUIE LIQUEUR CO.)

Akerman, Betts was himself a glass-cutter having started as a mirror grinder and he always described himself in his advertisements as 'the Real Workman'. It is possible that he may also have been a glass-engraver.

It is known that Betts employed a Bohemian cutter or engraver, Andrew Pawl, who stayed with him until 1744. Pawl's departure prompted Betts to place the following notice in the *Daily Advertiser,* 18 October 1744: 'Whereas Andrew Pawl went away from his Master, Thomas Betts, at ye King's Arms Glass Shop, opposite Pall-Mall,

Colour Plate 41. Jacobite wine glass engraved with a crest, which is probably that of Fairfax. H. 16cm. [A]. (COURTESY DRAMBUIE LIQUEUR CO.)

Charing Cross, on the 7th Instant, whoever harbours or entertains him after the publication hereof, be it at their peril.

He is tall, has a thin meagre look, is very much Pockfretten, with very small grey eyes, and a large scar on his Forehead; he had on when he went away, a Cinnamon Colour Coat, and a Dutch Frize Waistcoat.

Note… He is a Bohemian, and speaks good English.'[4]

It is not known what became of Pawl after he left Betts.

When Thomas Betts died on 7 January 1765 he left no will and the whole of his estate became the subject of a probate inventory. A copy of the inventory, which took six appraisers eight days to compile, remains in the Public Record Office and includes details of all Betts's stock in trade, his working tools and his personal possessions.[5]

It reveals that above the premises in Cockspur Street there was a first-floor workshop which contained an engraving tool with two mandrels and a bench with a number of other assorted tools. Also in this workshop there was a book on heraldry and another book which was probably a book of engraving patterns. In the garret above the premises there was another 'engraving tool with foot wheel bench and small wheels with a stand…with other necessaries compleat, a small flatting iron, and an engraving mandrel and frame with some spindles'. The flatting iron would be used to flatten the copper engraving wheels.

Amongst the huge stock of quality glass of all kinds were some 10,000 drinking glasses, over 1,600 of which were engraved.

Maydwell. Glisson Maydwell, a London glass-seller, was Master of the Glass-Sellers' Company in 1739. There was also a George Maydwell who, in Charleston's opinion, was probably Glisson's brother.[6] The firm later became Maydwell and Windles, at The King's Arms, against Norfolk Street in the Strand. Their trade card of circa 1760 advertised 'Engraving on Glass of ev'ry kind in the Newest Taste at ye most Reasonable Rates.'(Plate 124). The firm flourished in the Strand until 1778.

Benjamin Payne had a shop in Fleet Street called the Glass Sellers Arms. Payne had been apprenticed to Glisson Maydwell in 1725 and he specialized in heraldic engraving. In June 1735 he advertised in the *London Evening Post* '… With the Arms of all the Royal Family finely engraved on glasses. By Benjamin Payne'.[7] Later the same year in the *Daily Journal* his advertisement read 'The Glass Sellers Arms. Where are to be had the best Double Flint Glass, Diamond-Cut and Plain, with several curiosities engraved on Glass.'[8]

Jerome Johnson is possibly the most colourful of all the London glass-sellers. A contemporary and neighbour of Thomas Betts, he was first at Duke Street in 1739 and then at the Entire Glass Shop at the corner of St Martin's Lane in the Strand. There he remained until about 1757, when he moved to the Cockpit White Flint Glasshouse near the Falcon Stairs, Southwark.

A man of flare, he was the first London glass-seller to describe himself as 'Glass Engraver' and he was the first to use the term 'flowered Glasses' when describing some of his engravings. This reference occurred in an advertisement in the *Daily Advertiser* in December 1742.[9] He was self-taught and, like Betts, he described himself as the 'Real Workman', and would sometimes refer to himself as the 'Maker' or the 'Inventor'. As well as his retail outlet, Johnson had a thriving wholesale business supplying many of the smaller shops and he also exported to the Continent.

It is probably due to Jerome Johnson, more than any other London glass-seller, that glass engraving departed from the formal baroque designs and developed the free-flowing designs which became typical of English engraving. It seems quite likely that he was himself a glass engraver, and he certainly employed apprentices.

An interesting court case is recorded when, on 10 July 1736, Charles William Stutley protested that his master, Jerome Johnson, had failed to instruct him in the art of a Glass Engraver. The apprenticeship had been to learn glass engraving but for two years Johnson had concealed the art and given the work to another. Stutley had only been taught glass scalloping (cutting the edge of a glass vessel in a series of convex rounded projections, like the edge of a scallop-shell) and he claimed that his health had suffered as a result.[10]

In November 1756, presumably just prior to his move to Southwark, Johnson placed an advertisement in the *London Evening Post* selling his whole stock in trade and his working tools which included 'Glass Flowerers' and 'Engraving Tools'.[11] This confirms that glass engravers worked on the premises.

These, then, are the principal London glass-sellers connected with glass-cutting and engraving, and it is worth noting that the number coincides with the number of major Jacobite engravers. It is tempting to assume that each of the five principal glass-sellers employed one of the five major Jacobite engravers. One can go even further and speculate that Jerome Johnson might be Engraver A or that Benjamin Payne, with his interest in coats of arms, might be Engraver B, but this is, perhaps, assuming too much. Thomas Betts and Jerome Johnson certainly did engraving on the premises and Benjamin Payne claimed that he engraved 'the Arms of all the Royal Family' but, even if these men were engravers it is likely that they ceased to be the 'real workmen' as their business grew and they trained apprentices. It is quite probable that all five of the principal glass-sellers did employ an engraver on the premises but they may also have commissioned work from independent craftsmen. It should be remembered, however, that prior to 1750, glass engraving was still a relatively new art and good engravers were probably few in number.

Plate 124. Trade card of Maydwell and Windle, c.1760-75

A picture is now starting to emerge which conflicts with some of the old ideas about Jacobite glasses: that these treasonable engravings were executed by craftsmen in different parts of the country, working in great secrecy. There is a need to consider the glasses in the context of life in eighteenth century London.

At the beginning of the eighteenth century the largest provincial town in England was Norwich with a population of barely 30,000. The population of the whole country was only five million, and half a million of those lived in the capital. London was the only conurbation of any size; it was the centre of government, commerce, finance, the arts and the sciences. Many aspects of life in eighteenth century London would seem unjust today: birthright determined one's position in the social order; important public appointments, seats in parliament, commissions in the army and the navy, were acquired through wealth and property; advancement was by privilege and patronage. Abstract niceties, such as social equality, were for future generations to consider. For the majority life was hard, it was coarse and it could be brutal. Heavy drinking, gambling and blood-sports were popular pastimes. It was a man's world and sex inequality was gross. Life was cheap, three out of four children failing to survive to adulthood. Justice could be cruel: an adolescent might be sent to the gallows for pickpocketing and executions were a common sight.

Yet, even with an average life expectancy of only thirty-five, people contrived to live life to the full. The English revelled in being an island race and there was an intense pride in being British. England was smaller in size and population than any of

Colour Plate 42. Jacobite wine glass engraved with a rose, two buds and, on the reverse, a butterfly. H. 21.5cm. [F]. (COURTESY DRAMBUIE LIQUEUR CO.)

her European rivals, the population of France being three times that of England. The English saw themselves as small and tough; fair-minded, but fierce in adversity. Above all else, the Englishman cherished his freedom. In the sixteenth century Parson William Harrison was proclaiming 'as for slaves and bondmen we have none'.[12] It was his proud boast that simply to set foot on English soil was to be liberated. In a class-conscious society the Englishman might accept that he was not equal to his master but he considered himself to be as free.

Visiting foreigners often marvelled at the freedom enjoyed by the English. Towns and villages could be entered without hindrance; no gates barred the way and there were no sentries to be passed. Free speech was unbridled, censorship non-existent. One only has to see the cartoons of James Gillray, and the like, to realize that the satire levelled at

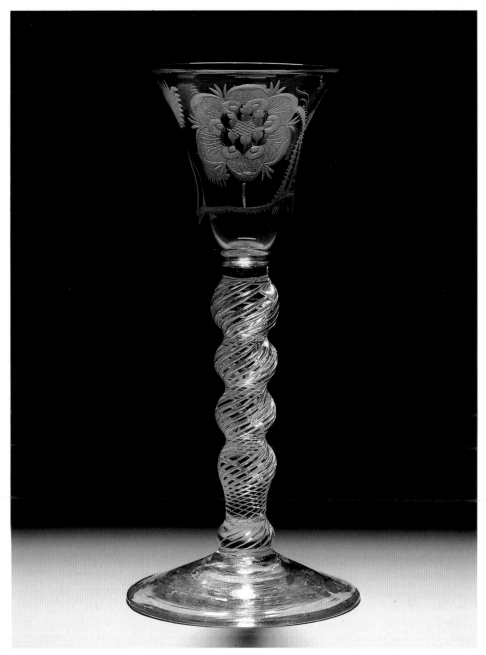

Colour Plate 43. Jacobite wine glass engraved with a rose, a single closed bud and, on the reverse, an oak leaf. H. 15.2cm. [D]. (COURTESY DRAMBUIE LIQUEUR CO.)

present-day public figures is nothing compared to that which their eighteenth century counterparts had to endure. Prints depicting a reigning monarch or a prime minister defecating would, today, be considered wholly unacceptable yet, such prints of George II and Walpole were often on display in shops in eighteenth century London.

This sense of freedom bred confidence and foreign visitors were often struck by the way the Englishman, although prepared to pay respect to his betters, frequently displayed unaccustomed familiarity. Pepys records that in 1663 the Lord Mayor, whom Pepys considered to be a 'bragging Bufflehead', was concerned that 'Noblemen, Ladies, Gentlemen and persons of quality' were being discouraged from shopping in the city by reason of the 'rudeness, affronts and insolent behaviour' of, among others, 'Hackney-coachmen, Carmen, Draymen, Colliers'.[13] The Englishman showed little inclination to bow and scrape and would quickly resort to violence if he sensed injustice. Unpopular politicians would be jostled in the streets or have their carriages pelted with mud. The reaction of the London mob was always a factor to be considered. 'I am here in a country which hardly resembles the rest of Europe,' wrote Montesquieu in 1729. 'This nation is passionately fond of liberty...every individual is independent.'[14]

The sense of freedom permeated all levels of society; even so, drinking the health of the Pretender or sporting emblems of Stuart sympathy around the time of the 1715 rising could bring severe penalties. However, the long period of peace and prosperity under Walpole seems to have bred complacency because the attitude of the government appears to have changed by the time of the 'Forty-five. Since the penalties for drinking the health of the Pretender had, at one time, been severe it is natural to assume that treasonable artifacts, such as wine glasses engraved with Jacobite emblems, must have been produced by craftsmen dedicated to the Jacobite cause and working in great secrecy. Yet, it seems likely that the majority of Jacobite glasses were produced in London by craftsmen who were employed by the major London glass-sellers. There is no reason to suppose that any of these craftsmen would have had strong Jacobite sympathies or that the glasses were produced in any secrecy. They were probably engraved to order as part of the everyday output of the workshop. The authorities must have known about them, and they must have known the source because around 1745 the number of competent engravers in the country was very small. This complacency may have arisen out of a feeling of confidence that the Jacobite threat was no cause for concern. Equally, there may have been a willingness to allow the Englishman to indulge his precious freedom of speech, preferring to be aware of where the glasses were coming from, rather than risk driving the source underground.

If it was complacency born of confidence, it did not last for very long. Jacobite hopes, which stirred as Walpole's peace started to disintegrate with the War of the Austrian Succession, must surely have taken flight when it became known that Prince Charles was in Paris in 1744. If Jacobite glasses started to appear in the early 1740s, the period of greatest demand is likely to have been 1744 and the early part of the 1745 rebellion. One can imagine the government being quietly confident after the collapse of the planned French invasion in 1744. Charles's appearance in Scotland in July 1745 was unexpected but, even so, the authorities were not overly concerned. A price of £30,000 was placed on the Prince's head and they felt certain that the rebels would soon be brought to heel. The defeat at Prestonpans, however, sent shock-waves through London and the complacency rapidly evaporated when they saw the rebels in control of Scotland. As the government recalled troops from the Continent, to meet what had come to be recognized as a real threat, the Jacobite engravers probably grew bolder and the portrait glasses started to appear. With the retreat from Derby and Cumberland's victory at Culloden, the Whigs heaved a sigh of relief and, suspending habeas corpus, they determined to stamp out the threat of Jacobitism once and for all. Prince Charles's escape back to France made this difficult; the Pretender had become a popular romantic figure with admirers in this country and on the Continent following his every move. The hero worship had to be stifled and the portrait glasses may have been more than the government was prepared to tolerate. Jacobite engraving came to an abrupt end in 1746-47. A state of near-martial law existed and whether there was an official visit to the individual glass-sellers advising them of the likely consequences if Jacobite engravings continued to appear, or whether the engravers themselves became nervous as the heads started to appear on the spikes at Temple Bar, may never be known. However, something occurred which caused all five of the major engravers to stop producing Jacobite glasses. Either way it shows that the government's reaction to the 'Forty-five was anything but complacent. They realized it had been close and they had been given a fright. Others may interpret the evidence a different way but this seems the most likely sequence of events.

The 1745 rising was an embarrassment for the Whigs. Prince Charles's arrival in Scotland took everyone by surprise and there was little the government could have done to foresee or prevent it. But, once the standard had been raised, the Whigs should have been much more alive to the dangers. The only field commander on the government side to come out of the rising with even a modicum of credit was Cumberland himself and, though he returned to London 'the conquering hero', Cumberland hardly covered himself with glory. At Derby he had been hoodwinked by Lord George Murray's simple diversionary tactic, leaving the capital exposed; at Culloden he had so many factors in his favour that he would have been hard pressed not to emerge the victor; and, in the aftermath of the battle, his cruelty tarnished his reputation for evermore. Throughout history rulers have always crowed about their achievements and blamed their shortcomings on their predecessors. The problem for the Whigs was that they had been in power so long that they had no one to blame but themselves, so they did the next best thing portraying the rising as a desperate, pathetic venture and the rebels as barbaric Highlanders led by an irresponsible adventurer. But, their conduct after the 'Forty-five revealed the extent to which their confidence had been shattered. The leniency shown after the 1715 rebellion was not repeated after the 'Forty-five. In Scotland alone the repressive measures resulted in 50,000 Highlanders emigrating to North America. The executions and deportations were at least treble those which followed the 1715 rising. It was 1747 before the Bill of Pardon was passed, and as late as 1753 the capital was shocked by the brutal execution of the well-loved Dr Archibald Cameron, who bravely met his death when he was hanged and had his heart torn out and burned at Tyburn on the 7th of June. Nor was the Bill of Pardon the token of complete forgiveness it is sometimes made out to be; there were eighty-seven exceptions and it excluded anyone who had taken up arms during the rising.

This is the real secret of the Jacobite glasses. It is not whether the butterfly represents the 'return of the soul', or whether this or that flower, other than the rose, has some tenuous link with Jacobitism. It is the fact that the engravings have something to say about the history of the times. They reveal aspects of the true perspective of Jacobitism in the eighteenth century and they confirm what modern historians have been saying for the last two decades: that the 'Forty-five rebellion may not have been the glamorous adventure of popular fiction but neither was it an irrelevant skirmish. Given the circumstances and the characters involved, there appears to be a certain inevitability about the 'Forty-five and it is easy, with the benefit of hindsight and knowledge of the tragic consequences, to view it as a rash, hopeless enterprise doomed to failure from the start. However, the outcome was far from being a forgone conclusion. Reckless or not the Young Pretender had come close to changing the course of British history, the establishment had been badly shaken and, for an instant, the Hanoverian dynasty had held its breath.

Colour Plate 44. *Jacobite wine glass, the bowl of which is engraved with a rose, two buds, a star and the mottoes 'Turno Tempus Erit' and 'Fiat'. The foot is engraved with a thistle and the motto 'Redeat'. H. 15.5cm. [A]. (Courtesy Drambuie Liqueur Co.)*

Colour Plate 45. *Large Jacobite wine glass engraved with a seven-petal rose, two buds, oak leaves, a star, a compass and the motto 'Fiat'. H. 21.2cm. [B].*
(Courtesy Drambuie Liqueur Co.)

CHAPTER 7
The Jacobite Rose

Red roses under the Sun,
For the King who is lord of lands,
But he dies when his day is done,
For his memory careth none
When his glass runs empty of sands.

White roses under the Moon
For the King without lands to give;
But he reigns with the reign of June
With his rose and his blackbird's tune,
And he lives while Faith may live![1]

A golden rose was the badge of Edward I. His descendants adopted different coloured roses as their badges: the House of Lancaster a red rose and the House of York a white one. Henry VII combined the red and white roses when he married Elizabeth of York to form the five-petal Tudor rose (Plate 125) and it is this rose, surmounted by a crown, which is the royal badge of England today.

Tudor rose

Red rose of Lancaster

White rose of York

Plate 125. The heraldic rose

a. Old Pretender, James   b. James II   c. Young Pretender, Charles

Plate 126 a, b, c. An improbable interpretation of the Jacobite rose. [E]

Badges are heraldic devices, distinct from arms or crests. Warrior chiefs throughout history often displayed devices on their shields as a form of identity on the battlefield and a symbol to which their supporters could rally. In England heraldry began in the twelfth century with the Crusades. Knights wore distinctive decorative devices on their shields. These shields of arms are often called coats of arms because the same device would be displayed on the surcoat of the armour, which was a long flowing tunic, usually of white linen, worn over the armour. The family coat of arms passed from father to son, and descendants in a legitimate male line were entitled to bear arms, the device being modified slightly to be distinctive for each member of the family. A rose was the emblem of the seventh son. As the coat of arms was associated with the shield, so the crest was a device worn on the helm of the armour. The coat of arms was a personal device unique to the individual; he alone displayed it on his shield, his surcoat, his lance pennon and his banner. His followers did not wear his arms but they needed to display some emblem which showed their allegiance to their leader, and it was for this reason that badges came into use in the fourteenth century. A heraldic badge therefore is an insignia distinctive of a person but which is not associated with the shield or the helm and which can be worn by retainers or supporters of that person. It would often be part of the livery of retainers and would also be displayed on household furniture and plate.

Exactly how or when the white rose came to be adopted as the badge of the Old Pretender is not known, but that it was his badge is beyond doubt. The suggestion that it was adopted by the Jacobites because James II had at one time been Duke of York, and the white rose was the Yorkist badge in the Wars of the Roses, does not bear scrutiny. Certainly the Jacobite white rose has nothing whatever to do with the Tudor rose of the sixteenth century and indeed, as a Stuart emblem, it probably goes back much further. Katharine Thompson in her *Lives of the Jacobites*, 1845, claims that the white rose is an ancient Scottish badge having been adopted by David II in the fourteenth century at a tournament at Windsor where he was held prisoner after the battle of Neville's Cross. Muriel Steevenson also makes the point that, apart from being an ancient Stuart badge, the white rose also signifies strict legitimacy and had been used by Richard II of England to show his right to the throne.[2] Recalling that the Whigs had endeavoured to discredit the birth of the Old Pretender by spreading the rumour that the royal baby had been smuggled into Mary of Modena's bedchamber in a warming pan, this would make the white rose an ideal choice of badge for James.

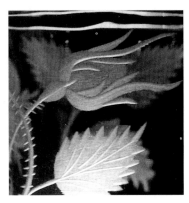

a   *b. Old Pretender, James*   *c. Prince Charles*

Plate 127 a, b, c. The 'old' interpretation of the single-bud Jacobite rose. [D]

Many ballads, poems and street songs from the first half of the eighteenth century contain references to the Old Pretender and the white rose, and the history of the Jacobite period is littered with incidents when Stuart supporters, wearing white roses, were attacked by Whigs. This usually happened on the 10th of June, the Old Pretender's birthday. Nor were these incidents always light-hearted frolics. In 1716 the guards were called out in London to prevent the wearing of white roses; this resulted in a printer being shot in Newgate Street and others being wounded.[3] In Edinburgh in 1721 soldiers were ordered to remove all white roses and again two men were killed.[4]

It is not clear why the rose on Jacobite glasses is usually a six-petal rose. Seven-petal, eight-petal and multi-petal roses occur but are much less frequent. The five-petal rose is so unusual as to be regarded as an aberration; it is almost as if the engravers were avoiding the five-petal rose and this may well have been the intention, otherwise the Jacobite rose might have been confused with the Tudor rose. The white rose upon which the Jacobite rose is supposed to be based is the *rosa alba maxima*.

The emblems occurring on Jacobite glasses, such as oak leaves, stars and thistles, can be interpreted with reasonable certainty. However, the precise interpretation of the most important emblem, the rose, has always puzzled students of Jacobite glass and has been a continuous source of debate and argument. The reason is that no theory to date answers all the questions.

One theory suggested that the rose represented James II and the open and closed buds the Old and the Young Pretenders respectively (Plate 126). There is really no reason why James II should have been revered in this way by the Jacobites and this theory never had many supporters.

The second theory could be called the 'old theory' because it was held as being correct until about fifty years ago. This theory is that the rose is the white rose, the badge of the Old Pretender, James, the two buds representing his sons Prince Charles and Prince Henry. In many ways this is the obvious interpretation of the emblems and it has the added advantage that if the rose is the badge of the Old Pretender, then the placement of the buds is correct in that they follow heraldic principles. When two members of a family are represented on any heraldic device the senior member is always placed on the dexter side (i.e. to the left when viewed from the front) of the junior member. Thus on single-bud glasses the closed bud is said to represent Charles and is always placed on the sinister side (i.e. to the right when viewed from the front) of his father (Plate 127). When three members of a family are represented the most senior is placed in the centre with the junior members on either side, the more senior of the two juniors occupying the dexter position. Therefore, on the two-bud glasses representing Charles and Henry, the more senior of the two, Charles, would be

a. Prince Charles
b. Old Pretender, James
c. Prince Henry

Plate 128 a, b, c. The 'old' interpretation of the two-bud Jacobite rose. [A]

a
b. Crown of England
c. Old Pretender, James

Plate 129 a, b, c. Horridge's interpretation of the single-bud Jacobite rose. [E]

represented by the opening bud and placed on the dexter side of James, and the more junior, Henry, by the closed bud on the sinister side (Plate 128).

This all sounds very reasonable and one might be forgiven for wondering why the rose emblems should present a problem. Difficulties have been encountered, however, because the Jacobite rose glasses are frequently thought of as occurring in three distinct groups: an early group of single-bud glasses, a large group of glasses in the middle period having two buds and a group of late glasses with a single bud. This representation is not strictly correct. There is certainly a group of early glasses with a single bud. These are often light baluster glasses and they usually display no emblems other than the rose, and there seems little doubt that Jacobite engravings started in this way. The group of late single-bud glasses, however, is far less distinct; in reality there is a scattering of single-bud glasses throughout the middle and later Jacobite periods. Problems have arisen in interpreting the single-bud glasses and also in explaining the large number of two-bud glasses, which outnumber the single-bud glasses by about two to one. This is because it is generally assumed that Prince Henry would have

a. Prince Charles	b. Crown of England	c. Old Pretender, James

Plate 130 a, b, c. Horridge's interpretation of the two-bud Jacobite rose. [B]

been ignored after he deserted the Jacobite cause in 1747, to become a cardinal in the Church of Rome, and would not have been represented on the glasses.

The early single-bud glasses are readily explained. If the glasses started to be engraved in the early 1740s, all hopes at this time were pinned on Prince Charles because Prince Henry was still a young boy of fifteen or sixteen. Although Henry did not attain his majority until 1746 there is no reason why he should not have been represented on the glasses by an additional bud two or three years earlier. Jacobite expectations must have reached fever pitch when it became known that Charles was in Paris in 1744 and in 1745 Henry was in Paris trying to persuade the French to give active support to his brother who had just defeated Cope at Prestonpans. Henry's following may well have declined sharply after he became a cardinal in 1747 but it is interesting to note that it did not disappear completely. The Jacobites in the letter (p. 69) were still drinking his health in 1759 and two 'Amen' glasses with the date 1749 carry dedications to Prince Henry.

The theory that the rose represented the Old Pretender, James, and the buds his sons Charles and Henry held until 1944 when Horridge read a well-reasoned paper to the Glass Circle.[5] Horridge had extensive knowledge of Jacobite history, as well as possessing a large collection of Jacobite glasses. War time conditions made it difficult for him to view large numbers of glasses personally. However, he based his paper on some forty glasses in his own collection and another fifty glasses he had viewed in museums and various collections. To these he added details from glasses illustrated in books and sale catalogues until the glasses in his study totalled two hundred. He too found that the proportion of two-bud glasses to single-bud glasses was approximately two to one. Believing that the majority of Jacobite glasses were engraved after 1750, for reasons already explained (pp. 158-9), he felt that another explanation for the rose emblems had to be found. He could not accept that Prince Henry would have continued to attract such support after he became a cardinal in 1747.

Horridge developed the theory that Henry was not represented on any of the glasses. The rose represents the Triple Crown and the buds the Old Pretender and the Young Pretender (Plate 130). With the early single-bud glasses the closed bud represents James (Plate 129) but as Charles became the central figure in Jacobite aspirations another bud was added and, as the son was seen to have superseded the father, Charles was given the more advanced open bud.

Barrington Haynes pursued Horridge's theory and modified it slightly.[6] He

a   *b. Crown of England*   *c. Old Pretender, James*

Plate 131 a, b, c. Barrington Haynes's interpretation of the single-bud Jacobite rose. [A]

a. Old Pretender, James   *b. Crown of England*   *c. Prince Charles*

Plate 132 a, b, c. Barrington Haynes's interpretation of the two-bud Jacobite rose. [D]

believed, like Horridge, that on the early single-bud glasses the closed bud represented James (Plate 131) but on the two-bud glasses that James took the senior open bud and Charles the closed bud (Plate 132). When James died in 1766 all the engraver had to do was to omit the open bud and this accounted for the late single-bud glasses. Haynes too believed that the rose represents the Crown of England and in commending Horridge's interpretation said that 'The traditional connexion needs no stressing when there is a 'Rose and Crown' in half the villages of England.'[7] This view appears to miss the whole point of the Jacobite rose. Certainly a rose has been associated with the Crown since medieval times, but this rose is always the five-petal Tudor rose which, together with a crown, forms the royal badge of England (Plate 133). It is this badge which is represented on the inn signs across the country. The Tudor rose, however, has no connection whatever with the Jacobite white rose.

The theory that the rose represents the Crown of England is the one now accepted in all the textbooks. The present author, however, favours the 'old theory' that the rose represents James and the buds his two sons. In the first place, if the majority of Jacobite glasses were engraved before the opaque-twist glasses first appeared in 1747-48, then the factors which worried Horridge and Haynes do not arise; the glasses would have been engraved *before* Henry became a cardinal and there would be no reason to exclude him and indeed every reason to represent him. After all he was in Paris assisting his brother's cause, and if Charles had been killed the whole responsibility for the Stuart restoration would have fallen on Henry's shoulders. Secondly, it is well recognized that the white rose was James's badge and the representation of the buds

Plate 133. Royal badge of England

follows accepted heraldic principles. Finally, there is not a distinct group of late single-bud glasses but a scattering of single-bud glasses throughout the whole Jacobite period and these are explained as belonging to supporters who simply favoured Prince Charles and continued the early single-bud theme, excluding Henry for any number of reasons.

In conclusion, there is one fact which is difficult to explain by any theory; namely, that a six-petal rose usually appears on the reverse side of Hanoverian glasses sporting the White Horse of Hanover (Plate 134). Horridge's theory probably scores better

a

b

Plate 134 a, b. Typical Hanoverian wine glass

here because he explained this particular rose by saying that the Hanoverians displayed it to show that they already possessed the Crown which the Jacobites were striving to capture. If this is so, then how does one interpret the sentiments expressed on the Hanoverian glass (Plate 135), which not only sports a six-petal rose but also a closed bud on the sinister side and, what appears to be, a severed bud on the dexter side? As was said at the beginning, it is often better to travel hopefully than to arrive.

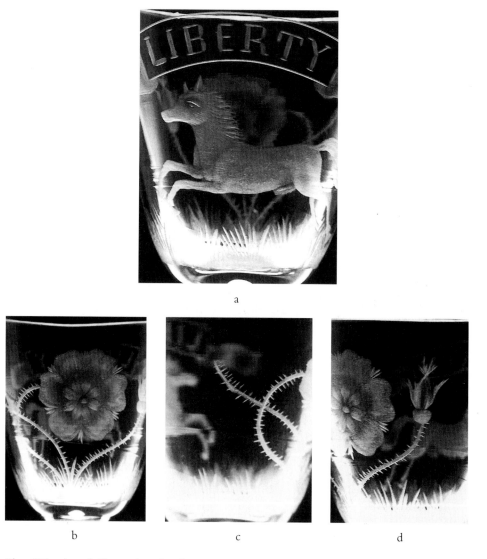

a

b   c   d

Plate 135 a, b, c, d. Hanoverian wine glass

CHAPTER 8
The 'Amen' Glasses

The 'Amen' glasses are in a class of their own; they have a fascination which is unique. If monetary worth is any measure then these wine glasses are, without question, the most highly prized of all Jacobite glasses. Many are in museum collections across the world but a few remain in private hands and, on the rare occasion when one appears for sale, there is always a buzz of excitement. The £66,000 paid for the Spottiswoode 'Amen' glass at Sotheby's in April 1991 made it the highest price ever paid for a Jacobite glass and one of the highest for any eighteenth century drinking glass. What is it that makes a simple wine glass attain the value of a fine painting or an exquisite piece of furniture? It is not craftsmanship for, although the engraving on an 'Amen' glass may be quite good, it is not exceptional. Nor is it rarity because over thirty 'Amen' glasses are known to exist and there are a number of less valuable Jacobite glasses much rarer than that. It is the value placed on historical sentiment. Each one of these glasses is an instrument of treason, a tangible piece of history.

Engraved in diamond-point, they leave no room for doubt about the sentiments expressed. There is no obscure symbolism: no roses, no buds, no oak leaves or butterflies, and no mottoes from Latin poetry. The Jacobite anthem spells out the message in plain unequivocal English and it is sealed under the cipher of the Pretender and his crown with the word 'Amen'. Some, going even further, hammer the message home by including the name of some loyal Scottish hero of the Stuart cause and one is immediately transported across the centuries.

The cipher, JR (Jacobus Rex), direct and reversed, is that of the Old Pretender, James. The figure 8, which is usually a small 8 in the lower part of the cipher or, more rarely, a large 8 intertwined with the cipher, refers to the fact that the Old Pretender would have been James VIII of Scotland had he regained the throne that was his by right (Plate 136).

The verses of the Jacobite anthem are enclosed in calligraphic scroll cartouches and the full anthem consists of four verses:

God Save the King, I pray
God Bliss the King, I pray
  God Save the King
Send him Victorious
Happy and Glorious
Soon to Reign over us,
  God Save the King.

God Bliss the Prince of Wales,
The True-born Prince of Wales,
  Sent us by Thee.
Grant us one Favour more,
The King for to Restore,
As Thou hast done before,
  The Familie.

God Save the Church, I pray,
God Bliss the Church, I pray,
  Pure to remain.
Against all Heresie,
And Whig's Hypocrisie,
Who strive maliciouslie,
  Her to defame.

God Bliss the Subjects all,
And Save both great and small
  In every Station.
That will bring home the King,
Who hath best right to reign,
It is the only thing,
  Can save the Nation.

                                       Amen

The majority of the *'Amen'* glasses only have the first two verses. When the full hymn is engraved the third and fourth verses appear either low down on the bowl or on the foot of the glass. The hymn probably dates back to James II, the reference to the 'true-born Prince of Wales' being a refutation of the rumours concerning the birth of the baby James Francis Stuart which were promulgated by the Whigs. The first verse of the Jacobite anthem, which is always engraved either side of the crown and cipher, is familiar because of the similarity it bears to our present National Anthem. The Georgian national anthem used today was first performed in September 1745 at the Theatre Royal in Drury Lane and there is a certain irony in it having been paraphrased from the opposing Jacobite anthem. The music was by the musical director at Drury Lane, Dr. Arne.

The *'Amen'* glasses were admirably suited to the drinking customs of the day. After dinner, when the time came for toasts, it was a common practice in Scotland for a single glass to be used and when a toast was called the glass would be passed around the table from person to person. In this way several bottles of wine might be drunk from a single glass circling the table. The *'Amen'* glass would be used for the loyal toasts to 'The King' and 'The Prince of Wales'. And they often carry other toasts such as 'To His Royal Highness Prince Henry' or 'To The Increase of The Royal

Plate 136 a, b, c. The Murray-Threipland 'Amen' glass showing: b the crown above the cipher and a and c the first verse of the Jacobite anthem. (No.22)

a

b

Family', as well as those to specific families or supporters such as 'Prosperity to The Family of Traquair' or 'A Bumper. To The Memory of Mr David Drummond'. Glasses such as these, with dedications to loyal Stuart adherents, exemplify the individuality of the *'Amen'* glasses.

There follows a list of all the *'Amen'* glasses known at the present time. When compiling such a list it is necessary, first of all, to decide which glasses are going to be included under the heading *'Amen* glass' because there are a few glasses which are atypical. Originally the glasses which are now known as *'Amen'* glasses were called Old Pretender glasses; then, in the 1920s, the term *'Amen* glass' started to be used for glasses with two or more verses of the Jacobite anthem and the title Old Pretender was reserved for a few glasses which were engraved with the crown and the cipher and which sometimes only had part of the first verse of the anthem and sometimes omitted the word *'Amen'*. Since, as will be shown later, all these glasses were the work of one engraver it seems reasonable to include them all under one heading and the Old Pretender glasses have been incorporated in this list.

The present author is indebted to Charleston's *'Tentative handlist of recorded 'Amen' glasses'*[1] for many of the details, particularly of provenances. However, the glasses in the following list have been grouped differently and those which are considered to be

Plate 136

c

forgeries have been omitted, but will be discussed in the next chapter. As Charleston points out in the introduction to his handlist, there are still some gaps and, doubtless, some errors but the details are as complete as present-day knowledge allows and the author would be grateful for any corrections or additions.

Plate 137a, b, c and d illustrates the variations in the crowns. These are: no shading at base (Plate 137b), solid shading to base (Plate 137a), lined shading to base (Plate 137d) and speckled shading to base (Plate 137c).

Plate 137a and b illustrates the two types of figure 8: the small 8 in the lower part of the cipher (Plate 137a) and the large intertwined 8 (Plate 137b).

Plate 137a, b, c, d and e also illustrates the different types of scrollwork: the circle and loop scrollwork around the rim of the bowl (Plate 137b, c and d) and the elaborate calligraphic scrollwork (Plate 137e). Plate 137a shows less elaborate calligraphic scrolls around the rim of the bowl. The different types of scrollwork are often combined on the same glass. For example, a glass with circle and loop scrollwork around the rim of the bowl will usually have the less elaborate calligraphic scrolls separating the verses of the anthem (Plate 137c).

The 'variations' refer to variations of the version of the Jacobite anthem on Page 185.

The quality of the engraving is graded: good, fair and poor.

FOUR-VERSE 'AMEN' GLASSES

(1) THE BREADALBANE I[2]

Photographed by the author (Plate 138).

Description: Trumpet-shaped bowl with plain drawn stem enclosing two tears, plain conical foot. H. 20cm.

Engraving: The bowl is engraved with a crown (lined shading to base), cipher with small 8 in lower part, four-verse anthem and 'Amen'. The reverse of the bowl also carries the dedication: 'To His Royal Highness Prince Henry Duke of Albany and York.'

Elaborate calligraphic scrollwork.

Quality of engraving: Good.

Variations: 'Long to Reign' instead of 'Soon to Reign'. The first and second lines of the first verse are transposed; similarly the first and second lines of the third verse.

Provenance: One of two 'Amen' glasses coming to light in the last ten years. At one time in the possession of the 2nd Marquis of Breadalbane at Taymouth Castle, the glass came by descent to Colonel Morgan Grenville and then to his daughter, Lady Ironside. The glass was sold at Christie's 25-11-1986, lot 123.

Notes: At the time of the 1745 rebellion the earldom was held by John Campbell, 2nd Earl of Breadalbane, but he was not a Jacobite so it is unlikely that the glass was given to him. He had been involved in the 1715 rebellion but had been summoned to surrender thus escaping punishment, and thereafter he supported the Whigs. The 3rd Earl succeeded his father in 1752 but he too had supported Walpole's administration and had been appointed a Lord of the Admiralty in 1741. It is likely that the glass was

a

The Baird of Lennoxlove (No.10)

b

The Russell (No.13)

c

The Fisher of Ham Common (No.6)

d

The Beves (No.2)

*Plate 137 a, b, c, d, e. The 'Amen' glasses.
Variations of the cipher, crown and scrollwork*

e

The Perry of Mambeg (No.29)

b

c

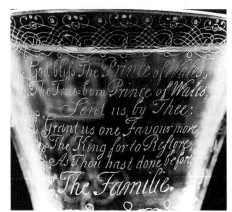

d

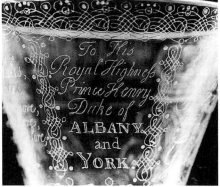

e

Plate 138 a, b, c, d, e. The Breadalbane I 'Amen' glass showing the first two verses of the anthem and the dedication to Prince Henry. (No.1). H. 20cm.

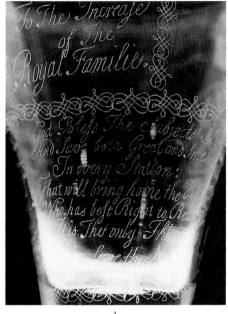

a   b

Plate 139 a, b. The Beves 'Amen' glass showing the third and fourth verses of the Jacobite anthem. (No.2)

acquired as a collector's item in the nineteenth century by either the 1st or 2nd Marquis of Breadalbane. Both were keen collectors, especially the 2nd Marquis who spent lavishly collecting works of art and furnishing the family seat at Taymouth Castle. The 1st Marquis died in 1834. When his son, the 2nd Marquis, died without an heir in 1862 the marquisate became extinct.

(2) THE BEVES[3]

Photographed by the author (Plates 137d, 139 and 168d).
Description: Trumpet-shaped bowl with plain drawn stem enclosing a pear-shaped tear, plain conical foot. H. 18cm.
Engraving: The bowl is engraved with a crown (lined shading to base), cipher with small 8 in lower part, four-verse anthem and *'Amen'*. The reverse of the bowl also carries the inscription: 'To His Royal Highness The Duke of Albany and York. And To The Increase of The Royal Familie.'
Circle and loop scrollwork around the rim of the bowl, calligraphic scrolls separating the verses of the anthem.
Quality of engraving: Good.
Variations: 'Bless' instead of 'Bliss', 'has done before' and 'has best Right to Reign' instead of 'hast done before' and 'hath best Right to Reign'. The first and second lines of the third verse are transposed.
Provenance: Formerly in the collection of Donald H. Beves, Cambridge. 1961 Fitzwilliam Museum, Cambridge. Sold by the Syndics of the Fitzwilliam Museum, Sotheby's 11-5-1964, lot 152. Sold Sotheby's 6-3-1984, lot 161.

(3) THE MESHAM[4]

Not photographed by the author; detailed photograph available (Plate 140).
Description: Trumpet-shaped bowl with plain drawn stem enclosing an oval tear, plain conical foot (chipped). H. 21.7cm.

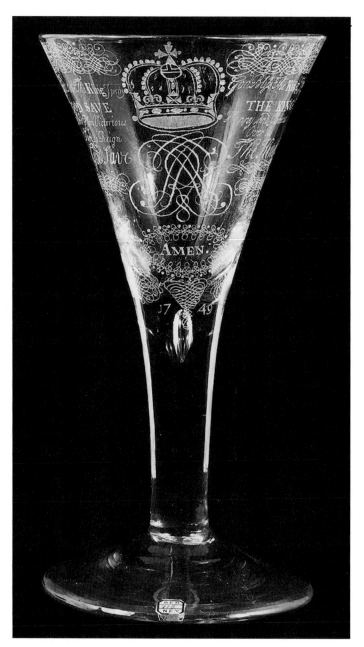

Plate 140. The Mesham 'Amen' glass. (No.3). H. 21.7cm.

Engraving: The bowl is engraved with a crown (solid shading to base), cipher with small 8 in lower part, four-verse anthem and *'Amen'*. There is also the additional inscription: 'To His Royal Highness Prince Henry Duke of Albany and York.' and the date '1749'. Elaborate calligraphic scrollwork.

Quality of engraving: Good.

Provenance: The Lindsey family of Fife. Then belonged to Colonel Mesham and was sold by his daughter to Messrs. Arthur Churchill who sold it to George F. Berney. Sold Christie's 30-6-1936, lot 130, and again at Christie's 26-4-1937, lot 116. Then owned by Jerome Strauss and now in the Corning Museum of Glass, New York, U.S.A.

Exhibited: Wine Trade Loan Exhibition 1933.

Notes: The Mesham glass is one of the six *'Amen'* glasses known to Albert Hartshorne in 1897. Like the Drummond Castle glass, which it closely resembles, the significance of the date '1749' is not known but may be the date when the glass was engraved.

Plate 141. The Drummond Castle 'Amen' glass. (No.4). H. 19.9cm.
(COURTESY PHILADELPHIA MUSEUM OF ART, U.S.A.)

(4) THE DRUMMOND CASTLE[5]

Not photographed by the author; detailed photographs available (Plates 141, 154, 170a, 175 and 177a).

Description: Trumpet-shaped bowl with plain drawn stem enclosing a long tapering tear, folded foot. H. 19.9cm.

Engraving: The bowl is engraved with a crown (solid shading to base), cipher with small 8 in lower part, four-verse anthem and *'Amen'*. There is also the additional inscription: 'To His Royal Highness Prince Henry Duke of Albany and York.' and the dates: 'Tenth of June', 'XX December' and '1749'.

Elaborate calligraphic scrollwork.

Quality of engraving: Good.
Variations: 'Bless' instead of 'Bliss'.
Provenance: Earl of Ancaster, a descendant of the Duke of Perth, whose seat was Drummond Castle. In 1921 the glass was in the possession of G.F. Berney. It was later owned by George H. Lorimer and is now in the Philadelphia Museum of Art, U.S.A.
Notes: Illustrated in detail in Joseph Bles's *Rare English Glasses of the 17th and 18th Centuries*.
The 10 June and 20 December are the birthdates (Old Style) of the Old Pretender and the Young Pretender respectively. The significance of the date 1749 is not known but could be the date when the glass was engraved.

(5) THE PALMER DOUGLAS[6]

Not photographed by the author; detailed photograph available.
Description: Trumpet-shaped bowl with plain drawn stem enclosing a large tapering tear, plain conical foot. H. 17.8cm.
Engraving: The bowl is engraved with a crown (solid shading to base), cipher with small 8 in lower part, three verses of the anthem and *'Amen'*. On the bowl there is the additional inscription: 'To His Royal Highness The Duke and the Increase of The Royal Family.' The fourth verse of the anthem is engraved on the foot.
Circle and loop scrollwork around the rim of the bowl and the edge of the foot; calligraphic scrolls separating the verses of the anthem.
Quality of engraving: Good.
Variations: 'Bless' instead of 'Bliss'.
Provenance: Mrs. Archibald Palmer Douglas, of Midgard, Hawick, Roxburghshire. Sold Christie's 15-12-1936, lot 28. In 1941 owned by Steuben Glass, New York. Now in the Metropolitan Museum of Art, New York, U.S.A.

(6) THE FISHER OF HAM COMMON[7]

Photographed by the author (Plates 137c, 142, 168b, 169a, c and e, 171).
Description: Trumpet-shaped bowl with plain drawn stem enclosing a small tear, plain conical foot. H. 17.8cm.
Engraving: The bowl is engraved with a crown (speckled shading to base), cipher with large 8 intertwined, the first two verses of the anthem and *'Amen'*. On the bowl are the additional inscriptions: 'To His Royal Highness The Duke.' and 'To The Increase of The Royal Family.' The third and fourth verses of the anthem are engraved on the foot.
Circle and loop scrollwork around the rim of the bowl, calligraphic scrolls round the edge of the foot and separating the verses of the anthem.
Quality of engraving: Good.
Variations: 'Bless' instead of 'Bliss', 'has done before' and 'has best Right to Reign' instead of 'hast done before' and 'hath best Right to Reign'.
Provenance: Mrs. John Fisher, Ham Common, Richmond, Surrey. Sold Sotheby's 27-6-1924, lot 38. Then owned by Joseph Bles and sold Christie's 16-7-1935, lot 34. Owned by Sir Bernard Eckstein and now in the Ashmolean Museum, Oxford.
Notes: This glass is illustrated in detail in Joseph Bles's book *Rare English Glasses of the 17th and 18th Centuries*. Bles also refers to the large intertwined 8 as being 'An extremely rare variation'.

Plate 142 a, b, c, d. The Fisher of Ham Common 'Amen' glass showing on the foot: b, c the third verse and d the fourth verse of the Jacobite anthem. (No.6). H. 17.8cm.

THREE-VERSE 'AMEN' GLASSES

(7) THE RISLEY[8]

Not photographed by the author; detailed photograph available (Plate 143).
Description: Trumpet-shaped bowl with drawn M.S.A.T. stem on a plain conical foot.
H. 17.2cm.
The bowl of the glass is cracked and the foot is badly damaged with a piece, accounting for about one quarter of the circumference, missing.

Plate 143. The Risley 'Amen' glass. (No.7). H. 17.2cm.

Engraving: The bowl is engraved with a crown (solid shading to base), cipher with small 8 in lower part, the first two verses of the anthem and *'Amen'*. The third verse is engraved on the foot. Originally there may have been the first line of the fourth verse on the piece of the foot that is missing; now only the word 'subject' remains.

Circle and loop scrollwork around the rim of the bowl, calligraphic scrolls separating the verses of the anthem.

Quality of engraving: Good.

Variations: 'has done before' instead of 'hast done before'.

Provenance: Purchased in Yorkshire and sold to Sir John Risley sometime prior to

1920. Later owned by MacBean and sold at auction in 1931 to Capt. Craig. Left to National Gallery of Victoria, Melbourne in 1960 as part of the Felton Bequest.

(8) THE OGILVY OF INSHEWAN

Not photographed by the author; no photographs available.
Description: Trumpet-shaped bowl with drawn M.S.A.T. stem. H. 17cm.
Engraving: The bowl is engraved with a crown, cipher, figure 8, two-verse anthem and *'Amen'*. The bowl also carries the additional inscription: 'Prince Henry Duke of Albany and York.' The foot is engraved with the third verse of the anthem and 'God Bliss all Loyall Subjects. Amen.'
Quality of engraving: Not known.
Provenance: John Ogilvy of Inshewan. Sold Sotheby's 27-6-1924, lot 39, to Mrs. Aspin.

(9) THE KEITH-DOUGLAS[9]

Photographed by the author (Plate 144).
Description: Trumpet-shaped bowl with drawn M.S.A.T. stem on a plain conical foot. H. 16.8cm.
The foot, which is badly damaged, has been repaired in three pieces held together by a silver mount. Two of the pieces, which are thinner, have come from another glass.
Engraving: The bowl is engraved with a crown (solid shading to base), cipher with small 8 in lower part, the first two verses of the anthem and *'Amen'*. The bowl is also engraved with the additional inscription: 'Prince Henry Duke of Albany and York.' On the foot the remaining segment of the original glass is engraved in the same hand with part of the first half of the third verse of the anthem:

> 'God Bliss The Church
> And Save The Church I pray
> Pure to Remain'

The two thinner segments from another glass are engraved in a different, less experienced, hand: one with the second half of the third verse, 'against all heresy and Whig Hypocrasy who strive Maliciously Her to defame', and the other with, 'God bless all Loyal Subjects'.

   Circle and loop scrollwork around the rim of the bowl, calligraphic scrolls separating the verses of the anthem.
Quality of engraving: Good.
Variations: The first and second lines of the first verse are transposed.
Provenance: From George, 10th Earl Marischal to Bishop Keith, Primate of Scotland. The glass then descended to Mr. Stewart Marischal Keith-Douglas when it was one of the six *'Amen'* glasses known to Albert Hartshorne in 1897. It was then owned by Cecil Davis (1926) and after that by Capt. W. Horridge. Sold by Jackson, Stops and Staff 30-11-1959, lot 367. Owned by Dr. Peter Plesch and sold Sotheby's 6-12-1971, lot 159. Owned by K.A. Alexander. Now on loan to the Glasgow Museums and Art Galleries.
Exhibited: Circle of Glass Collectors Commemorative Exhibition, Victoria and Albert Museum, 1962.

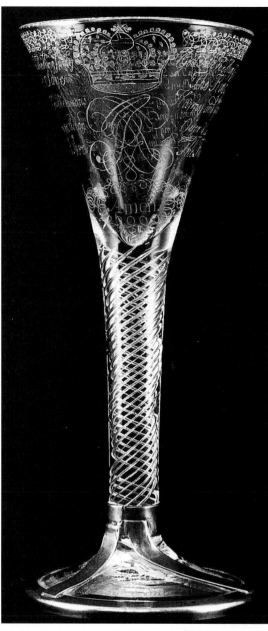

*Plate 144 a to i. The Keith
Douglas 'Amen' glass. (No.9).
H. 16.8cm.*

a

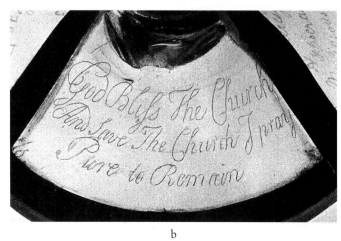

b

c

d

e

f

g

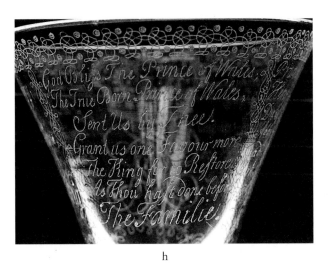

h

i

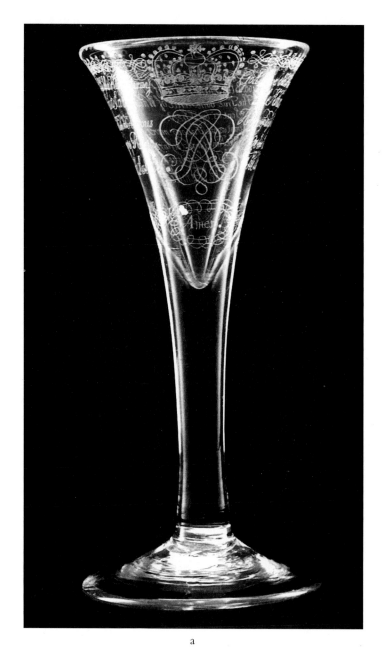

a

Plate 145 a, b, c, d. The Baird of Lennoxlove 'Amen' glass. (No. 10). H. 17.6cm. (See also plate 137a.)

TWO-VERSE *'AMEN'* GLASSES

(10) THE BAIRD OF LENNOXLOVE[10]

Photographed by the author (Plates 137a and 145).
Description: Trumpet-shaped bowl with plain drawn stem on a folded foot. H. 17.6cm.
Engraving: The bowl is engraved with a crown (solid shading to base), cipher with small 8 in lower part, two-verse anthem and *'Amen'*.
Moderately elaborate calligraphic scrollwork around the rim of the bowl and separating the verses of the anthem.
Quality of engraving: Good.

| b | c | d |

Variations: 'Long to Reign' instead of 'Soon to Reign'. The first and second lines of the first verse are transposed.

Provenance: The Lords Blantyre, of Lennoxlove, Haddington, and their successors the Bairds of Newbyth. Owned by Robert Baird and sold Christie's 18-12 1947, lot 113 when it was acquired by Messrs. Arthur Churchill. The present owner is K.A. Alexander and the glass is on loan to the Victoria and Albert Museum.

Exhibited: By the Baird family at the Scottish Exhibition of National History, Art and Industry held in Glasgow in 1911; by Messrs. Arthur Churchill at the Antique Dealers' Fair in 1948; the Victoria and Albert Museum Exhibition of English Glass in 1968.

(11) THE BREADALBANE II

Not photographed by the author; detailed photograph available.

Description: Trumpet-shaped bowl with plain drawn stem enclosing an elongated tear, plain conical foot. H. 17cm.

Engraving: The bowl is engraved with a crown (lined shading to base), cipher with small 8 in lower part, two-verse anthem and *'Amen'*.

Elaborate calligraphic scrollwork.

Quality of engraving: Good.

Provenance: This glass, like the Breadalbane I *'Amen'* glass, has only been recorded in recent years and it has the same provenance. Sold Christie's 16-10-1990, lot 148.

(12) THE ATTWOOD[11]

Not photographed by the author; detailed photograph available.

Description: Trumpet-shaped bowl with plain drawn stem enclosing a pear-shaped tear, folded foot. H. 19.7cm.

Engraving: The bowl is engraved with a crown (lined shading to base), cipher with small 8 in lower part, two-verse anthem and *'Amen'*.

Elaborate calligraphic scrollwork.

Quality of engraving: Good.

Provenance: G.E. Attwood. Sold Puttick and Simpson 12-4-1912 to Law Foulsham and Cole. Owned by R. Drane and sold Sotheby's 29-6-1916. Owned by Wilfred Buckley and then acquired by Victoria and Albert Museum. This glass was broken during the 1939-45 War.

a   b

Plate 146 a, b. The Russell 'Amen' glass. (No.13)

Notes: Albert Hartshorne in his book, *Old English Glasses* (1897), refers to an *'Amen'* glass owned by Mr. G.E. Attwood which corresponds to the above description. He also records a legend attached to the glass, namely, that it was given by Prince Charles to a Bond Street silversmith, named Collier, for entertaining him on one of the occasions about the middle of the eighteenth century when Charles is said to have visited London incognito.

(13) THE RUSSELL[12]

Not photographed by the author; detailed photograph available (Plates 137b and 146).
Description: Trumpet-shaped bowl with a drawn M.S.A.T. stem on a plain conical foot. H. 17.7cm.
Engraving: The bowl is engraved with a crown (no shading to base), cipher with large 8 intertwined, two-verse anthem and *'Amen'*. In addition the bowl carries the inscriptions: 'To His Royal Highness Prince Henry.' and 'To The Increase of The Royal Familie.'.
Circle and loop scrollwork around the rim of the bowl, calligraphic scrolls between the verses of the anthem.
Quality of engraving: Good.
Variations: 'Bless' instead of 'Bliss' and 'has done before' instead of 'hast done before'.
Provenance: Owned by A.J. Russell, Edinburgh (1887) and then the Misses Russell. Sold Christie's 16-6-1949, lot 9. Owned by Mr. C.A. Hamilton (1950). (Charleston believes this glass belonged to Major Hamilton of Murrayfield and was sold to J. Gordon and Gordon, Edinburgh, 1953). Then owned by Walter F. Smith, Jnr., Trenton, U.S.A. Sold Sotheby's 4-12-1967, lot 206. Now in Harvey's Wine Museum, Bristol.
Exhibited: Edinburgh 1950: Exhibition of Rare Scottish Antiquities.
Notes: The Russell *'Amen'* glass is a good example of how an unrecorded item of historical importance can suddenly appear and yet still have a reliable provenance; a subject which is discussed in more detail in the next chapter. When this glass appeared at auction in 1949 it was entirely unknown, yet the owners were able to trace the glass back to it being in the possession of their grandfather, Mr. A.J. Russell, who died in 1887. He had acquired it from an unknown source.

The Spottiswoode 'Amen' glass. (No.14). H. 20.8cm. See also frontispiece.

(14) THE SPOTTISWOODE

Not photographed by the author; detailed photograph available. (See frontispiece and above.)

Description: Trumpet-shaped bowl with drawn M.S.A.T. stem on a plain conical foot. H. 20.8cm.

Engraving: The bowl is engraved with a crown (lined shading to base), cipher with small 8 in lower part, two-verse anthem and *'Amen'*. The bowl carries the additional

inscription: 'His Royal Highness Prince Henry Duke of Albany and York.'
Elaborate calligraphic scrollwork.
Quality of engraving: Good.
Provenance: This glass is said to have descended through the family of Spottiswoode of Spottiswoode in Berwickshire from the eighteenth century. Sold Sotheby's 25-3-91, lot 31. Now owned by the Drambuie Liqueur Co. Ltd., Edinburgh.
Notes: At auction the glass came in a nineteenth century, red morocco leather bound, green velvet lined, casket. The key to the casket has a luggage label attached with the inscription: 'Jacobite Glass and Thornydike Cup are in a red Box which is on the oak chest under the stair March 1867'. The label also has the name 'Mrs Spottiswoode' printed upon it.

The assertion that this *'Amen'* glass has descended through the Spottiswoode family from the eighteenth century is made in the sale catalogue, which also claims that the Spottiswoodes were staunch Jacobites and participated in the 1715 and 1745 risings. All of this is disputed by Mrs Dorothy Dore (née Spottiswoode), who, as a member of the Spottiswoode Society, is extremely knowledgeable about her family history. She claims the glass was bought at auction in the nineteenth century by Lady John Scott, whose maiden name was Spottiswoode. In her will Lady Scott clearly refers to the 'morocco case' containing 'valuable Jacobite relics' and also states that they were 'bought with Lord John Scott's money'. She bequeathed the Jacobite relics to the Duke of Buccleuch but, for some reason, they never reached the intended recipient and were left behind in the Spottiswoode estate. This is, presumably, how the label which accompanies the *'Amen'* glass comes to bear the name 'Mrs Spottiswoode'. Mrs Dore's evidence is very compelling and it would appear that the only real Spottiswoode connection is that this happened to be the maiden name of Lady Scott. Since it is quite clear from the will that Lady Scott was married when she bought her 'valuable Jacobite relics' it would really be more fitting for the glass to be known as the Scott *'Amen'* glass but it is unlikely that it will be renamed.

(15) THE CORNING

Not photographed by the author; detailed photograph available.
Description: Trumpet-shaped bowl with plain drawn stem enclosing a long pear-shaped tear, plain conical foot. H. 17.1cm.
Engraving: The bowl is engraved with a crown (lined shading to base), cipher with small 8 in lower part, two-verse anthem and *'Amen'*.
Elaborate calligraphic scrollwork.
Quality of engraving: Good.
Variations: 'Bless' instead of 'Bliss'.
Provenance: Steuben, New York. Now in the Corning Museum of Glass, New York, U.S.A.
Exhibited: Royal Ontario Museum, Toronto, 1950.

(16) THE TRAQUAIR[13]

Photographed by the author (Plate 147).
Description: Trumpet-shaped bowl with plain drawn stem enclosing an elongated tear, plain conical foot. H. 16.1cm.

a

b

c

d

Plate 147 a, b, c, d. The Traquair 'Amen' glass. (No.16). H. 16.1cm.

Engraving: The bowl is engraved with a crown (solid shading to base), cipher with small 8 in lower part, two-verse anthem and *'Amen'*. The foot carries the further inscription: 'Prosperity to The Family of TRAQUAIR.'
Elaborate calligraphic scrollwork.
Quality of engraving: Fair.

Variations: The first three lines of the second verse agree with the usual version but the remainder is different:

'God Bliss the Prince of Wales
The true-born Prince of Wales
Sent Us by Thee.
Send Him soon over
And kick out hannover
And then we'll recover
Our Old Libertie.'

Provenance: Traquair House, Peebleshire. Present owner F. Maxwell-Stuart.
Exhibited: Bute House, Edinburgh, 1949.
Notes: This *'Amen'* glass is still to be found in Traquair House together with several other Jacobite glasses and an important collection of miniatures, which include portraits of the 6th and 7th Earls of Traquair; the Old Pretender, James, his wife, Princess Clementina Sobieska and their sons, Prince Charles Edward and Prince Henry.

In the first half of the eighteenth century Traquair House became the centre for Jacobite activities in the south of Scotland. The 4th Earl of Traquair spent some time imprisoned in Edinburgh Castle for his Jacobite sympathies and was involved in the 1715 rising, being a member of a Jacobite conspiracy known as the Braemar Hunting Party.

The 4th Earl's wife was the only daughter of the 4th Earl of Nithsdale; it was her sister-in-law, Lady Nithsdale, who travelled to London after the 1715 rebellion and threw herself at the king's feet pleading for the life of her husband, the Earl of Nithsdale, who was condemned to death for his part in the rebellion. Her entreaties failed but she managed to get permission to visit her husband in the Tower and on the eve of his execution she became the heroine of a famous daring exploit. Having made meticulous preparations she succeeded in organizing her husband's escape from the Tower by disguising him as her maid. The couple fled to France and finally settled in Rome.

The 5th Earl of Traquair was another ardent Jacobite and was sentenced to two years in the Tower for his role in the 1745 rebellion. It is the 5th Earl who is associated with one of the romantic legends of Scottish history. One of the entrances to Traquair House is 'The Steekit Yetts'. This is at the end of a long avenue flanked by trees. Legend tells of the iron gates being closed by the 5th Earl one day in 1745, after he bade farewell to his guest, Prince Charles Edward, and never being opened since. The Earl vowed that the gates would remain closed until a Stuart was restored to the throne.

Dool an' sorrow hae fa'en Traquair,
An' the Yetts that were shut at Charlie's comin'
He vowed wad be opened nevermair
Till a Stuart King was crooned in Lunnon.

(17) THE MORTON

Not photographed by the author; detailed photograph available (Plate 148).
Description: Trumpet-shaped bowl with plain drawn stem enclosing a tear, folded foot. H. 17.4cm

Plate 148. The Morton 'Amen' glass. (No.17). H. 17.4cm. (COURTESY NATIONAL GALLERY OF VICTORIA, MELBOURNE, AUSTRALIA)

Engraving: The bowl is engraved with a crown (solid shading to base), cipher with small 8 in lower part, two-verse anthem and *'Amen'*.
Less elaborate calligraphic scrollwork.
Quality of engraving: Good.
Provenance: In the possession of the Morton family 'for as long as it can be recalled'. Mrs. M.H. Morton. Sold Christie's 11-12-1961, lot 30. Then owned by Gordon Russell, Sidney, Australia. Now in the National Gallery of Victoria, Melbourne, Morgan Endowment 1973.

Plate 149. The Erskine of Cardross I 'Amen' glass. (No.18). H. 16.3cm.

(18) THE ERSKINE OF CARDROSS I

Photographed by the author (Plate 149).

Description: Trumpet-shaped bowl with plain drawn stem enclosing an elongated tear, plain conical foot. H. 16.3cm.

Engraving: The bowl is engraved with a crown (solid shading to base), cipher with small 8 in lower part, two-verse anthem and *'Amen'*.
Elaborate calligraphic scrollwork.

Quality of engraving: Fair.

Provenance: Sir David Erskine of Cardross, a descendant of Chancellor Erskine, whose forebears were ardent Jacobites. Probably owned by G.F. Berney, then owned by O.S.N. Turnbull (1921). Now owned by the National Trust, Mompesson House, Salisbury.

a   b

Plate 150 a, b, c. The Erskine of Cardross II
*'Amen' glass. (No.19). (*COURTESY GLASGOW ART
GALLERY AND MUSEUM*)*

(19) THE ERSKINE OF CARDROSS II

c

Not photographed by the author; detailed photographs available (Plate 150)
Description: Trumpet-shaped bowl with plain drawn stem, plain foot. H. 17.1cm.
Engraving: The bowl is engraved with a crown (solid shading to base), cipher with
small 8 in lower part, two-verse anthem and *'Amen'*.
Less elaborate calligraphic scrollwork.
Quality of engraving: Good.
Variations: The first and second lines of the first verse are transposed.
Provenance: Sir David Erskine of Cardross (as for the Erskine of Cardross I) although
Charleston notes, 'The connexion of this glass with Sir David Erskine seems uncertain.'
Owned by G.F. Berney (1921) and then Sir Hugh Dawson (1942). Sold Sotheby's 21-10
1960, lot 49. Owned by J.F. Wells. Now with the Glasgow Museums and Art Galleries.

(20) THE LOCHIEL[14]

Photographed by the author (Plate 151)

Description: Trumpet-shaped bowl with plain drawn stem enclosing a tear, folded foot. H. 16.5cm.

Engraving: The bowl is engraved with a crown (solid shading to base), cipher with small 8 in lower part, two-verse anthem and *'Amen'*. The foot is engraved: 'A Bumper To The Prosperity of The Family of Lochiell.'
Circle and loop scrollwork around the rim of the bowl, calligraphic scrolls between the verses of the anthem.

Quality of engraving: Fair.

Variations: 'Bless' instead of 'Bliss' and 'hath done before' instead of 'hast done before'.

Provenance: This glass was unrecorded until 1952 but was probably owned by the Camerons of Lochiel. Sold in Edinburgh 1952. Acquired by the Royal Scottish Museum, Edinburgh, (Now the National Museums of Scotland).

Notes: The Camerons of Lochiel were staunch Jacobite supporters throughout the Jacobite period. Colonel John Cameron of Lochiel declared for Viscount Dundee after James II was driven into exile and his Highlanders were largely responsible for Dundee's victory at Killiecrankie in 1689.

In 1745 it was the decision of Donald Cameron of Lochiel to fall in behind Prince Charles Edward which formed the backbone of Jacobite support in the early days of the rising. 'Gentle' Lochiel remained loyal to the Prince throughout the 'Forty-five and sailed back to France with him on his final escape. He did his best to give Charles the benefit of his wise counsel during the troubled period in Paris but Lochiel died of meningitis in 1748, just before the Prince was arrested by the French.

(21) THE AIRTH CASTLE

Not photographed by the author; detailed photograph available.

Description: Trumpet-shaped bowl with plain drawn stem enclosing a small pear-shaped tear, plain conical foot. H. 17.7cm. The bowl of this glass is damaged.

Engraving: The bowl is engraved with a crown (lined shading to base), cipher with small 8 in lower part and two-verse anthem. By accident or design the *'Amen'* has been omitted.
Circle and loop scrollwork around the rim of the bowl, calligraphic scrolls below the anthem.

Quality of engraving: Good.

Variations: 'Bless' instead of 'Bliss'.

Provenance: The glass came to auction at Sotheby's 17-4-1978, lot 83, as, 'A hitherto unrecorded *'Amen'* glass.'

Notes: It had been found at Airth Castle by the owner who had acquired the property from the Graham family. This family had occupied the Castle since its acquisition by Judge Graham in 1717. The Judge's second wife was Lady Mary Livingstone, daughter of the Earl of Callendar by Falkirk, whose family estate was forfeited after the 'Forty-five.

a

b

c

d

Plate 151 a, b, c, d. The Lochiel 'Amen' glass. (No.20). H. 16.5cm.

(22) THE MURRAY-THREIPLAND[15]

Photographed by the author (Plates 136 and 152).
Description: Trumpet-shaped bowl with drawn M.S.A.T. stem above a beaded basal knop on a domed foot. H. 19cm. A triangular piece has been broken from the bowl and replaced.
Engraving: The bowl is engraved with a crown (solid shading to base), cipher with small 8 in lower part, two-verse anthem and *'Amen'*.
Elaborate calligraphic scrollwork.
Quality of engraving: Good.
Variations: 'has done before' instead of 'hast done before'.
Provenance: Mr. P. Murray Threipland of Fingask Castle, Aberdeenshire (1822); then Mr. W. Murray Theipland (1897); then P.W. Murray Threipland, FRGS, FSA (Scot.). Then acquired by the National Museum of Antiquities, Edinburgh, (Now the National Museums of Scotland).
Notes: One of the six *'Amen'* glasses known to Albert Hartshorne in 1897.

(23) THE PEECH[16]

Not photographed by the author; detailed photograph available.
Description: Trumpet-shaped bowl with drawn M.S.A.T. stem above a beaded basal knop and a domed foot. H. 19cm.
Engraving: The bowl is engraved with a crown (solid shading to base), cipher with small 8 in lower part, two-verse anthem and *'Amen'*. The bowl also carries the additional inscription: 'To The Increase of The Royal Family.'
Elaborate calligraphic scrollwork.
Quality of engraving: Good.
Provenance: Henry Peech. Sold Sotheby's 19-3-1926, lot 30. Owned by Hamilton Clements and then Sir Harrison Hughes. Sold Sotheby's 24-6-1963, lot 64.

(24) THE DUNVEGAN[17]

Photographed by the author (Plate 153).
Description: Trumpet-shaped bowl with plain drawn stem enclosing a pear-shaped tear, plain conical foot. H. 17.7cm. The bowl is broken and most of the upper part is missing.
Engraving: The crown and most of the cipher is missing. There is a small 8 in the lower part of the cipher and the bowl is engraved with the remains of the two-verse anthem and *'Amen'*. The foot, which is the most interesting part of the glass, is intact and carries the inscription: 'Donald MacLeod of Gualtergil in The Isle of Skye. The Faithful PALINURUS. ÆT.69. Anno 1747.'
Elaborate calligraphic scrollwork.
Quality of engraving: Fair on bowl; good on foot.
Variations: 'Long to Reign' instead of 'Soon to Reign'.
Provenance: Dunvegan Castle, Isle of Skye.
Notes: This glass is in Dunvegan Castle together with a number of other Jacobite relics. The Castle has been the ancestral home of the Chiefs of the Clan MacLeod

Plate 152. The Murray-Threipland 'Amen' glass. (No.22). H. 19cm.

since the thirteenth century, but it is not known how the glass comes to be there, for during the 'Forty-five the MacLeods of Dunvegan were anti-Jacobite. The glass refers to a MacLeod from another part of Skye: Donald MacLeod of Galtrigill, the old boatman who, scorning the reward on the Prince's head, 'speeded the bonny boat' and risked his life to guide and protect Charles Edward, evading the government frigates which were searching for them. Hence the reference to Palinurus, the mythological steersman of Aeneas.

a

Plate 153 a, b, c, d, e, f, g. The Dunvegan 'Amen' glass. (No.24). H. 17.7cm.

The old boatman was also given a silver snuff-box by John Walkinshaw who had served the Old Pretender and was the father of Clementina Walkinshaw, the girl who became Charles's mistress. The snuff-box is recorded as being engraved with exactly the same inscription as that on the foot of the *'Amen'* glass except that the date was 1746 and the age of Donald MacLeod correspondingly 68. It has been inferred from this that John Walkinshaw also gave Donald MacLeod the *'Amen'* glass, but it seems unlikely that Walkinshaw, having made one gift of appreciation, would feel the need

b

c

d

e

f

g

to make another. However, it is quite possible that the inscription on the glass was copied from that on the snuff-box and it does seem to confirm that the date on the glass is genuine and contemporary. The old boatman died in poverty in 1749.

Among the other relics at Dunvegan Castle are Donald MacLeod's spectacles and a Jacobite portrait glass. There is also an embroidered waistcoat said to have belonged to Prince Charles and a lock of his hair. Flora MacDonald returned to her native Skye towards the end of her life. She died in Dunvegan in 1790 at the age of 68 and some of the relics in the Castle belonged to her.

(25) THE BRUCE OF COWDEN[18]

Not photographed by the author; detailed photograph available (Plate 154).
Description: Trumpet-shaped bowl with plain drawn stem enclosing a small slender tear, plain conical foot. H. 17.7cm.
Engraving: The bowl is engraved with a crown (lined shading to base), cipher with small 8 in lower part, two-verse anthem and *'Amen'*.
Elaborate calligraphic scrollwork.
Quality of engraving: Good.
Variations: 'Long to Reign' instead of 'Soon to Reign'.
Provenance: The family of Bruce of Cowden, Clackmannanshire. Margaret Bruce married the 4th Earl of Airlie. The glass passed to her son, the Hon. John Bruce Ogilvy, and then to his great nephew, the Hon. Bruce Ogilvy. Sold Sotheby's 14-2-1924, lot 199. Owned by G.F. Berney and then George H. Lorimer. The glass is now in the Philadelphia Museum of Art, U.S.A.

(26) THE NEWTON OF BALLYMOTE[19]

Not photographed by the author; detailed photograph available (Plate 154).
Description: Round funnel bowl on an incised twist stem and plain conical foot. H. 16.7cm.
Engraving: The bowl is engraved with a crown (lined shading to base), cipher with small 8 in lower part, two-verse anthem and *'Amen'*.
Elaborate calligraphic scrollwork.
Quality of engraving: Good.
Provenance: Lady Newton of Newtown Park House, Ballymote, Co. Sligo. Owned by Mrs. H.F. Thomas (1927), then G.F. Berney (1930), and then George H. Lorimer (1934). Now in the Philadelphia Museum of Art, U.S.A.

(27) THE HOWARD[20]

Not photographed by the author; detailed photograph available (Plate 154).
Description: Round funnel bowl on a double series air-twist stem with a multi-ply spiral band enclosing a pair of spiral threads, plain conical foot. H. 19.5cm.
Engraving: The bowl is engraved with a crown (solid shading to base), cipher with small 8 in lower part, two-verse anthem and *'Amen'*. In the first verse the engraver has made a mistake: 'Send Him Victorious' has been repeated for the fifth line instead of the usual 'Happy and Glorious'. Realizing the error the engraver has inserted 'Happy and Glorious' beneath the last line of the verse. On the foot there is the inscription: 'God Bliss and Restore the Son of the Father we had before'.
Elaborate calligraphic scrollwork.
Quality of Engraving: Good.
Provenance: T.N.S.M. Howard, C.D., D.S.O. to whom it allegedly descended from a Scottish branch of the family. Sold Sotheby's 1926. Owned by G.F. Berney and then George H. Lorimer (1936). Now in the Philadelphia Museum of Art, U.S.A.
Exhibited: Wine Trade Loan Exhibition, 1933.

(28) THE VAILLANT[21]

Not photographed by the author; no photographs available.
Description: Trumpet-shaped bowl with drawn air-twist stem. H. 16.5cm.
Engraving: The bowl is engraved with a crown, cipher, two-verse anthem and *'Amen'*. On the bowl there is the additional inscription: 'To His Royal Higness The Duke And To The Increase of The Royal Family.' On the foot is engraved: 'A Bumper To The Noble and True Patriot of his Countrey The Right Hon^le George Earle Marshal etc. etc. Hereditary Earl Marshal of Scotland.'
Quality of engraving: Not known.
Provenance: This is one of the six *'Amen'* glasses known to Albert Hartshorne and it is to him that we owe details of the provenance. The glass originally belonged to Ann, daughter of Richard Harcourt and his wife Henrietta, daughter of Henry Browne, Viscount Montagu of Cowdray. Ann's parents had followed the fortunes of the Stuarts into France; she died 2nd March 1800. Her effects were sold at auction and the glass remained in Boulogne throughout the nineteenth century. When Hartshorne was

writing (1897) the glass was owned by M.V.-J. Vaillant at Boulogne. Nothing is known of its subsequent whereabouts.

Notes: George Keith, born 1693, the 10th and last hereditary Earl Marischal of Scotland was a devoted Jacobite supporter. He took an active part in the 1715 rising and on 23 December 1715 received the Old Pretender at his house in Newburgh. After the failure of the rebellion he followed James to France. He was wounded in Scotland in the 1719 rising but again escaped to the Continent. He served James in Rome and, together with the Duke of Ormonde, was the Old Pretender's representative in Madrid.

When the French were planning the invasion of England under Marshal Saxe in 1744, James appointed Marischal the Captain General of the Jacobite forces in Scotland. He was with Prince Charles at Dunkirk when the invasion plans collapsed. From then onwards Marischal's attitude seems to have been one of detachment. He was not overly fond of Charles Edward and, ever mindful of his own career, he had little time for what he perceived as the Prince's hare-brained schemes. The Prince, for his part, was impatient with the older man's cautious pessimism. Charles would have

Plate 154 Left to right. The Bruce of Cowden. (No.25). H. 17.7cm. The Drummond Castle. (No.4). H. 19.9cm. The Newton of Ballymote. (No.26). H. 16.7cm. The Howard. (No.27) H. 19.5cm. (Courtesy Philadelphia Museum of Art, U.S.A.)

valued Marischal's presence in Scotland, for the Earl's standing in the Scottish Highlands, and amongst the English Jacobites, was second to none. But Marischal remained in France where he made some efforts to get French support for the Jacobite cause. He strongly disapproved of Charles's behaviour in Paris after the failure of the rebellion.

He finally retired, with his brother, to Prussia where he served the King, Frederick the Great. He gained the confidence of the King and in 1751 was appointed Frederick's minister to the French Court in Paris. He always contrived to remain at the centre of Jacobite affairs and kept Frederick informed about the details of the Elibank Plot. He was pardoned by George II in 1759 and he died in 1778.

(29) THE PERRY OF MAMBEG[22]

Photographed by the author (Plates 137e and 155).
Description: Trumpet-shaped bowl with plain drawn stem enclosing an elongated tear, plain conical foot. H. 15.8cm.
Engraving: The bowl is engraved with a crown (solid shading to base), cipher with small 8 in lower part, two-verse anthem and *'Amen'*.
Elaborate calligraphic scrollwork.
Quality of engraving: Fair.
Provenance: Belonged to Dr. Perry and then to Mrs. Perry of Mambeg, Garelochhead. Sold Sotheby's 27-6-1924, lot 36. Owned by George Henderson. Sold Knight, Frank & Rutley 2-10-1952, lot 60. Later owned by T.S. Lucas of Haxby Hall and M. Bucks. Sold Sotheby's 10-2-1956, lot 22. Owned by J.D. Fox. Sold Sotheby's 16-10-1972, lot 194, to C. Davis Ltd. Now on loan to the Glasgow Museums and Art Galleries.
Exhibited: Glasgow Archaeological Society, November 1905.

(30) THE BURN MURDOCH[23]

Not photographed by the author; detailed photograph available.
Description: Trumpet-shaped bowl with plain drawn stem enclosing a long divided tear, plain conical foot. H. 18.1cm.
Engraving: The bowl is engraved with a crown (solid shading to base), cipher with small 8 in lower part, two-verse anthem and *'Amen'*.
Moderately elaborate calligraphic scrollwork.
Quality of engraving: Good.
Variations: 'Long to Reign' instead of 'Soon to Reign'.
Provenance: Owned by Dr. T. Burn Murdock, Gartincaber, Doune, Perthshire. Sold Sotheby's 27-6-1924, lot 37. Then owned by Hamilton C. Clements and later by Capt. W. Horridge. Sold Plaish Hall, Cardington, Church Stretton, Salop., by Jackson, Stops & Staff, 30-11-1959, lot 368. Owned by Dr. Peter H. Plesch. Sold Christie's 4-6-1980, lot 153. Now in the Birmingham Museum and Art Gallery.
Exhibited: V and A Exhibition of English Glass, 1968.

(31) THE HADDINGTON[24]

Photographed by the author (Plates 156 and 158).
Description: Round funnel bowl with four-sided moulded pedestal stem enclosing a

Plate 155. The Perry of Mambeg. (No.29). H. 15.8cm.　　*Plate 156. The Haddington. (No.31). H. 12.6cm.*

tear at base, folded foot. H. 12.6cm. The bowl is badly cracked and has been repaired.
Engraving: The bowl is engraved with a crown (no shading to base), cipher with small 8 in lower part, two-verse anthem and *'Amen'*. The bowl is also engraved with two dates: '1716' in the scrollwork surrounding *'Amen'*, and '1745' in the scrollwork below the second verse.
Circle and loop scrollwork around the rim of the bowl, calligraphic scrolls between the verses.
Quality of engraving: Writing – Fair. Scrollwork – Poor.
Variations: 'Bless' instead of 'Bliss' and 'has done before' instead of 'hast done before'.
Provenance: Bought at Haddington in 1876. Known to Albert Hartshorne in 1897 when the glass was already in the National Museum of Antiquities, Edinburgh, (Now the National Museums of Scotland).

Plate 157. The Steuart. (No.32). H. 16.1cm.

OTHER *'AMEN'*-TYPE GLASSES

(32) THE STEUART[25]

Photographed by the author (Plates 157 and 159).

Description: Bell-shaped bowl with solid base enclosing a tear, plain stem and plain conical foot. H. 16.1cm.

The bowl and the foot are badly cracked and have been repaired.

Engraving: The bowl is engraved with a crown (lined shading to base), cipher with small 8 in lower part, the second half of the first verse of the anthem and *'Amen'*:

Send Him Victorious	Happy and Glorious
Soon to Reign	Over Us
God Save	The King

Amen

The lower part of the bowl is engraved: 'Prosperity to The Bank of Scotland.' The foot is engraved: 'A Bumper. To The Memory of Mr David Drummond. 1743'

Plate 158 a, b, c, d. The Haddington 'Amen' glass. (No.31)

Circle and loop scrollwork around the rim of the bowl, calligraphic scrollwork on the lower part of the bowl and round the edge of the foot.

Quality of engraving: On bowl – Poor. On foot – Good.

Provenance: Descended in unbroken line in the Steuart family. Miss Sylvia Steuart. Acquired by National Museum of Antiquities, Edinburgh, (Now the National Museums of Scotland).

Exhibited: Circle of Glass Collectors, Commemorative Exhibition 1937-62, London (1962).

Notes: It is interesting that James Steuart V.W.S., who became a member of the Old Edinburgh Club (pp. 132-3) in 1909 and wrote about the eighteenth century meetings held at the house of his ancestor in Edinburgh, also mentions this glass. He records

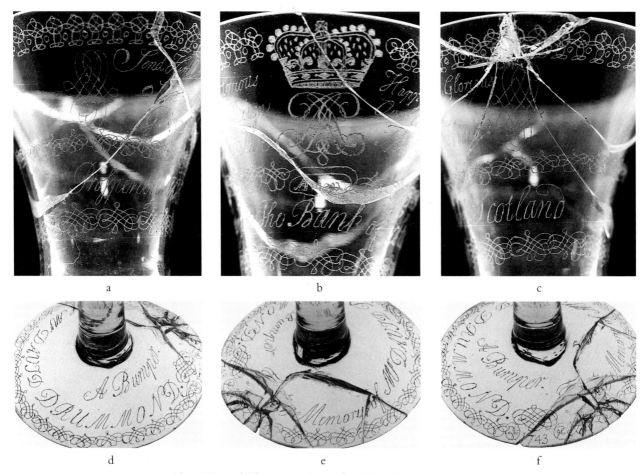

a   b   c

d   e   f

Plate 159 a to f. The Steuart 'Amen' glass. (No.32)

the occasion when Thomas Erskine produced six enamel portrait glasses for drinking the Prince's health and states that this *'Amen'* glass was used at the same meeting. Indeed the memory of David Drummond was toasted, together with that of the Prince, on each occasion until the last of the annual meetings was held in 1787.

David Drummond was the Treasurer of the Bank of Scotland from 1700 to 1740 and was the son of the Rev. David Drummond, minister of Moneydin, Perthshire. He was also an advocate and a loyal Jacobite. He is said to have acted as custodian of the funds raised for the defence of Jacobites captured in the 1715 rebellion. He was Deputy Lord of the High Court of Scotland and President of the Council of the Royal Company of Archers. He was highly respected and when he died in 1741, at the age of 85, great tribute was paid to him.

(33) THE GREGSON OF TILLIEFOUR[26]

Not photographed by the author; detailed photograph available.
Description: Bell-shaped bowl with solid base enclosing a small tear, plain stem and conical folded foot. H. 24.2cm.
Engraving: The bowl is engraved with a crown (lined shading to base), cipher with small 8 in lower part and the following inscription:

> 'Send Him soon home   To Holyruood House
> And that no Sooner   Than I do Wish
> Vive La Roy'

The unnecessary 'u' in Holyrood is erased.

Plate 160. The Fraser of Ford. (No.35)

Circle and loop scrollwork around the rim of the bowl.
Quality of engraving: Good.
Provenance: Major Gregson of Tilliefour, Aberdeenshire. Sold Christie's July 1919. Owned by Henry Peech. Sold Sotheby's 19-3-1926, lot 16. Owned by Hamilton Clements and then Sir Harrison Hughes. Sold Sotheby's 24-6-1963, lot 63. Sold Sotheby's 14-4-1992, lot 68.

(34) THE KER

Not photographed by the author; detailed photograph available.
Description: Trumpet-shaped bowl with plain drawn stem enclosing a long thin tear, folded foot. H. 28.7cm.
Engraving: The bowl is engraved with a crown (lined shading to base), cipher with small 8 in lower part, second half of the first verse of the anthem and *'Amen'*.
A few calligraphic scrolls around the rim of the bowl and below the inscription.
Quality of engraving: Poor.
Variations: 'Long to Reign' instead of 'Soon to Reign'.
Provenance: James Ker (1750-1819) of Blackshiells, to his grandson, John Archibald Ker (1819-1915). Then owned by Brigadier T.F.K. Howard. Present owner W.N.J. Howard. The glass is now on loan to the Victoria and Albert Museum.

(35) THE FRASER OF FORD

Not photographed by the author; detailed photograph available (Plate 160).
Description: Trumpet-shaped bowl with plain drawn stem enclosing an irregular tapering tear, folded foot. H. 14.6cm.
Engraving: The bowl is engraved with a crown (solid shading to base),cipher with small 8 in lower part, and the second half of the first verse of the anthem. (*'Amen'* is omitted).
There is no scrollwork.
Quality of engraving: Poor.
Provenance: According to tradition the glass was given by the Dowager Duchess of Gordon to William Fraser sometime before 1760. Fraser was the solicitor and confidant

a Steuart

b Lochiel

Plate 161 a to p. A series of interconnecting features of the writing on the 'Amen' glass to show they are the work of one diamond-point engraver.

c Lochiel

d Traquair

e Traquair

f Dunvegan

g Dunvegan

h Beves

i Beves

j Keith Douglas

k Keith Douglas

l Lennoxlove

m Lennoxlove

n Haddington

o Haddington

p Steuart

of Lord Lovat who was executed in 1747. The glass was then passed down in the family to the present owners, Dr. and Mrs. H. McGiles.

The same questions need to be asked about these thirty-five glasses as were asked about the wheel-engraved Jacobite glasses: Where were they engraved, who engraved them and when?

Where were the *'Amen'* glasses engraved?

When Hartshorne was pondering this question he decided that they had probably been engraved in France.[27] He seems to have based this conclusion, principally, upon the frequent use of the word 'bliss' instead of the English 'bless'.[28] He may also have been influenced by the fact that of the six glasses known to him, one, the Vaillant, dedicated to Earl Marischal, was known to have been in France since the eighteenth century, and another, the Keith Douglas, also had connections with Marischal. However, as Grant Francis points out,[29] it was quite usual in Scotland in the eighteenth century to use the spelling 'bliss' for 'bless' and, now that more glasses are known, the evidence for any French connection is very slender. Everything about the glasses points to Scotland: the cipher with the figure 8 referring to James VIII, and the dedications to notable Scottish adherents such as Lochiel and Traquair. There seems no reason whatever to suppose that the glasses were not engraved in Scotland; precisely where may never be known and it might be best to consider this in conjunction with the next question.

Who engraved the *'Amen'* glasses?

This too is unknown but it is possible to make a few reasonable deductions.

Firstly, since the glasses are so unique in their concept and design, could they all be the work of one engraver? At first, this might seem unlikely because the quality of the engraving varies considerably and there are numerous variations in the spelling and phrasing of the Jacobite anthem. However, there is a distinct uniformity in the style of the writing which could mean that the glasses are the work of the same hand gradually improving over a period of time. Plate 161 seeks to illustrate this by selecting words and features which interconnect the different glasses.

The writing on the *'Amen'* glasses photographed by the author has been closely studied by a forensic handwriting expert from the West Midlands Forensic Science Laboratory. The conclusion was that they are all, quite definitely, the work of one

a

Plate 162 a to f. Jacobite wine glass with engraved silver foot. H. 17.4cm.

engraver and there seems little doubt that all thirty-five glasses listed are the work of the same hand.

There was clearly a learning curve with the engraver making a shaky start with glasses such as the Ker and the Fraser of Ford, then progressing through glasses such as the Steuart and the Dunvegan where the engraver is still having difficulties on the curved bowl but is more confident on the flat surface of the foot, to finally achieving the fine quality engraving on glasses such as the Keith Douglas and the Drummond Castle. He did not make his task any easier by selecting the drawn trumpet as his preferred shape of bowl; writing on a sharply curved surface must be difficult enough, but one which is convex in one direction and concave in the other must be even more so.

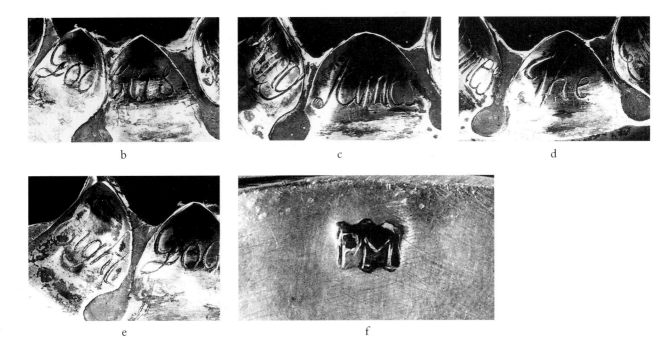

b   c   d

e   f

The engraver obviously had some calligraphic skills before he tried his hand at diamond-point engraving because, as already mentioned, the writing on the flat surface of the foot is expert and well-formed, even on the early glasses. Also the scrollwork on the *'Amen'* glasses is reminiscent of the calligrapher's art and it seems likely that the engraver could well have had his training in this discipline.

In the past it has been suggested that the *'Amen'* glasses may be the work of a silver engraver. It is difficult to see the reasoning behind this belief unless it stems from the fact that the engraving on the sixteenth century Verzelini glasses is thought to have been the work of Anthony de Lysle who also engraved on pewter. But the crafts of diamond-point engraving and silver engraving have little in common; the tools and techniques are quite different.

An interesting Jacobite glass which has some silver engraving is the one illustrated in Plate 162. This glass, with a trumpet-shaped bowl and plain drawn stem, has had the foot broken off and replaced in silver. There is no engraving on the glass but where the silver joins the stem the scalloped edge of the silver is engraved: 'God Blis King James The Eight'.

The glass has a reliable provenance from the family of Bruce of Cowden in the County of Clackmannan and it was sold at Sotheby's in 1924 when it appeared in the same sale as the Bruce of Cowden *'Amen'* glass.

It was not an uncommon practice to break a wine glass after drinking the health of the King, thus denying its use for any less noble toast, and traditionally this glass is said to have been broken by Prince Charles after drinking the health of his father.

The silver has never been assayed so there is no date mark but the maker's mark, 'PM', is on the underside of the foot. The mark is not recorded but it has been suggested that the silver work might be that of a Stirling goldsmith by the name of Patrick Murray, a Jacobite who was hanged for treason in 1746. This may well be so, but it has also been suggested that Patrick Murray might have been responsible for the *'Amen'* glasses and this latter theory does not bear close scrutiny. Apart from the difficulty in explaining how he could have been engraving glasses such as the Dunvegan *'Amen'* glass a year after he had been executed, the engraving on the silver does not match the writing on the *'Amen'* glasses. Nor does it follow that the silversmith who fashioned the foot also did the silver engraving because the crafts were often separate.

The glasses used for the *'Amen'* engravings may well have come from one of the glassmaking centres near to Scotland, such as Newcastle, and Charleston suggests,[30] that the *'Amen'* engraver may have been one of the travelling glass sellers touring the country. In sparsely populated areas this was the usual means by which glassware was distributed. Alternatively the *'Amen'* engraver may have worked in a large centre such as Edinburgh.

The Dunvegan *'Amen'* glass (pp. 212-15) is interesting in this respect although it does not resolve the question of whether the *'Amen'* glasses were the work of a resident or a travelling craftsman.

Donald MacLeod, the old boatman, was a tenant of the MacLeods of Dunvegan. He lived at Galtrigill, a remote hamlet in northern Skye, about ten miles from Dunvegan Castle. He was imprisoned after the 'Forty-five and was released in June 1747. Upon his release in London John Walkinshaw presented him with the silver snuff-box, dated 1746. Donald arrived in Edinburgh in August and remained there until late October when he returned to his native Skye. His stay in Edinburgh is recorded in detail because it forms part of the 'Journal of Donald MacLeod' written by Robert Forbes for the Scottish History Society.[31] Forbes, who was with Donald during his stay in Edinburgh and was actually responsible for raising the money to pay for his return to Skye, describes the snuff-box in great detail but at no time mentions any commemorative wine glass. Therefore, if the date on the *'Amen'* glass is genuine and it was the work of a travelling glass seller in Skye, it must have been commissioned in November or December of 1747. Since Forbes makes no mention of Donald having any commemorative glass in Edinburgh, and since, indeed, there is no evidence that he ever actually possessed the *'Amen'* glass, it raises the possibility of someone having had the glass engraved for their own use simply because they admired the old boatman. If this was so then a resident engraver begins to look more probable and points to Edinburgh as the most likely place of work. Because the inscriptions on the snuff-box and the *'Amen'* glass are the same apart from dates and ages the glass would have to have been commissioned by someone who had seen and studied the snuff-box. Since the glass now resides in Dunvegan Castle this raises an interesting, albeit unlikely, possibility. It is known that Donald's clan chief, Norman MacLeod, was also in Edinburgh during the autumn of 1747. He, like the other great clan chief of Skye, Sir Alexander MacDonald of Sleat, had originally promised support for Charles but, when the Prince arrived without French troops had refused to 'come out'. Norman MacLeod's loyalties were clearly divided and it is just possible that he may have commissioned the *'Amen'* glass while in Edinburgh having had a pang of conscience towards his old tenant. However, for this to have occurred the Laird would have to have met Donald in Edinburgh and seen the snuff-box and there is no record of any such meeting. Indeed, Forbes writes that one day, while in Edinburgh, Donald passed his Laird in the street and made to enquire about his welfare but Laird MacLeod refused to acknowledge the old boatman.

When were the *'Amen'* glasses engraved?

It used to be thought that the *'Amen'* glasses dated from about 1720 and that they were made to celebrate the birth of Prince Charles. However, it is now generally agreed that they were engraved in the 1740s.

The earliest dated glass is the Steuart *'Amen'* glass. Here the date, '1743', is clearly incorporated into the scrollwork indicating that it is not a later addition. The quality of the engraving suggests that this was one of the engraver's early attempts and it seems quite likely that 1743 is the date when the glass was engraved. It also probably represents the approximate date when the series of *'Amen'* glasses commenced.

The next glass with an engraved date is the Haddington *'Amen'* glass. Indeed, there are two dates: '1716' in the scrollwork around the *'Amen'* (Plate 158c) and '1745' in the scrollwork below the second verse of the anthem, although the second date is not very clear on the photograph (Plate 158d). Again, neither date appears to be a later addition and the glass does seem to fit into the series around 1745. The quality of the engraving on the bowl is better than the 1743 Steuart glass but not as good as the next glass bearing a date, the Dunvegan *'Amen'* glass. There seems no reason to suppose that the '1747' on this glass is not contemporary with the engraving on the bowl; it corresponds with the age of Donald MacLeod and the inscription on the foot, apart from the date, is the same as that on the snuff-box presented to the old boatman by John Walkinshaw (pp. 228-29).

The last date to be engraved on an *'Amen'* glass is 1749, and this date occurs on both the Mesham and the Drummond Castle glasses. The significance of 1749 is uncertain, unless it is simply the date when the engraving was executed. Both glasses have four-verse anthems and the engraving is of good quality, so they could represent the tail-end of the *'Amen'* engraving period. It seems unlikely that the same identical date would be a later addition on two independent glasses.

The evidence therefore seems to point to the *'Amen'* glasses having been engraved between about 1742 and 1750. It is interesting that the engraving on the bowl of the 1747 Dunvegan glass is still rather crude, suggesting that most of the *'Amen'* glasses were engraved after the 1745 rebellion. It is also worth noting that the engraver still had a high regard for Prince Henry because no fewer than eleven of the thirty-five glasses listed carry a dedication to the Prince. All the four-verse glasses have such a dedication, and indeed all the glasses with a dedication have good quality engraving, indicating that they are later than the 1747 Dunvegan glass. This is significant because 1747 is the year when Prince Henry is said to have alienated himself from any Jacobite sympathy by becoming a cardinal in the Church of Rome.

Much mystery still surrounds the *'Amen'* glasses and there are many questions yet to be answered. There may well be other *'Amen'* glasses waiting to be discovered and, who knows, they may provide further pieces of the jig-saw to help complete this fascinating puzzle.

CHAPTER 9
The Snake in the Grass

'Beware all thieves and imitators of other people's labour and talent ——'.
Albrecht Dürer 1511

The art of duplicity is as old as art itself. Ever since man first started to use his skills to produce things of beauty there have been those who have coveted and collected them and others, less gifted, who have faked and forged to satisfy the collector's appetite. The perpetrators of fakes often possess considerable skill in their own right which, when directed towards honest means, can produce genuine works of distinction. But they frequently lack original artistic creativity, and there is always that temptation to emulate the master. The motive is often monetary gain but can sometimes be a desire to dupe the scholars in a particular field. When the art establishment is seen paying homage to original art of dubious merit the faker, having talent but lacking originality, may feel compelled to produce another 'Corot' to confound the experts.

The faker has the covetousness of his victim to assist him because the collector is always looking for the rarity and in his quest is inclined to see what he wants to see. The difficulty is getting a fake work of art past the impartial expert whose critical judgement may be more acute. The specialists employed by the museums and major auction houses carry the responsibility of authenticating and valuing the works of art which pass through their hands. But, however great their expertise, mistakes are made and every now and again the experts are deceived. The difficulties are then compounded because the fake, by getting this far, has gained respectability; it has acquired a provenance. The next time it appears it will be 'from so and so's collection' or 'last sold in these rooms' and there is less and less inclination to doubt its authenticity.

Vincent Van Gogh, during his most productive years, 1880–1890, produced some two thousand paintings and drawings. A rather cynical joke tells that at least three thousand of these are now in America. This quip may have more than a grain of truth in it for we are led to believe that most art galleries across the world unwittingly display some paintings and works of art which are probably faked. Eric Hebborn, a self-confessed faker of Old Master drawings and possessing formidable technical skills, freely admits that his works are represented in many such museums and galleries world-wide.[1] When, a few years ago, the British Museum mounted an exhibition of bogus works of art, entitled 'Fakes?', he wondered, rather mischievously, why they had not shown any of his Old Master drawings since they had several from which to choose.

Hebborn now lives in Italy on the fruits of his labours. It is easy to feel a certain admiration for a talent such as his, and to feel contempt for the crooked art dealers who have knowingly traded in his work. Patience wears thin, however, when Hebborn attempts to justify the way he has used his gifts by asserting that there is no such thing as a fake work of art, only fake experts, because they are unable to spot every spurious item which passes through their hands.[2]

Hebborn would execute a drawing in the style of an Old Master on genuine old

Plate 163. Reproduction with no intention to deceive. 'Pretender' glass from the pattern book of Stevens and Williams, c.1900.

paper and then offer it to Sotheby's or Christie's or a specialist dealer. He never sold direct to the general public and he was clever enough not to present the drawing as an authentic original; he would simply submit it for appraisal. If the bait was taken and the drawing was accepted then it was the expert who was the fake and Hebborn considered himself to be absolved from any responsibility. Apart from showing that he was a clever faker he was only demonstrating what most intelligent beings know already: that expertise in any field of human activity is never infallible. It was all an exciting, not to say rewarding, game; pitching his skills against those of the best authorities in his field and one can see the attraction of the challenge. But, where was his conscience? Hebborn does little to conceal his self-satisfaction and he does not consider himself to be a criminal.[3] Fakers such as him feel free to write about their adventures on the fringes of the law because they know, only too well, that the experts they have hoodwinked prefer to let sleeping dogs lie rather than have their lapses of competence exposed to the glare of publicity. If it pleases Hebborn to think there was nothing dishonest in his activities, so be it. But there must always have been a loser and it was never him. He has no hesitation in casting the crooked dealers as the villains of the piece but he was all too ready to avail himself of their services when it suited his purpose.[4] His advice that art, whether genuine or fake, should be appreciated and bought for what it is seems too naïve to be taken seriously.[5] This completely disregards what most purchasers know to be true, namely that there are several factors which contribute toward the value of a work of art other than technical talent: rarity, originality, antiquity and, perhaps most of all, authenticity, to name but a few. Why else do fakers such as Hebborn go to the trouble of forging signatures and using old paper contemporary with the artist they are seeking to imitate?

Nevertheless, this does raise a moral question. If a fake is so good that it deceives the best in its field and everyone believes it to be genuine, where is the harm? Does it really matter? The answer is that if art and truth mean anything at all then of course it matters; it matters a great deal. Just because the recognized authorities are deceived it does not mean that no harm is done. The genuine works of art are diminished and honesty is devalued. If it is acceptable to pass a fake wine glass, why not counterfeit bank notes? And, sooner or later a fake will probably be exposed to someone's detriment.

A work of art is said to be a fake when it is produced in the style of a master craftsman or a certain period. A forgery is when something is slavishly copied. It is not against the law to make a copy of any object, painting or document, nor to produce these items in the style of some other artist or period, and many works of art are copied as genuine reproductions with no intention to deceive. (See plate 163). However, when such an item is presented as an authentic original and used for gain then the crime becomes that of fraud.

The general glass collector is probably troubled less by fakes than collectors in many other fields. The reasons for this are self-evident. Although it is quite possible to produce glass similar in consistency to that made in a particular period, such as the eighteenth century, it is not easy. The production of the metal requires expertise and expensive equipment, to say nothing of the skills and the teamwork necessary to produce the finished article. Most fake antique drinking glasses are reproductions made with modern glass. The underside of the foot will usually have been abrased to simulate wear and the majority of these glasses are not too difficult to detect, although there are exceptions.

The glass collector does not have hallmarks, maker's marks or date stamps to assist in identification, and in many ways this is one of the fascinations. When presented with a drinking glass purporting to be, for example, English eighteenth century, there are a number of checks to be made which, with practice, become second nature.

(1) THE METAL

Is it lead glass? This is the first and most important fact to establish. If it is soda or potash glass it does not mean that there is necessarily anything amiss but we need to know. Eighteenth century lead glass does not have the brilliance of modern, highly purified, lead crystal; it has a distinctive limpid clarity. Early eighteenth century glass may even have a greyish tone to its colour, a feature much prized by collectors. It is the lead in the glass which increases its density and enhances the power of the glass to refract and disperse light. On picking up a glass one becomes accustomed to expect a certain weight of metal. Soda glass invariably feels lighter than expected; it may also have a slight greenish tinge and usually contains numerous small bubbles.

It is reassuring to flick the bowl of a wine glass with the finger nail and elicit the prolonged ringing tone typical of lead glass. However, this does depend upon the shape of the bowl and the thickness of the glass, which means that as a definitive test of lead glass it is of limited value.

The foregoing description of lead and soda metal is a generalization and it has to be said that some modern non-lead glass can be very deceptive. If confirmation of the type of metal is needed the glass should be subjected to ultra-violet light. Lead glass fluoresces bluish-purple, soda glass a greenish-yellow. Modern pure lead glass fluoresces a deeper blue than eighteenth century glass.

(2) THE STYLE

The overall proportions of a wine glass must be considered. Is the size and shape of the bowl in balance with the type of stem and the foot? This requires experience and it is always reassuring to find a textbook illustration of a similar glass.

The diameter of the foot of an eighteenth century wine glass should at least equal, and usually exceeds, the diameter of the bowl. If the foot is measured between the finger and thumb then the bowl should pass through with space to spare. When the glass has a folded foot there is no problem, but if the foot is plain and the diameter is less than the bowl then it is likely that the foot has been chipped and subsequently trimmed. This is not a disaster but it will affect the value. Much more serious is when the bowl looks out of proportion and one suspects that the rim of the bowl has been ground down.

If the glass has an opaque-twist stem the enamel should be a dense opaque white and not the milky transparent white sometimes seen on reproductions.

The glass should then be examined for signs of having been crafted by hand. An eighteenth century glass will have a pontil mark. Later in the century, as the feet of drinking glasses became less conical in shape, the pontil on the better quality glasses was frequently ground and polished. Tooling marks will also be visible on the bowl of the glass. These are surface striations caused by the tool used for shaping the bowl and there may be a slight swelling at one point on the rim produced by the final cut of the trimming shears.

(3) THE WEAR

On an old wine glass wear occurs at three sites:

(a) The underside of the foot. There is pitting of the glass and irregular scratches where the foot makes contact with the surface upon which it stands. When efforts are made to simulate wear on the foot of a glass it is usually done by rubbing the glass on some abrasive surface. This produces scratch marks which are parallel to one another and, with the use of a hand-lens, they can usually be detected without too much difficulty.

(b) The rim of the bowl. There is minute pitting of the glass around the rim. This has been caused by the glass catching the teeth of the drinker or by it being stood upside down. These marks can be seen with a hand-lens and they can be felt by running the thumb nail round the rim of the bowl. On fake drinking glasses these marks are often absent.

(c) Around the edge of the foot. Again, this is pitting similar to that round the rim of the bowl and can be detected in the same way with the thumb nail. Because the foot of an eighteenth century wine glass is usually wider than the bowl, when glasses are stood together the foot of one glass tends to impinge upon that of its neighbour causing these minute marks. On a genuine glass the absence of these marks is another sign that the foot may have been trimmed.

With a little experience most reproduction eighteenth century-style drinking glasses can be detected without too much trouble, but when it comes to fake decorations on glass the opposite applies; it can be extremely difficult. The most common form of decoration on glass is wheel-engraving and here the problems are considerable. Because it is a technique which involves the removal of material there is no analytical test which can be applied and if the faker uses a genuine eighteenth century glass for the engraving it can be impossible to prove that the glass has been fake engraved. Some experts have claimed to be able to distinguish an old engraving from a recent one, stating that old engravings have a patina. But glass is too hard a substance to develop a patina and the texture of an engraving depends entirely upon the fineness of the abrasive which was used to create it in the first place. Also, in the mistaken belief that engravings darken with age, glasses have sometimes been soaked in hot coffee and other liquids likely to produce the desired effect. All these tricks are quite unnecessary because a wheel-engraving that is two hundred years old can look as clean and as fresh as one done twelve months ago.

The problems encountered with Jacobite engravings are greater than with any other type of commemorative glass, and it is not difficult to see why this is so. A simple air-twist stem glass can have its value quadrupled if it is engraved with a Jacobite rose. If it is also engraved with a motto, particularly one of the rarer ones such as *'Redi'* or *'Redeat'*, its value can be increased tenfold. And, if it should be engraved with a portrait of the Young Pretender, then it may be increased twenty or thirty-fold. With returns of this order the faker has few qualms about using a genuine eighteenth century glass in the exercise of his skills. Add to this the fact that the value of the majority of Jacobite glasses rests in rarity and historical sentiment, not craftsmanship, most Jacobite engravings falling well within the competence of an average wheel-engraver, and the unscrupulous craftsman has a recipe for fraud on a grand scale which may be difficult to resist.

However, all is not lost. It may not be possible to prove that a Jacobite wheel-engraving is a fake but, by recognizing the styles of the principal eighteenth century engravers, it is possible to authenticate most of the genuine glasses. Jacobite wheel-engravings which do not conform to a recognized eighteenth century style and which lack a reliable provenance should be left to wither on the vine.

In the present series of 487 Jacobite glasses, 459 are wheel-engraved. Of these the five major engravers account for 61.3 per cent. Of the remaining wheel-engraved glasses there are a number of smaller groups which might also be considered genuine: The minor engravers F, G, H and I (6.1 per cent); the isolated glasses which do not fit into the other groups but which seem to be authentic, either because of the unusual character of the engraving or because they have a reliable provenance (5.8 per cent); the glasses thought to be of Jacobite significance displaying sunflowers, beehives etc., subjects which are probably less likely to appeal to the faker (8.4 per cent). If these groups are added to the 61.3 per cent of the major engravers the total becomes 81.6 per cent. If the benefit of the doubt is then given to the remaining enamel-twist stem and facet stem glasses not already accounted for (6.1 per cent), on the grounds that they were engraved later in the eighteenth century when there were many more engravers working, and also that a modern engraver wanting to fake a Jacobite glass is probably less likely to choose an opaque-twist or a facet stem glass, the total becomes 87.7 per cent. With all these allowances this still leaves 12.3 per cent of wheel-engraved Jacobite glasses for which there is no satisfactory explanation and in the present author's opinion most of these are probably fakes.

With fake wheel-engraving one is wrestling with the impossible problem of trying to prove a negative. However, when the diamond-point engraving on the *'Amen'* glasses comes to be considered the situation is quite different, because writing is involved and this can be analyzed enabling some positive conclusions to be reached.

In the 1930's a few *'Amen'* glasses were in circulation which were of doubtful origin and this doubt usually stemmed from an inadequate provenance. With any object of historical significance the provenance is always of paramount importance. New discoveries are made all the time; in the last ten years two previously unrecorded *'Amen'* glasses have come to light. But, when a discovery such as this is made it usually means that it is brought to the notice of the art world; the owners themselves may have known about it for decades but may not have been aware of its importance or may not have wished it to be publicized for any one of a variety of reasons. Some priceless relic which may have languished in a hat-box in someone's loft will cause a stir when it is offered for sale. It may well be an unrecorded work of art but the owner will have known of its existence and will probably know a good deal about its previous history. However, the story must be a convincing one.

Plate 164. The Fitzwilliam glass. H. 19.0cm.

In 1930 an unrecorded *'Amen'* glass appeared for sale with Hankinson's Auctioneers, Bournemouth. The vendor was a Miss. D. Graham who claimed that she was one of the Scottish Grahams and that the glass had always been in her family who were Jacobites.

The glass has a trumpet-shaped bowl with a plain drawn stem on a plain conical foot. H. 19.0cm.

The bowl is engraved with a crown (speckled shading to base), cipher with large 8 intertwined, the first and second verses of the anthem and *'Amen'*. The bowl also carries the additional inscriptions: 'To His Royal Highness The Duke.' and 'To The Increase of The Royal Family.' The third and fourth verses of the anthem are engraved on the foot.

The glass was bought by Mrs. W. D. Dickson and in 1945 was given to the Fitzwilliam Museum, Cambridge.

This glass will be referred to as the Fitzwilliam glass (Plate 164) and corresponds to the Graham glass, No. 24 in Charleston's classification.

In 1933 a gentleman, calling himself Robert Ferguson, walked into Sotheby's in London with another unrecorded *'Amen'* glass and asked them to sell it for him. When questioned about the provenance Mr. Ferguson was unable to contribute anything of any substance, saying that the glass had come down through his wife's family, her maiden name being Urquhart, and he knew little of its previous history. Again, the glass is a genuine eighteenth century wine glass, having a trumpet-shaped bowl, a plain drawn stem and a folded foot. H. 18.2cm.

The bowl is engraved with a crown (speckled shading to base), cipher with large 8 intertwined, two verses of the anthem and *'Amen'*. The bowl also carries the additional inscription: 'To His Royal Highness Prince Henry Duke of Albany and York.'

The engraving looked authentic enough and Sotheby's accepted the glass for sale, 7-4-1933, lot 76. It was purchased by Cecil Higgins, a well-known collector of his day. When Cecil Higgins died in 1949, his house in Bedford with his collection of works of art was opened to the public as the Cecil Higgins Art Gallery and Museum. However, there was still doubt about the *'Amen'* glass, due to the lack of a reliable provenance, so it was withdrawn from public view and has been held in store at the Museum ever since.

This glass will be referred to as the Cecil Higgins glass (Plate 165) and corresponds to the Ferguson I glass, No. 22 in Charleston's classification.[7]

In 1937 Mr. Ferguson presented two more unrecorded glasses at Sotheby's in London, with the same story: that they had come down through his wife's side of the family. The fact that Mr. Ferguson seemed to be chancing upon more than his fair share of unrecorded *'Amen'* glasses appears not to have sounded any alarm bells. But, again, both glasses were genuine eighteenth century wine glasses and the engraving appeared authentic, so Sotheby's accepted them both for sale.

One, an Old Pretender glass, has a bell-shaped bowl with solid base, a plain stem and a folded foot. H. 18.6cm. The bowl is engraved with a crown (speckled shading to base), cipher with small 8 in lower part and the inscription:

'Caelum non animum mutant
Qui trans mare currunt'.
(Horace *Epistles* 1-11 27)

The translation of which is: 'They change clime, not heart, who speed across the sea'.

Sold Sotheby's 12-3-1937. Now in the Cinzano Glass Collection.

This glass corresponds to the Ferguson glass, No. 38 in Charleston's classification.[8]

The other, an *'Amen'* glass, has a trumpet-shaped bowl with a plain stem, enclosing a small pear-shaped tear, on a folded foot' H. 18.9cm.

The bowl is engraved with a crown (speckled shading to base), cipher with large 8 intertwined, four verses of the anthem and *'Amen'*. In addition, the bowl carries the inscription: 'To His Royal Highness Prince Henry Duke of Albany and York.' and the date '6th March 1725'. This is the birthdate (New Style) of Prince Henry.

Sold Sotheby's 12-3-1937. It was purchased by Sir Harrison Hughes and was sold again at Sotheby's, 24-6-1963, lot 65, and at Sotheby's yet again, 19-6-1972, lot 144, when it too was acquired for the Cinzano Glass Collection.

Plate 165. The Cecil Higgins glass. H. 18.2cm.

Plate 166. The Cinzano glass. H. 18.9cm.

This glass will be referred to as the Cinzano glass (Plate 166) and corresponds to the Ferguson II glass, No. 23 in Charleston's classification.[9]

The three *'Amen'* glasses (Fitzwilliam, Cecil Higgins and Cinzano) are all included in the present series and have been photographed by the author. Some similarities are immediately apparent. All three are engraved with a crown having speckled shading to the base and they all have a cipher with the large 8 intertwined, features which are extremely rare on other *'Amen'* glasses. Also they all have circle and loop scrollwork around the rim of the bowl with calligraphic scrolls separating the verses of the anthem. The writing on each of the three glasses is the same (Plate 167) and is very similar to that on the other *'Amen'* glasses, yet it lacks the flowing quality of the writing on the other glasses and there is not the same expert use of the available space. The writing on these three glasses resembles that on the other *'Amen'* glasses too

a *Fitzwilliam*

b *Cecil Higgins*

c *Cinzano*

Plate 167 a, b, c. Showing the writing on the three glasses to be by the same hand. Note improvement in the quality of the engraving, especially on the Cinzano glass.

closely for them to be regarded as the work of a totally independent engraver. The forensic handwriting analyst (pp. 225-26) confirmed that the three glasses were by the same hand but a different one to that responsible for the rest of the 'Amen' glasses. Furthermore, he was in no doubt that the writing had been copied from that on the other 'Amen' glasses. However, it does not necessarily follow that they are forgeries. The glasses themselves are genuine eighteenth century drinking glasses and the engraving could be contemporary; it might possibly be the work of an apprentice copying his master. If only one of the glasses had a reliable provenance it would authenticate the other two. The fact that all three glasses lack a sound provenance is decidedly odd and Mr. Ferguson's discovery of two of them does seem to be stretching credibility. Moreover, if they are the work of an eighteenth century engraver, why go to the trouble of copying the other engraver's writing? Using a diamond-pointed tool on a surface which is concave in one direction and sharply convex in the other must be difficult enough without trying to copy another person's handwriting.

Of the three glasses, the last to appear, the Cinzano glass, is undoubtedly the best. The quality of the engraving is good and it takes a handwriting expert to identify the

a Cecil Higgins　　　　　　　*b Fisher of Ham Common*

(Note lower case 't's)

c Fitzwilliam　　　　　　　*d Beves*

(Note upper case 'T's)

Plate 168 a, b, c, d. Differences in the letter 'T'. a and b lower case; c and d upper case.

small but consistent differences between the copied writing and that on the other *'Amen'* glasses.

The letter 'T' will serve to demonstrate this point. Plate 168 illustrates the differences between the lower case 't' and the capital letter 'T' on the authentic glasses and the copies. On the majority of *'Amen'* glasses the cross on the lower case letter 't'

a Fisher of Ham Common

b Fitzwilliam

c Fisher of Ham Common

d Fitzwilliam

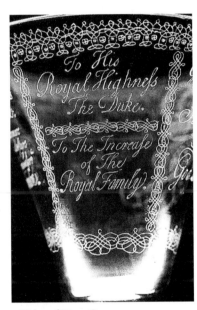

e Fisher of Ham Common

f Fitzwilliam

Plate 169 a to f. Similarities between the Fisher of Ham Common 'Amen' glass and the Fitzwilliam glass

is always on a level with the top of the other letters (Plate 168b), while on the copies it is always at a level higher than the top of the other letters (Plate 168a). Again, on the authentic glasses the cross on the upper case 'T' always stops short of the next letter. For example, with the combination 'Th' the cross on the 'T' does not pass over the top of the 'h' (Plate 168d). On the copies, however, the cross on the capital 'T' extends over the top of the succeeding letter (Plate 168c). There are similar consistent differences in some of the other letters and also some of the scrollwork which a trained eye can detect.

Two of the three glasses are very similar to two other existing *'Amen'* glasses. The Fitzwilliam glass bears a striking resemblance to the Fisher of Ham Common *'Amen'* glass in the Ashmolean Museum, Oxford (Plate 169), and the Cinzano glass to the

Drummond Castle *'Amen'* glass in the Philadelphia Museum of Art (Plate 170). The Drummond Castle glass has a small 8 in the cipher, more elaborate scrollwork and a different date but otherwise the glasses are almost identical.

Given an eighteenth century wine glass and the tools for the job, it is no mean calligraphic feat to produce a presentable copy of an *'Amen'* glass. The working surface is a difficult shape, the writing is small and there is little room for error. Also, how could one hope to have possession of an *'Amen'* glass for long enough to make such a copy? In the absence of a genuine *'Amen'* glass the only other way would be to obtain, by some means or other, detailed close-up photographs. In the late 1920's and early 1930's about twelve *'Amen'* glasses were known and most were in private hands; this certainly applied to the Fisher of Ham Common glass, which was in the personal collection of Joseph Bles, and the Drummond Castle glass, which was in the collection of G.F. Berney. It is Joseph Bles who supplies the answer to the question.

In 1926, knowledge of Jacobite glass took a leap forward with the publication of Grant Francis's *Old English Drinking Glasses* in which a substantial chapter is devoted to the subject. In the same year Joseph Bles's *Rare English Glasses of the 17th and 18th Centuries* appeared. This book was published by Geoffrey Bles, a publishing firm founded in 1923; Geoffrey Bles the publisher being the son of Joseph Bles the author. Bles's book added little to the overall knowledge of Jacobite glass but it does contain large detailed photographs. Three *'Amen'* glasses are illustrated and with two of them the writing is photographed in close-up detail. It has to be significant that these two glasses are the Fisher of Ham Common and the Drummond Castle *'Amen'* glasses.[10] Even so, although suspicion continues to build-up, this still proves nothing.

When looking at the photographs of the Fitzwilliam glass and the Fisher of Ham

a Drummond Castle. (Courtesy Philadelphia Museum of Art, U.S.A.)   b Cinzano

Plate 170 a, b. Similarities between Drummond Castle 'Amen' glass and the Cinzano glass

Plate 171. Foot of the Fisher of Ham Common glass

Common glass (Plate 169), the extent to which the one is a replica of the other is very striking; every twist and flourish of the writing appears to have been copied. And yet, there is one notable difference between the two. The third and fourth verses of the anthem are engraved on the foot of each glass but, whereas the Fisher of Ham Common glass has the verses engraved on the **top** of the foot (Plate 171), as is usual with all the *'Amen'* glasses which have writing on the foot, the Fitzwilliam glass, for some inexplicable reason, has the same verses engraved on the **underside** of the foot (Plate 172). This does not occur on any other *'Amen'* glass, so why engrave in this way? In Bles's book there is a small photograph (Plate 173) which provides an explanation.[11] This is Bles's illustration of the foot of the Fisher of Ham Common *'Amen'* glass. Bearing in mind that the engraving is on the **top** of the foot, this photograph does not make any sense; because, with the bowl of the glass in the way, it is quite impossible to obtain a single vertical view of the whole of the top of the foot, and this photograph clearly shows the foot of the glass seen from below.

Bles was economizing on his illustrations. To cover the verses on the top of the foot he would have needed three separate plates, so he has employed some trick photography. The foot of the glass has been photographed from below, that is, showing the writing as back-to-front mirror writing which has then been corrected by reversing the negative when printing. The result is a photograph of the foot of the glass, seen from below, but with the writing appearing the right way round.

Plate 172. Foot of the Fitzwilliam glass

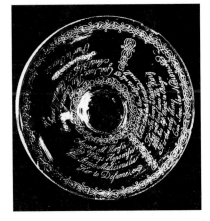

Plate 173. Bles's illustration of the foot of the Fisher of Ham Common glass

a   b

Plate 174 a, b. The Cecil Higgins glass

This *lapsus calami* is the forger's undoing; a silly mistake after taking so much care. He has unwittingly copied Bles's photograph and put the third and fourth verses of the anthem on the underside of the foot of the Fitzwilliam glass. This shows that the forger had never seen the Fisher of Ham Common *'Amen'* glass and was working from the photographs in Bles's book.

The first glass to appear, the Fitzwilliam (1930), is a direct copy of the Fisher of Ham Common *'Amen'* glass. The next glass, the Cecil Higgins (1933), is a compilation (Plate 174); the crown, cipher and first two verses of the anthem being very similar to the Fisher of Ham Common glass, but the dedication to Prince Henry resembling that on the Drummond Castle *'Amen'* glass. The last glass to appear, the Cinzano (1937), is the most ambitious and the most competent, with all four verses engraved on the bowl.

Plate 175. The Drummond Castle 'Amen' glass.   *Plate 176. The Cinzano glass*
(Courtesy Philadelphia Museum of Art, U.S.A.)

The forger has made a few alterations (Plates 175 and 176): he has changed the date and has used the crown with speckled shading to the base, the large intertwined 8 and simple scrollwork, as on the Fitzwilliam and Cecil Higgins glasses, but the remainder of the glass is a superb copy of the Drummond Castle *'Amen'* glass. And here, yet another strange fact emerges which requires an explanation.

There is one portion of the Drummond Castle *'Amen'* glass which is not illustrated in Bles's book. This is the panel on the reverse of the bowl showing the dedication to Prince Henry. There is no known illustration of this part of the Drummond Castle glass. So, how did the forger overcome this hurdle? The dedication is recorded in the text and, if he was going to include it, he could simply have made the panel to his own design. The Philadelphia Museum of Art very kindly supplied a close-up photograph of this portion of the Drummond Castle glass and, comparing the two (Plate 177), there is no question of the dedication to Prince Henry on the Cinzano glass having been composed independently; the one is a very close copy of the other.

So, here is someone who, when copying one glass, makes the elementary error of engraving on the underside of the foot, and yet when copying another glass appears to have precise detailed knowledge of a little known part of the glass. It is almost certain that when the Drummond Castle glass was photographed for the book it would have been photographed from every angle. Bles would then have had to select the photographs he wanted to use. There would have been several close-up photographs of the Drummond Castle *'Amen'* glass which were never used in the book and the most likely explanation is that the forger was someone who had access to these photographs, possibly someone connected in some way with the publication of the book.

In June 1993 another glass, the Henry Brown, appeared for auction. It was shown to

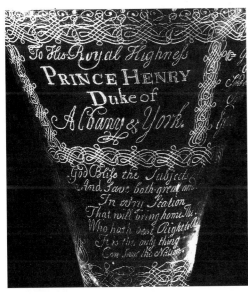 

a Drummond Castle. (Courtesy Philadelphia Museum of Art, U.S.A.)   *b Cinzano*

Plate 177 a, b. The dedication of Prince Henry, which is not illustrated in Bles's book

be by the same hand as the Fitzwilliam, Cecil Higgins and Cinzano glasses and, once this was realized, was withdrawn from the sale. It has many features similar to the Cinzano glass and seems to have been the forerunner of this glass having been presented at Christie's in 1936, a year before the Cinzano glass was presented at Sotheby's.

The Henry Brown glass has a trumpet-shaped bowl with a plain drawn stem, enclosing a large tear, above a folded foot. H. 18.7cm.

The bowl is engraved with a crown (speckled shading to base), cipher with large 8 intertwined, four-verse anthem and *'Amen'*. The reverse of the bowl carries the further inscription: 'To His Royal Highness Prince Henry Duke of Albany and York'. and also 'XX Decem.'. As with the other three copies, there is circle and loop scrollwork around the rim of the bowl and calligraphic scrolls separating the verses of the anthem.

The glass was sold at Christie's 7-5-1936, lot 16, with the provenance that it was from the collection of David R.S. Crabb, Scotland, and had previously been in the collection of C.B.O. Clarke. It was purchased by Henry Brown and subsequently sold at Sotheby's 14-11-1947, lot 279. Owned Francis L. Dickson and sold Sotheby's 26-7-1965, lot 95. Present owners Capt. and Mrs L. Stahl, Florida, U.S.A.

A sad note upon which to end this brief review of what was, in so many ways, an exciting and formative period in British history. Nevertheless, it serves to illustrate that those who fall prey to the spell of the White Rose, and who seek to possess a relic of this period, should exercise a degree of caution. *Caveat emptor* is advice which would have been endorsed, one feels sure, by the Old if not the Young Pretender.

APPENDIX

Total number of Jacobite glasses photographed 487

 Drinking glasses 472
 Decanters 7
 Finger bowls 4
 Jelly glasses 2
 Bowl stands 1
 Flasks 1

   Total **487**

The Drinking Glasses

 Wine, cordial and dram glasses 453
 Ale glasses 8
 Tumblers 7
 Rummers 1
 Tankard 1
 Water glasses 1
 Loving cup 1

   Total **472**

Decorative Techniques

 Wheel-engraving 459
 Diamond-point engraving 19
 Enamelling 5
 Coin glasses 3
 Plain glass with engraved silver foot 1

   Total **487**

WHEEL-ENGRAVED GLASSES

 Wine, cordial and dram glasses 425
 Ale glasses 8
 Tumblers 7
 Decanters 7
 Finger bowls 4
 Jelly glasses 2
 Bowl stands 1
 Rummers 1
 Tankards 1
 Flasks 1
 Loving cups 1
 Water glasses 1

   Total **459**

Wheel-Engraved Drinking Glasses with Stems

Wine, cordial and dram glasses 425
Ale glasses 8
Rummers 1
Water glasses 1
Loving cups 1

Total **436**

Stem Forms

M.S.A.T. 125
M.S.A.T. with two knops 87
M.S.A.T. with one knop 19
M.S.A.T. with five knops 1
S.S.A.T. 15
D.S.A.T. 8
Mercury twist 7
Plain stem 56
D.S.O.T. 53
S.S.O.T. 6
Colour twist 7
Light baluster 17
Facet 13
Incised twist 8
Composite 6
Moulded pedestal 1
Baluster 2
Rudimentary 5

Total **436**

Note: Total No. of air-twists 262
       Total No. of opaque and colour twists 66

Bowl Shapes

Round funnel 153
Trumpet 120
Bell 69
Ogee 41
Bucket 26
Ovoid 6
Pantopped round funnel 6
Waisted bucket 5
Waisted round funnel 4
Conical 3
Waisted ogee 3

Total **436**

Foot Forms

Plain conical	380
Folded conical	23
Firing	14
Domed	12
Folded domed	7
Total	**436**

Wheel-Engraved Rose Glasses (including Portrait Glasses)

Drinking glasses with air-twist stems	242
" " " plain stems	51
" " " opaque-twist stems	48
" " " light baluster stems	16
" " " incised-twist stems	7
" " " colour-twist stems	6
" " " facet stems	6
" " " composite stems	5
" " " rudimentary stems	5
" " " baluster stems	2
" " " moulded pedestal stems	1
Decanters	7
Tumblers	7
Bowls	4
Jelly glasses	2
Bowl stands	1
Tankard	1
Loving cup	1
Flask	1
Total	**413**

Number of Petals

Roses with 5 petals	4
" " 6 "	313
" " 7 "	41
" " 8 "	18
Multi-petalled roses	27
Stylized roses difficult to classify	10
Total	**413**

Number of Buds

Roses with 1 bud	143
" " 2 buds	244
" " 3 buds	2
Total	**389**

Note 1. 24 glasses engraved with a rose had no buds. Some of these are of doubtful Jacobite significance.

Note 2. Of the 143 single buds, 10 would be described as 'empty buds'. These are often associated with a multi-petalled rose. For a discussion on 'The Empty Bud' see Glass Notes, Arthur Churchill Ltd. No. 11, pp. 18-21.

Other Wheel-Engraved Flowers

Sunflowers	11
Carnations	4
Daffodils	3
Honeysuckle	2
Foget-me-nots	1
Mixed floral spray	12
Total	**33**

Some Other Wheel-Engraved Emblems

Oak leaf	131
Star	91
Thistle	76
Butterfly or moth	72
Fleur-de-lis	25
Insect	24
Crown	17
Bird	13
Family crest	6
Compass	5
Beehive	2

Wheel-engraved mottoes

Fiat	98
Audentior ibo (portrait glasses)	28
Audentior ibo (non-portrait glasses)	1
Revirescit	8
Reverescit (misspelt)	1
Redeat	4
Redi	5
Reddas incolumem	2
Radiat	1
Redi & Fiat	1
Turno Tempus Erit, Redeat & Fiat	3
Turno Tempus Erit & Fiat	1
Hic Vir Hic Est	1
Success to the Society	4
Sir Watkin Williams Wynn	2

Wheel-engraved mottoes (continued)

The Friendly Hunt 2
Health to all our Fast Friends 1
Health to all True Blues 1

Wheel-Engraved Portraits of Prince Charles

Conventional portraits with bonnet and tartan 36
Portraits with star and riband of garter on
   right breast (Plate 96) 13
Augustan portraits (Plate 95) 2
Full-length portrait (Plate 97) 1
Hic Vir Hic Est portrait (Plate 89b) 1
Disguised portraits (Plate 100b) 2

        Total **55**

ENAMELLED GLASSES

Portrait glasses 4
Glass with enamelled rose (Plate 39) 1

        Total **5**

DIAMOND-POINT ENGRAVED GLASSES

'Amen' glasses 16
Blackbird and dragonfly (Plate 101) 1
Crown and thistle 1
Rose and moth 1

        Total **19**

THE 'AMEN' AND 'AMEN'-TYPE GLASSES

Total number known at present time 35

Bowl Shapes Trumpet 30
               Round funnel 3
               Bell 2

Stem Forms Plain 24
               M.S.A.T. 8
               D.S.A.T. 1
               Incised twist 1
               Moulded pedestal 1

Foot Forms Plain 22
               Folded 9
               Domed 2
               Not known 2

Illustrations Attributed To:

Engraver A
Colour plates: 14, 20, 22, 27, 40, 41, 44.
Plates: 4, 9, 15, 16, 19, 30, 32, 36, 46, 62, 64, 66a, 69, 70, 71, 79, 80a, 81, 93b & c, 96b, 103, 106, 107, 122b, 128, 131.

Engraver B
Colour plates: 15, 16, 25, 36, 45.
Plates: 5, 13, 43, 55, 65, 66b, 72, 76, 78, 85, 91, 92?, 99, 108, 109, 116a,b & c, 122a, c, d, e, f, 130.

Engraver C
Colour plates: 19, 21, 26, 37.
Plates: 11, 12, 14, 17, 31, 33, 37, 41, 42, 45, 48, 54, 61, 63, 66c, 77, 80b, 82, 89, 93d, 110, 111, 116d,e & f.

Engraver D
Colour plates: 18, 31, 43.
Plates: 18, 20, 23, 34, 47, 52, 53, 57, 58, 60, 96a, 97, 102, 104, 112, 113, 127, 132.

Engraver E
Colour plates: 24, 28, 35.
Plates: 10, 21, 24, 35, 49, 50, 66d, 75, 80c, 93a, 95, 100?, 114, 115, 126, 129.

Engraver F
Colour plates: 38, 42.
Plates: 26, 59, 117, 118.

Engraver G
Plates: 27, 38, 119.

Engraver H
Colour plate: 39.
Plates: 88, 120.

Engraver I
Plate: 121.

NOTES

INTRODUCTION

1. Youngson, A.J., *The Prince and the Pretender. A Study in the Writing of History.*
2. Churchill, Sir Winston S., *A History of the English-Speaking Peoples* Vol.III, *The Age of Revolution* p. 110.
3. Berwick, 1st Duke of, *Memoirs,* Vol.II, pp. 199-205.

CHAPTER ONE: THE CAUSE

1. *Memoirs of Sir Ewan Cameron of Lochiel* by his grandson, Drummond of Balhaldie; Bannatyne Club 1737. p. 268.
2. Berwick, 1st Duke of, *Memoirs,* Vol.II, p. 473.
3. This is a much quoted description of the Old Pretender and, in some respects, it seems to coincide with the overall impression of his character. However, it is only one person's observation and, as mentioned in the opening introduction, we should be wary of accepting it without reservation. In several other particulars quoted in the article the anonymous author of *A True Account of the Proceedings at Perth* has been shown to be inaccurate and unfair.

     Choosing to remain anonymous and to be known only as 'A Rebel', the author has caused speculation as to his true identity. Some have said that he was the Master of Sinclair, others that he was Daniel Defoe. Many of the events recorded occurred after Sinclair had left which seems to render his nomination untenable.
4. Speck, W.A., *The Butcher. The Duke of Cumberland and the Suppression of the '45,* p. 181.

CHAPTER TWO: CHARLES EDWARD STUART

1. McLynn, Frank, *Charles Edward Stuart,* pp. 205-6.
2. Ibid., p. 206.
3. Cruickshanks, Eveline, *Political Untouchables. The Tories and the '45,* pp. 106-8.
4. Doran, Dr, F.S.A., *London in The Jacobite Times,* Vol.II, pp. 267-8.

CHAPTER THREE: THE JACOBITE CLUBS

1. Firth, Sir Charles, *Oliver Cromwell and the Rule of the Puritans in England,* pp. 216-7.
2. Lochiel Memoirs, op. cit., pp. 270-1.
3. Cruickshanks, Eveline, *The House of Commons 1715 - 1754* Preface, Vol.I, p. ix.
4. Steevenson, Muriel, *Glass Circle Paper No.7* 19-1-1939. Also *Glass Circle Papers Nos.59, 60 & 61,* 1945.
5. Steevenson, Muriel, *Glass Circle Paper No.116.*
6. Lole, F.P., 1745 Association, *A Check List of Jacobite Clubs.*
7. Lole, F.P., *The Jacobite No.81,* 1993, 'The Scottish Jacobite Clubs', p. 11.
8. Steevenson, Muriel, *Glass Circle Paper No.116,* p. 2.
9. Steevenson, Muricl, *Glass Circle Paper No.7* p. 3.
10. The Ballad of 'The White Rose over the Water, 1744'. See Hartshorne, *Old English Glasses,* pp. 363-4.

11. Steevenson, Muriel, *Glass Circle Paper No.116,* p. 4.
12. Doran, Dr., F.S.A., *London in The Jacobite Times* Vol.I, p. 328.
13. Ibid., p. 306.
14. Hartshorne, op. cit., p. 363, Note 1.
15. Steevenson, Muriel, *Glass Circle Paper No.17,* 11-7-1940, p. 3.
16. Ibid., p. 6.
17. Steevenson, Muriel, *Glass Circle Paper No.101,* p. 2.
18. Steevenson, Muriel, *Glass Circle Paper No.61,* 1945, Addenda.
19. Steevenson, Muriel, *Glass Circle Paper No.116,* p. 3.
20. Cruickshanks, Eveline, *Political Untouchables,* pp. 106-7.
21. Doran, op. cit., Vol.I, pp. 263-4.
22. Ibid., pp. 91-2.
23. Steevenson, Muriel, *Glass Circle Paper No.61,* 1945, Addenda.
24. Ibid., p. 1. See also *Glass Circle Papers Nos.7 & 116.*
25. Steevenson, Muriel, *Glass Circle Paper No.116,* pp. 3-4.
26. Steevenson, Muriel, *Glass Circle Paper No.101,* p. 3 and *No.7,* pp. 11-12.
27. Petrie, Sir Charles, *The Jacobite Movement,* p. 441.
28. Hartshorne, op. cit., p. 370. See also *Glass Circle Papers Nos.7 & 101.*
29. Steevenson, Muriel, *Glass Circle Paper No.101,* p. 3.
30. Francis, Grant.R., *Old English Drinking Glasses,* pp. 179-81.
31. Cycle of the White Rose. Not to be confused with the White Rose Society. The latter may have been quite a large Jacobite society but little is known about it and its sphere of activity is obscure.
32. Hartshorne, op. cit., pp. 363-8.
33. Steevenson, Muriel, *Glass Circle Paper No.101,* p. 1.
34. Phillips, John Pavin, *Notes and Queries, Series III, Vol.II,* p. 1.
35. Churchill, Arthur, Ltd., *Glass Notes No.10,* Dec. 1950, pp. 15-7.
36. Steevenson, Muriel, *Glass Circle Paper No.116,* p. 2.

CHAPTER FOUR: ENGLISH GLASS IN THE EIGHTEENTH CENTURY

1. Evelyn, John, *The Diary of John Evelyn,* Vol.III, p. 246.
2. Watts, D.C., *The Glass Circle 2,* 1975, 'How did George Ravenscroft discover lead crystal?', pp. 71-84.
3. Thorpe, W.A., *A History of English and Irish Glass,* p. 205. See also, Thorpe, W.A., *Connoisseur,* 1933, 'The Dagnia Tradition in Newcastle Glass', pp. 13-25.
4. Ross, Catherine, *The Glass Circle 5,* 1986, 'The Flint Glass Houses on the Rivers Tyne and Wear during the 18th century', pp. 75-82.
5. Charleston, R.J., *English Glass,* p. 147, and Plate 39a.
6. Ibid., p. 142.
7. Buckley, Francis, *A History of Old English Glass,* p. 57.
8. Smith, Sheenah, *The Glass Circle 2,* 1975, 'Glass in 18th century Norwich', p. 54.
9. Buckley, op. cit., p. 58.
10. Charleston, op. cit., p. 146.
11. Thorpe, W.A., *English Glass,* 1961, p. 201.
12. Thorpe, W.A., *A History of English and Irish glass,* p. 213.
13. Hughes, G.Bernard, *English Glass for the Collector, 1660-1860,* p. 41.

14. Buckley, op. cit., p. 58.
15. Ibid., p. 58.
16. Ibid., p. 60.
17. Thorpe, W.A., *English Glass,* 1961, p. 212.
18. Charleston, op. cit., p. 151.
19. Ibid., p. 142 & p. 151.
20. Thorpe, W.A., *A History of English and Irish glass,* pp. 238-41.
21. Buckley, op. cit., p. 120, Note 1.
22. Ibid., p. 120, 8b.
23. Thorpe, W.A., *A History of English and Irish Glass,* pp. 241-3.
24. Buckley, op. cit., p. 120, 9c.
25. Ibid., p. 121, 9d.
26. Ibid., p. 48.

CHAPTER FIVE: SOME JACOBITE GLASSES

1. Francis, Grant.R., *Old English Drinking Glasses,* p. 173.
2. Lelièvre, F.J., *The Glass Circle 5,* 1986, 'Jacobite Glasses and their Inscriptions: Some Interpretations', pp. 68-74.
3. Doran, Dr., F.S.A., *London in The Jacobite Times,* Vol.II, pp. 177-81.
4. Steevenson, Muriel, *Glass Circle Paper No.11,* 2-5-1940, p. 5.
5. Francis, op. cit., p. 191.
6. Lelièvre, op. cit., p. 71.
7. British Museum glass, (2, 11-13, 86).
8. Bles, Joseph, *Rare English Glasses of the 17th & 18th Centuries,* p. 112, Plate 35.
9. Lelièvre, op. cit., pp. 71-2.
10. Haynes, E. Barrington, *Glass Through the Ages,* p. 172.
11. Francis, op. cit., p. 178.
12. Steevenson, Muriel, *Glass Circle Paper No.5,* May 1938, pp. 8-9. The portraits are in Lang, Andrew, *Prince Charles Edward,* opposite p. 32 & p. 189.
13. Robert Strange was an artist who accompanied Prince Charles during the 'Forty-five, and fought at the Battle of Culloden. He was later responsible for several royal portrait commissions. He was subsequently pardoned by George III and given a knighthood.
14. Francis, op. cit., pp. 193-5.
15. Churchill, Arthur,Ltd., *Glass Notes No.16,* p. 24.
16. Lole, F.P., *The Jacobite No.81,* 1993, 'The Scottish Jacobite Clubs', p. 14.
17. Francis, op. cit., p. 186, Plate LXIV, No.364.
18. Mortimer, Martin, *Amicorum No.3,* Spring 1993,'Discretion', p. 25.

CHAPTER SIX: THE JACOBITE ENGRAVERS

1. Charleston, R.J., *English Glass,* p. 174.
2. Buckley, Francis, *A History of Old English Glass,* p. 122, No.17a.
3. Charleston, op. cit., p. 175.
4. Werner, Alexander, *The Journal of The Glass Association,* Vol.I, 1985, 'Thomas Betts - an Eighteenth Century Glasscutter', p. 3.

5. Ibid., Appendix 2.
6. Charleston, op. cit., p. 152.
7. Buckley, op. cit., p. 120, No. 8a & Note 1.
8. Ibid., p. 120, No. 8b.
9. Ibid., p. 120, No. 9c.
10. Werner, op. cit., p. 4.
11. Charleston, op. cit., p. 154.
12. Harrison, William, *Description of England, 1577,* 3 Vols. (1887).
13. *The Diary of Samuel Pepys,* edited by Latham, R.C. & Matthews, W., Vol.IV, pp.77-8.
14. Porter, Roy, *English Society in the Eighteenth Century,* p. 253.

CHAPTER SEVEN: THE JACOBITE ROSE

1. Petrie, Sir Charles, *The Jacobite Movement,* p. 440.
2. Steevenson, Muriel, *Glass Circle Paper No.144,* March 1966, p. 3.
3. Steevenson, Muriel, *Glass Circle Paper No.12,* Sept. 1940, p. 1.
4. Steevenson, Muriel, *Glass Circle Paper No.144,* March 1966, p. 2.
5. Horridge, W., *Glass Circle Paper No.56,* Nov. 1944. 'The Rose and Emblems on Jacobite Drinking Glasses'.
6. Haynes, E. Barrington, *Glass Through the Ages,* p. 168.
7. Ibid., p. 168.

CHAPTER EIGHT: THE *'AMEN'* GLASSES

1. Charleston, R.J., *The Glass Circle 5, 'Amen' Glasses,* Appendix pp. 8-14.
2. Seddon, Geoffrey B., *Country Life,* 19-6-1986, 'For Treasonable Toasts, The Breadalbane *'Amen'* Glass', pp. 1786-7.
3. 'Cambridge Connoisseur', *Connoisseur,* June, 1960, p. 36, Fig. 18.
4. Hartshorne, Albert, *Old English Glasses,* p. 347, Plate 56.
   Churchill, Arthur, Ltd., *History in Glass, 1937,* Plate 8. No.30.
   Cat. of Old English Glass, 1937, p. 66, No. 530.
   Anon., *Antiques,* Aug. 1941, 'Glassmaking History in Drinking Vessels' p. 80.
   Connoisseur, Sept. 1942, pp. 47, 50, No. I.
   Haynes, E. Barrington, *Antiques,* March 1944, 'An Historic Relic'.
   Corning, *Glass Drinking Vessels from the Strauss Collection,* 1955, pp. 99-100, No. 247.
   Lloyd, Ward, *Investing in Georgian Glass,* p. 130.
5. Bles, Joseph, *Rare English Glasses of the 17th & 18th Centuries,* pp. 90-3, Plates 24 & 25. Fleming, Arnold, *Scottish and Jacobite Glass,* Plate XLIX. *Connoisseur,* Sept. 1942, pp. 47, 50, No. II.
6. Fleming, op. cit., p. 178. *Antiques,* Nov. 1941, Steuben Glass advert.
7. Bles, op. cit., pp. 94-7, Plates 26 & 27. Churchill, Arthur, Ltd., *Glass Notes No.12,* Dec. 1952, p. 13. *Connoisseur,* Sept. 1942, p. 49, No. V.
8. *Connoisseur,* Nov. 1919. Risley, Sir John S., *Burlington Magazine,* XXXVI, June, 1920, pp. 276, 281, Plate I, 1-3.
   Churchill, Arthur, Ltd., *Glass Notes No.9,* p. 7.
   Connoisseur, Sept. 1942, p. 49, No.IV.
   Ebbott, Rex, *British Glass of the 17th & 18th Centuries,* Melbourne, 1971, p. 13, No. 14.

9. Hartshorne, op. cit., p. 347-8.
   Davis, Derek C., *English and Irish Antique Glass,* Fig. 47.
   Plesch, Peter H., *Journal of Glass Studies,* VII, 1965, 'English and Continental Glass The Collection of Dr. and Mrs. Peter H. Plesch', p. 81, Fig. 7.
10. Churchill, Arthur, Ltd., *Glass Notes No.8,* Dec. 1948, p. 4.
11. Hartshorne, op. cit., p. 349.
    Risley, op. cit., pp. 276-7.
    Buckley, W., *The Art of Glass,* p. 280, No. 506.
    Connoisseur, Sept. 1942, p. 48, No. III.
    Honey, W.B., *Glass: A Handbook,* p. 108.
    Elville, E.M., *The Collector's Dictionary of Glass,* p. 121, Fig. 170.
12. Churchill, Arthur, Ltd., *Glass Notes No. 9,* Dec. 1949, pp. 6-7, Fig. 4.
    Churchill, Arthur, Ltd., *Glass Notes No.10,* Dec. 1950, p. 20.
13. Churchill, Arthur, Ltd., *Glass Notes No.11,* Dec. 1951, pp. 12-3.
14. Churchill, Arthur, Ltd., *Glass Notes No.12,* Dec. 1952, pp. 11-2.
    Robertson, R.A., *Chats on Old Glass,* 1954, Plate 34.
    Wilkinson, O.N., *Old Glass,* Plate 116.
    Wallis, W. Cyril., *Connoisseur,* Oct. 1952, 'An Unrecorded *'Amen'* Glass', p. 105.
15. Clark, R., *Account of the National Anthem,* 1822.
    Hartshorne, op. cit., p. 349.
16. *Connoisseur,* March, 1920, p. XIII.
    Risley, op. cit., p. 281.
    Bles, op. cit., p. 116, Plate 37, Fig. 50.
    Antique Collector, 17-10-1931, p. 587.
    Connoisseur, Sept. 1942, p. 50, No. VII.
    Crompton, S., *English Glass,* Plates 118-9.
17. Herraghty, Edward A., *SMT Magazine and Scottish Country Life,* XXX, No. 6, Dec. 1942, pp. 23-5.
    Connoisseur, Sept. 1942 and Sept. 1943.
    Haynes, E. Barrington, *Antiques,* March 1944, 'An Historic Relic'.
18. Francis, Grant R., *Old English Drinking Glasses,* p. 167, Plate LX, No. 351.
    Connoisseur, Sept. 1942, p. 49, No. VI. (19) ibid., p. 50, No. IX.
20. Ibid., p. 50, No. VIII.
21. Vaillant, V.-J., *Notes Boulonnaises, Variétés, etc., 1889,* p. 51.
    Hartshorne, op. cit., p. 348-9.
22. Risley, op. cit., p. 281.
    Bate, Percy, *English Table Glass,* p. 99, Plate LII, No. 200.
    Churchill, Arthur, Ltd., *Glass Notes No.12,* Dec. 1952, p. 12.
23. Buckley, Francis, *A History of Old English Glass,* Plate XVIII.
    Connoisseur, Sept. 1942, p. 51, No. X.
    Plesch, op. cit., p. 81, Fig. 6.
24. Hartshorne, op. cit., p. 349.
    Powell, Harry J., *Glass-Making in England,* p. 60, Fig. 49.
25. Churchill, Arthur, Ltd., *Glass Notes No.16,* Dec. 1956, pp. 24-5.
26. Risley, op. cit., pp. 276-7.
    Bles, op. cit., p. 98, Plate 28.
27. Hartshorne, op. cit., p. 349.

28. Ibid., p. 347, Note 1.
29. Francis, op. cit., p. 168.
30. Charleston, R.J., *The Glass Circle 5,* p. 8.
31. Forbes, Robert, *The Lyon in Mourning,* Vol.I, (SHS 1895-6), pp. 154-69.

CHAPTER NINE: THE SNAKE IN THE GRASS

1. Hebborn, Eric, *Drawn to Trouble. The Forging of an Artist.*
2. Ibid., p. 357.
3. Ibid., p. 355.
4. Ibid., p. 359 & pp. 364-77.
5. Ibid., p. 379-80.
6. Charleston, R.J., *The Glass Circle 5,* p. 12.
7. Ibid., p. 12.
8. Ibid., p. 14.
9. Ibid., p. 12.
10. Bles, Joseph, *Rare English Glasses of the 17th & 18th Centuries,* pp. 90-7, Plates 24, 25, 26 & 27.
11. Ibid., p. 96, No. 38a.

SELECT BIBLIOGRAPHY

Published in London unless stated otherwise.

HISTORY

General

Ashley, Maurice, *The Glorious Revolution of 1688* (Panther edition, Manchester, 1968).

Beddard, Robert, *A Kingdom without a King. The Journal of the Provisional Government in the Revolution of 1688* (Oxford, 1988).

Clark, J.C.D., *Revolution and Rebellion. State and society in England in the 17th & 18th centuries* (Cambridge, 1986).

Marwick, Arthur, *The Nature of History* (1989).

Miller, John, *Seeds of Liberty. 1688 and the Shaping of Modern Britain* (1988).

Plumb, J.H., *England in the Eighteenth Century* (Penguin Books, 1974).

Porter, Roy, *English Society in the Eighteenth Century* (Penguin Books, 1990).

Rudé, George, *Paris and London in the Eighteenth Century* (1974).

Jacobite

Black, Jeremy, *Culloden and the '45* (Stroud, 1990).

Chambers, Robert, *History of the Rebellion of 1745-6* (London & Edinburgh, 1869).

Cruickshanks, Eveline, *Political Untouchables. The Tories and the '45* (1979).

Cruickshanks, E. & Black, J.,(Editors), *The Jacobite Challenge* (Edinburgh, 1988).

Doran, Dr., F.S.A., *London in The Jacobite Times* 2 Vols. (1877).

Forbes, R., *The Lyon in Mourning* Vols I-III (Edinburgh 1895-6). Reprinted Scottish History Society, 1975.

Francis, Grant R., *Romance of the White Rose* (1933).

Kemp, Hilary, *The Jacobite Rebellion* (1975).

Lees-Milne, James, *The Last Stuarts* (1983).

Lenman, Bruce, *The Jacobite Risings in Britain 1689-1746* (1980).

Lenman, Bruce, *The Jacobite Cause* (Edinburgh 1986).

McLynn, Frank, *The Jacobites* (1985).

McLynn, Frank, *The Jacobite Army in England, 1745* (Edinburgh, 1983).

Petrie, Sir Charles, *The Jacobite Movement* (1958).

Selby, John, *Over the Sea to Skye* (1973).

Seton, Sir Bruce, and Gordon, Jean, eds., *The Prisoners of the '45,* Vols. I-III (Edinburgh 1928).

Sinclair-Stevenson, Christopher, *Inglorious Rebellion. The Jacobite Risings of 1708, 1715 and 1719* (1971).

Tayler, A. & H., *1715. The Story of the Rising* (1936).

Tayler, A. & H., *Stuart Papers at Windsor* (1939).

Youngson, A.J., *The Prince and the Pretender. A Study in the Writing of History* (Beckenham, 1985).

Biographies

James II

Earle, Peter, *The Life and Times of James II* (1972).
Haswell, Jock, *James II* (1972).
Miller, John, *James II. A Study in Kingship* (1989).
Trevor, Meriol, *The Shadow of a Crown* (1988).

Viscount Dundee

Murray Scott, Andrew, *Bonnie Dundee* (Edinburgh, 1989).

James Francis Edward Stuart

Miller, Peggy, *James* (1971).

Charles Edward Stuart

Daiches, David, *Charles Edward Stuart* (1973).
Erickson, Carolly, *Bonnie Prince Charlie* (1993).
Forster, Margaret, *The Rash Adventurer* (1973).
Kybett, Susan Maclean, *Bonnie Prince Charlie* (1988).
Lang, Andrew, *Prince Charles Edward* (Paris, 1900).
Maclean, Fitzroy, *Bonnie Prince Charlie* (1988).
Marshall, Rosalind K., *Bonnie Prince Charlie* (Edinburgh, 1988).
McLaren, Moray, *Bonnie Prince Charlie* (1972).
McLynn, Frank, *Charles Edward Stuart* (1988).

Duke of Cumberland

Speck, W.A., *The Butcher* (Oxford, 1981).

Lord George Murray

Tomasson, Katherine, *The Jacobite General* (Edinburgh, 1958).

GLASS

Bacon John M., *Glass Circle Paper No.30*, 'Notes on Jacobite Glass' (1942),
Bate, Percy, *English Table Glass* (1913).
Bickerton, L.M., *Eighteenth Century English Drinking Glasses. An Illustrated Guide* (1971).
Bles, Joseph, *Rare English Glasses of the 17th & 18th Centuries* (1926).
Buckley, Francis, *A History of Old English Glass* (1925).
Brooks, John, *The Arthur Negus Guide to British Glass* (1981).
Charleston, R.J., *English Glass* (1984).
Charleston, R.J., *The Glass Circle 5, 'Amen' Glasses. Introductory'*, pp. 4-14. (1986).
Churchill, Arthur, Ltd., *History in Glass* (1937).
Churchill, Arthur, Ltd., *Glass Notes No.7* (1947).

*Glass Notes No.8 (*1948).

*Glass Notes No.9 (*1949).

*Glass Notes No.10 (*1950).

Churchill, Arthur, Ltd., *Glass Notes No.11* (1951).

Glass Notes No.12 (1952).

Glass Notes No.13 (1953).

Glass Notes No.14 (1954).

Glass Notes No.15 (1955).

Glass Notes No.16 (1956).

Crompton, Sidney, *English Glass (*1967).

Dillon, Edward, *Glass (*1907).

Elville, E.M., *The Collector's Dictionary of Glass* (1961).

Fleming, Arnold, *Scottish and Jacobite Glass (*Glasgow, 1938).

Francis, Grant R., *The British Numismatic Journal,* Vol. XVI, 'Jacobite Drinking Glasses' (1925).

Francis, Grant R., *Old English Drinking Glasses. Their Chronology and Sequence* (1926).

*Glass at the Fitzwilliam Museum (*Cambridge).

*The Glass Circle Number 1 (*1972).

Number 2 (1975).

*Number 3 (*1979).

Number 4 (1982).

Number 5 (1986).

Number 6 (1989).

Number 7 (1991).

Hartshorne, Albert, *Old English Glasses* (1897).

Republished as *Antique Drinking Glasses (*New York, 1967).

Haynes, E. Barrington, *Glass Through the Ages (*Penguin Books, 1959).

Horridge, W. & Haynes, E.B., *Connoisseur,* Sept. 1942, 'The *'Amen'* Glasses', pp. 47-50.

Horridge, W., *Glass Circle Paper No.56,* 'The Rose and Emblems on Jacobite Drinking Glasses' (1944).

Hughes, G. Bernard, *Glass Circle Paper No.51* 'Jacobite Drinking Glasses' (1944).

Hughes, G. Bernard, *English, Scottish and Irish Table Glass* (1956).

Hughes, G. Bernard, *English Glass for the Collector 1660- 1860 (*1958).

Lazarus, Peter, *The Cinzano Glass Collection* (1978).

Lelièvre, F.J., *The Glass Circle 5* 'Jacobite Glasses and their Inscriptions: Some Interpretations' pp. 68-74 (1986).

Lewis, J. Sydney, *Old Glass and how to Collect it* (1928).

Lloyd, Ward, *Investing in Georgian Glass* (1969).

Powell, Harry J., *Glass-Making in England (*Cambridge, 1923).

Robertson, R.A., *Chats on Old Glass* (1954).

Seddon, Geoffrey B., *The Glass Circle 3* 'The Jacobite Engravers', pp. 40-78 (1979).

Seddon, Geoffrey B., *Country Life,* 19-6-1986, 'For Treasonable Toasts. The Breadalbane *Amen* Glass' pp. 1786-7.

Seddon, Geoffrey B., *The Glass Circle 5* 'The Engraving on the *Amen* Glasses' pp. 15-16 (1986).

Steevenson, Muriel, *Glass Circle Paper No.5,* 'The Historical Aspect of the Jacobite Glasses' (1938).

Paper No.7 'Jacobite Clubs' (1939).

Paper No.11 '*Amen*' and *Fiat*' (1940).

Paper No.12 'Jacobite Emblems: The Rose' (1940).

Paper No.13 'More Emblems of Jacobite Glass' (1940).

Paper No.17 'Some Jacobite Toasts' (1940).

Paper No.59 'Some Jacobite Clubs' (1945).

Paper No.60 'Some Jacobite Clubs' continued (1945).

Paper No.61 'Some Jacobite Clubs' continued (1945).

Paper No.87 'Afterthoughts' (1948).

Paper No.101 'More Clubs'.

Paper No.116 'The Jacobite Club'.

Paper No.144 'Pruning the Jacobite Rose' (1966).

Thorpe, W.A., *English and Irish Glass* (1927).

Thorpe, W.A., *A History of English and Irish Glass* (1929).

Thorpe, W.A., *English Glass* 3rd ed. (1961).

Vose, Ruth Hurst, *Glass* (1980).

Wilkinson, O.N., *Old Glass* (1968).

Wilkinson, R., *The Hallmarks of Antique Glass* (1968).

Wills, Geoffrey, *English and Irish Glass* (1970).

Wills, Geoffrey, *Antique Glass for pleasure and investment* (1971).

Yoxall, J.H., *Collecting Old Glass. English and Irish* (1916).

INDEX